D176ᴧ400

Comparing Empires

European Colonialism from Portuguese Expansion to the Spanish-American War

Jonathan Hart

palgrave
macmillan

COMPARING EMPIRES
Copyright © Jonathan Hart, 2003, 2008.

All rights reserved. No part of this book may be used or reproduced in any manner whatsoever without written permission except in the case of brief quotations embodied in critical articles or reviews.

First published in hardcover 2003 by
PALGRAVE MACMILLAN™
175 Fifth Avenue, New York, N.Y. 10010 and
Houndmills, Basingstoke, Hampshire, England RG21 6XS.
Companies and representatives throughout the world.

PALGRAVE MACMILLAN is the global academic imprint of the Palgrave Macmillan division of St. Martin's Press, LLC and of Palgrave Macmillan Ltd. Macmillan® is a registered trademark in the United States, United Kingdom and other countries. Palgrave is a registered trademark in the European Union and other countries.

ISBN-13: 978–0–230–60240–3
ISBN-10: 0–230–60240–1

Cataloging-in-Publication Data is available from the Library of Congress.

A catalogue record for this book is available from the British Library.

Design by Newgen Imaging Systems (P) Ltd., Chennai, India.

First PALGRAVE MACMILLAN paperback edition: April 2008

10 9 8 7 6 5 4 3 2 1

Printed in the United States of America.

BLACKBURN COLLEGE
LIBRARY

Acc. No BB52592
Class No.UCL 325.309 4 HAR
Date 9 -11 - 2012

To Charles, Gwendolyn, Deborah, Alan and Jennifer

A fin qu'en me tuant ie peuffe receuoir
Quelque peu de renom pour vn peu de fçauoir.

Pierre Ronsard, *Les POEMES*
(Paris, 1567), p. 57

Indeed, it is a strange disposed time:
But men may construe things after their fashion,
Cleane from the purpose of the things themselues.

Cicero in Shakespeare, *Julius Caesar*
(First Folio, London, 1623)

Contents

Note to the Paperback Edition

I would like to dedicate this paperback edition to the memory of my mother, Jean MacLean Jackman Hart (1922–2005) and to my father, George Edward Hart (who continues to write), while keeping my original dedication to my brothers and sisters, and to thank Farideh Koohi-Kamali (my editor), Brigitte Shull and others I thanked before at Palgrave. Stephen Ferguson, George Hart and Nicole Mallet deserve additional thanks to that given in the hardcover edition. My gratitude to the Library of Congress for permission to reproduce this version of the "Death of Wolfe" on the cover, a version that shows the variety, popularity and importance of West's painting. This edition involves some corrections. I would like to note that I chose originally, for better or worse, to show some of the material culture of the time and the migration back and forth between languages by keeping contemporary spellings and placing them into my own text. This included names. For instance, in some cases, I have used Calichut for Calicut, Candi for Kandy, Chillora for Kilwa, Combaia for Cambay, Guzerat and Guzerate for Gujarat, Malindi and Melinde, Ormus for Hormuz, and Zaffalle or Zofala for Sofala. Some facts are still controversial (dating and so on) and I have tried to stick with what seems to be the scholarly consensus at the time of printing. My gratitude to the Master and fellows of Churchill College, Cambridge, for welcoming me as a fellow. My final thanks to Palgrave for producing this paperback, which I hope will enable the book to reach more scholars, students and members of the reading public.

—Jonathan Hart, Cambridge, November 2007.

Preface and Acknowledgments

Having lived some of my youth in Québec, the comparison and clash of cultures and empires was something that was in the air, sometimes so much so that we could cut it with a knife. I had a friend, Louis Vaillancourt, who lived near the Plains of Abraham: this was a charged ground. When I studied history in French and English in school, I found that we did not hear much about the Portuguese, Spaniards, Dutch and others: that was someone else's ground. It was the battle for the heart of New France that was the crucial moment, almost as if just over 200 years after the fall of Québec and the death of Wolfe it were still 1759. In time I came to learn more about the Natives, always a central part of Canadian history, to find more of my own personal and cultural connections with the Anglo-American colonies, Britain and France and, in time, to come to the conclusion that comparative studies in history, even if suggestive and not exhaustive, helped to throw light on one's own turf and tradition.

The death of Wolfe is in many ways a diptych with the death of Montcalm, the French general who faced his British counterpart, a death equally poignant but more ghostly in its representation. This great battle was not something in isolation but a conflict that had its roots in the relations with local peoples in Africa that the Portuguese had initiated over 300 years before. The New World, even though John Cabot or Giovanni Caboto and Binot de Paulmier de Gonneville had been there in the first dozen years of European exploration, was not a place of English (British) and French precedence. The Spanish and later the Portuguese built up thriving permanent colonies well before those that England and France planted in lands beyond the practical reach of Spain and Portugal in the Americas. Wolfe and Montcalm were later rivals in an imperial expansion and conflict that had begun long before and continued after their deaths.

Here was a fulcrum. Just when Britain and France were fighting for supremacy in North America, their moment had passed. Within a few years, the British colonies in North America lay fractured and the United States, with the help chiefly of France, gained its independence. Within about 50 years many of the colonies on the mainland of the New World had achieved their independence. Canada, of course, was a key exception. Colonialism has never really died in this land: it has lingered more apparently than in other places where its traces and subterranean marks lie. The death of Wolfe never quite dies.

As C. P. Stacey—a leading military historian who was a presence at Massey College, where I once was affiliated—observed the basic facts of the painting: Benjamin West (1738–1820) exhibited it at the Royal Academy in 1771; Lord Grosvenor purchased the picture and his descendant, the second duke of Westminster, presented it to Canada, through Lord Beaverbrook, as a tribute to what that "dominion" had accomplished in World War I; this is the picture that is in the National Gallery of Canada, Ottawa, and is reproduced on this cover; West painted three copies of the painting—one for King George III (in Kensington Palace, London), another for the Monckton family (in the Sigmund Samuel Collection, Toronto) and yet another for the Prince of Waldeck (in the William L. Clements Library at Ann Arbor, Michigan); there are, among the four versions, significant variations. It seems that painterly interpretations of the death of Wolfe, even by the same painter, multiplied as did historical explanations. George Romney (1734–1802) represented Wolfe in 1762—the painting is lost—and Edward Penny had depicted Wolfe at least twice, one of his works, that of 1763, being in the Ashmoleon Museum in Oxford. Penny's picture of the death of Wolfe is not as epic and mythological in sweep as West's and probably gestures more toward historical accuracy than this later version. In the *National Gallery of Canada Bulletin* (*Bulletin* 7 (IV:1), 1966), Stacey provides a provocative and brief summary about West's painting:

> It seems to me that the picture's fame is actually an integral part of that interesting phenomenon of British history, the Wolfe Legend. Historical fact has little to do with the public reputation of General Wolfe and the campaign of Quebec. From the moment when the first reports of the Battle of the Plains of Abraham reached England in October 1759, with all their almost incredibly romantic accompaniments—the descent of the dark river, the midnight climb; the deaths of the two commanders ... in the dramatic conflict before the walls of Quebec—the episode was thought of in romantic rather than in historical terms, and in the popular mind it is so thought of still. West's imposing picture, with its glimpses of a strange new western world, appeared 12 years after the battle, at a time when American questions were prominent; and it was engraved in the year of the Declaration of Independence. It evidently fell in with a popular romantic mood in England and has been part of the Wolfe story ever since, almost as if it were a contemporary document. It is historically absurd, but really not much more so than a good deal of the 'historical' Literature about the 1759 campaign. In the years after 1759 a brave young fighting soldier, who had had extraordinary difficulty in making up his mind about a campaign plan and was really not better than a second-rate commander, came to be popularly remembered as one of the great British generals. By a parallel and related process, a picture which was doubtful as art and entirely contemptible as history became "probably the most famous of all historical paintings."

The mythology of history is a potent force. In this painting implicit comparisons, absences and occlusions reside. The French and their descendents, for instance, would have looked on Wolfe in quite a different fashion. Natives would likely not see themselves as adjuncts contemplating the death of a conquering general. This painting is a partial synecdoche and metonymy for the alliances, tensions and conflicts between European powers and between Natives and Europeans and their "American" descendents. Montcalm—another subject that recurs about the time of the American War of Independence—is compared to Wolfe. Woollett's well-known engraving after West's "The Death of General Wolfe" affected Louis-Joseph Watteau's drawing, "The Death of Montcalm," engraved and published in Paris in 1783. Whereas West was born and lived in North America, Watteau (1731–98) had never been there and so he based his Native peoples on barbarians in ancient Roman reliefs. The nudes in the lower right corner and the figure with the tomahawk in Watteau's drawing are thus figures of fancy or the translation of empire, a kind of classicism crying out in the wilderness. Moreover, in a kind of false exoticism, Watteau added a palm tree to the final engraving. The French (those living in the Saint-Lawrence valley were later called Canadians then French Canadians then Québecois), might dispute the events and the mythology of the events at that fateful battle in Québec, but, through a translation of study and art, they had themselves "translated" Wolfe into Montcalm. The French general was a simulacrum or double of his British counterpart while displacing him. Watteau reinscribes and challenges Wolfe as the only mythological historical figure at that turning point at Québec. There are Christian as well as classical aspects to these images: West placed the figures around Wolfe as though they lamented the death of Christ (the notes in the website of the National Gallery of Canada make this point and give other information, some of which I have drawn on here).

The death of Wolfe is partly a displacement of a religious martyr—the son of God sacrificed for the sake of humanity—to a secular sacrifice (the son of empire who made a sacrifice for the imperial cause). The figures in the military dress of the British, Anglo-American (ranger) and Native concentrate their gaze and thoughts on this heroic figure. This is the birth of British power even as Britain is about to lose its most populous colonies in America, even though those colonies will become a world and then the world power in another translation of empire.

The deaths of Wolfe and Montcalm coincide with the ascent of British India—Clive is a missing double from this myth—and the curtailment of French power outside Europe until the American and French Revolutions and the rise of Napoleon. This book does not discuss the events of the Seven Years' War (1756–63) directly, but this conflict is the moment of eruption for empire, colony and nation in North America. My method in *Comparing*

Empires is to examine texts closely and to place them into contexts, bringing to bear the Iberian experience in the Atlantic basin and beyond on the English (British) and French in a period from the fifteenth to the twentieth century and later. Coming after Portugal in Africa and India and Spain in the New World, the explorers and writers in English and French had to translate these previous texts and events into intertexts. My study can be oblique in the textual and contextual moments it discusses, providing an attempt to suggest a larger textuality and context. William Blake's seeing the world through a grain of sand might be more akin to this textual shard and its refractions.

In trying to recognize a pattern of interpretation in this material, I had a good deal of help along the way. When I began the specific research in this area in 1991, I did not realize, even when I started to give talks and write drafts, that it would take the direction it did. The first paper on the topic was at Kirkland House, Harvard, and it was the Co-Masters, Donald and Cathleen Pfister, and Alfred and Sally Alcorn, who kindly got me moving from reading to the exchange of ideas, although Bernal Díaz and Hernán Cortés, the primary subjects of that talk, have migrated into the pages of my other books. My various projects about the New World, which Palgrave has been publishing in a series, have taken on unintended shapes. Work that came up later or grew out of earlier research ended up being finished or published first. As I have thanked many people in *Representing the New World* and *Columbus, Shakespeare and the Interpretation of the New World*, I will keep these thanks relatively brief here, not from ingratitude but to avoid being too repetitive. My thanks go to those I have mentioned in those two acknowledgements. Some repetition will be necessary here: my thanks to the President or Masters, Fellows, Students and Staff at Clare Hall, Cambridge; at Kirkland House, Harvard and Wilson College, Princeton; faculty and students at the Faculties of History and English at Cambridge; at the Departments of English and Comparative Literature at Harvard; at the Departments of History and Comparative Literature and the Committee of Canadian Studies at Princeton for being generous and marvellous hosts and colleagues. University of Alberta has been supportive of my research and has generously provided me with leaves. Fellowships from the Social Sciences and Humanities Research Council, the British Council, the Fulbright Commission, Camargo Foundation and Princeton University funded me for this and other projects. My thanks to the directors, trustees, academic committees and staff of those organizations, without whose support I would have had difficulty completing this and other research.

Thanks in particular to Dale Miller, whose friendship, generosity, skill, and commitment to Canadian Studies and interdisciplinary studies, gave me time and wonderful circumstances to complete books in this series.

My gratitude also to Maria Luísa Leal and Maria Alzira Seixo for giving me a pretext to write chapter 2; to Anthony Pagden for his encouragement generally and in relation to chapter 3; to Peter Burke, Mark Kaplanoff and Nicholas Canny for their advice on this and related research. My particular gratitude to Anne Barton, Philip Ford, Kenneth Mills, Anthony Pagden, Gordon Teskey and Michael Worton for their kindness and support. Others deserve general thanks: Jeremy Adelman, Diane Barrios, Sandra Bermann, Jean Bessière, Peter Buse, Homi Bhabha, E. D. Blodgett, Miguel Centeno, Ross Chambers, Caroline Clancy, Patricia Demers, Olive Dickason, Jacques Dion, Robert Duplessis, Katy Emck, G. Blakemore Evans, Karen Fenton, Stephen Ferguson, Norman Fiering, Orlando Figes, Philip Ford, Marjorie Garber, Anthony Grafton, Judith Hanson, Shelagh Heffernan, Allan and Laura Hoyano, Peter Hulme, Barbara Johnson, Michèle Lamont, Hao Li, Rod Macleod, Julian Martin, Eric Marty, Steven Mobbs, François Moreau, Philip Nord, Kenneth Norrie, Douglas Owram, Stephanie Palmer, Donald and Cathleen Pfister, Ben Primer, Meg Sherry Rich, Peter Sinclair, Don Skemer, Nigel Smith, Marcia Snowden, Magali Sperling, Rod and Gilly Stratford, Pauline Thomas, Robert Tignor, Ming Xie, Robert Zaretsky, Jan Ziolkowski.

Thanks also to my hosts at Harvard, Oxford, Southampton, Hull, British Columbia, Samyung [Korea], Nanjing Normal, Hong Kong, Montpellier III, Cambridge, Deakin, Melbourne, Madeira, Salford and elsewhere since 1991 who heard me give various papers in the field and provided me with stimulating suggestions and questions. More thanks to the librarians, curators and archivists at Widener, Houghton and the other libraries at Harvard, the John Carter Brown, the Firestone, University archives and Mudd (Princeton), the Rutherford and Special Collections (Alberta), Robarts and Thomas Fischer (Toronto), the Baldwin Room (Metropolitan Toronto), the Royal Ontario Museum (Toronto), Museum London (Ontario), the Glenbow Museum (Calgary), the Provincial Museum of Alberta (Edmonton), the National Gallery (London), the Fitzwilliam Museum and the University Library (Cambridge), the Bodleian (Oxford), the British Library, the Bibliothèque Nationale (Paris), the Archive National in Paris, the Archive d'Outre Mer (Aix), the Bermuda Archives (Hamilton) and too many museums, libraries and galleries to note here in full. Thanks to the editors who encouraged earlier versions of some of the research that appears here (and which are acknowledged in the notes). Thanks also to the National Gallery of Canada for permission to reproduce Benjamin West's "The Death of General Wolfe" for the cover of the hardcover edition.

A particular thanks to Irene Sywenky for help with this and other projects. The encouragement and support from my editors at Palgrave, Kristi Long and Roee Raz, have been exemplary. Ian Steinberg, Mukesh V.S. and their colleagues in design and production have made the publication of this book even more of a pleasure. Palgrave Macmillan has made a big difference to my research and writing.

Many thanks to friends, family and my parents, George and Jean, and my wife, Mary, and our children, James and Julia. I dedicate this book with thanks to Charles, Gwendolyn, Deborah, Alan and Jennifer, many of whom were there before I knew speech or signs let alone that there was a New World and that it might be represented or that there were empires and that these could be compared. That the topic still has approaches, angles and horizons still unexpected and unexplored makes it all the more worth pursuing.

Chapter 1 ∼

Introduction

Comparing empires is an ongoing attempt to put into context a specific group of nations who expanded into countries with trading posts and colonies overseas. In approaching the expansion of western European nations beyond Europe, I am going back into an explanation of the title and reverse its terms by discussing "empire" before "comparing." The cultural connotations of the word "empire" and the related terms "imperialism" and "imperial" have probably always been laden with semantic intricacies and led to emotional responses depending on which side of the divide of power a person or culture inhabited. That there would be contradictory and ambivalent situations, responses and representations within Europeans and their states and within the people and peoples they encountered is something that complicates the idea of empire. The textual messiness—the descriptions, opinions, proclamations, asides and other forms of verbal record and report—makes difficult any single notion of imperial expansion. By comparing cultures in these empires and by comparing empires, some of the complexity of these expanding nations and the places and peoples they came into contact with begins to arise. Comparison can be useful in decentering national pride and shame while not taking away what each nation and culture has said and done. What seems like an accomplishment to one person, nation, generation might come to appear like an embarrassment to the next. In moving through comparisons of these empires from before the divide of about 1500 to empires still unwinding in our lifetimes and still with us, from Portugal, the begetter, to the United States, the inheritor, for better or worse, this study, by selecting a few key themes and moments, will attempt to take the measure of the ambivalence and shifts in empire. This comparing of empires is existential since our present encounters the past as an estrangement as well as itself through the past. Triumph and shame, accusation and imitation, principle and violence all coexist in the voices and events that appear in this study. "Coming after" a rival empire is, at the level of statehood, a little like coming after Columbus for the Europeans who explored the western Atlantic—they follow and they seek to displace. Empire, once a source of pride in the official ideology, is now reviled often as it is unpopular. These empires brought much good and ill, but while much of the ill was too often swept aside or rationalized, sometimes the denial of any good blinds us to the contradiction and ambivalence of culture and of the meetings of cultures during this age of imperial expansion. Rather than get involved in the rating of empires and pointing out what is good or ill in them, I have presented some of the vast messiness of the textual record. Many of the texts, particularly as they relate to occurrences away from Europe on sea and land, are up close and in the daily habitation of culture.

The term "empire" is used specifically here to mean those western European nations who, beginning with Portugal, began in the fourteenth and fifteenth centuries to expand offshore and later overseas. These European powers might have had affinities with other "empires" in Europe and elsewhere, but this is the particular sense in which the book is using the word and its cognates, except as it relates to *translatio imperii* or the translation of empire. This translating is literal, in the translation of study and particular texts, especially from the empires of the Greeks and Romans, and figurative, as in a carrying over, a making of ideological and mythological connections or affinities with the classical past and imperial culture and history. The colonial in the Middle Ages and Renaissance (or early modern period) was already postcolonial and it might well be that Greece and Rome were already colonies themselves before they became empires. Perhaps there is a regression beyond records of such a pattern of settlement and expansion. That is why it is important here to emphasize that the empires in question in this study are western European and seaborne and expand in succession from before Columbus to the twentieth century. The United States, more like Russia, became principally a country whose expansion was continental, although the Spanish-American War of 1898, where the book ends, resulted in gaining territories largely through naval power. This great colony became imperial with a difference. Between Portugal and the United States, Spain, England (Britain), France and the Netherlands fill out the principal matter of this comparison of empires.

Even though this study is using empire in a particular way under specific circumstances, which provides focus, there have been many studies of empire in various periods of history.[1] In the middle of this study, perhaps so much in relation to other empires that its ghostly presence alone is felt, is the British Empire. In writing about this empire, T. O. Lloyd noted the shift between empires before and after 1500:

> Loyalty and thrift were the principles that shaped the British Empire, and, now that they survive as private virtues rather than as forces to shape public

policy, the British Empire has passed from the scene. Until quite recently loyalty to an often distant monarch, rather than a geographical or linguistic devotion to a nation, was the force that held states together. Great empires could expand over vast distances and encounter no long-lasting resistance at anything more than a tribal level. Patriotic resistance would now make such expansion far more difficult than in the past, and can dissolve away all but the most ruthless of empires.

Until 1500 the empires created in this way were confined to single masses of land, and could only be continent-wide. About 500 years ago empires began to spread across oceans and became world-wide. Although the British Empire came closer than any other empire to establishing itself in every region of the globe, there were clearly occasions at which it might have expanded more vigorously. The restraint on expansion was the pressure of thrift.[2]

The role of the ships, sea and navy cannot be underestimated before the advent of air transport and air forces.[3] This seafaring began in earnest a movement to a global trade and culture. The last two decades of the fifteenth century and the first two decades of the sixteenth were pivotal in this sea change. The western Europeans were translated and their own cultures as well as those with which they came into contact were in time transformed utterly.

Although the translation of empire began before the Romans and it would be unwise not to mention the Greeks in this context, for the purposes of this study, it is best to begin with Rome and the Romans, the empire western Europeans looked back to the most and used as a measure of their own empires. The word "*imperium*," or empire, entered documents following the rise of Roman power in the Mediterranean as were conventional phrases like "*imperium orbis terrae*" (empire of the world), "*imperium populi Romani*" (the empire of the Roman people), "*nostrum imperium*" (our empire), "*vestrum imperium*" (your empire) and "*hoc imperium*" (this empire).[4] The expression *imperium populi Romani*, as Richard Koebner observed, was "not merely rhetorical. It defined the authority in the name of which Roman magistrates wielded power abroad. But like the other expressions it had a triumphant ring. Such a phrase could be emphatically enlarged: 'imperium orbis terrae, cui omnes gentes, reges, nationes partim vi, partim voluntate, concesserunt.' But a succinct reference to 'this empire' could suffice to impress an audience—as young Cicero knew when defending the countryman."[5] The enlargement of the phrase expressed an expanded power: "the empire of the world, to which all nations, kings, tribes—some under duress, some of their own will—have yielded." This Roman dominion went through different phases and served as a model for subsequent empires in eastern, central and western Europe. Before the period that this study examines, there were shifts in empire that also served as examples for the British,

French, Austrian, Russian and German empires: "The modern concept of Empire unfailingly recalls the Roman Empires of the past: the *Imperium populi Romani* of the Republic, the *Imperium Romanum* governed by the Emperor Augustus and his successors, the Holy Roman Empire which was vested in Charlemagne and later on in the kings elected by German princes."[6] The meaning of empire has specific contexts depending on the actual state in question, but some shared the qualities it had in Rome. The term *imperium* gathered meanings in new political contexts in Rome as Koebner has noted: "The original Latin conveyed the general meanings of command and power. It specifically denoted the legal power of command. Its purport was extended to include territories and populations subject to a dominant power. These meanings could be predicated by the word with regard to peoples outside as well as inside the orbit of Roman law and order."[7] On the Iberian Peninsula some of the rulers also took up titles that looked back at Rome. For instance, the kings of Leon insisted on the title of emperors and this claim was intensified when, after 1033, this territory was often united with Castile, a larger kingdom. In the opposition to Muslims, Alphonso VI, hoping for allegiance from small Christian principalities, called himself the "emperor of all Spain" in 1077 and in 1085, after his great triumph, assumed titles such as "Toletanus imperator" and "Toletani imperii magnificus triumphator," suggesting, as Koebner has remarked, that the *imperium* in Spain at that time was more about aggrandizing the person of the king and not that of the enduring realm as in the dominions of the king-emperor in Germany.[8] The Romans had eternal Rome but they also had the great *imperator*, so both these aspects of empire were in conflict early on. The extent of Spanish and Portuguese power, particularly after 1500, would give these kingdoms more leverage to be recognized as empires whether in name or in fact. These two nations, intertwined culturally, economically and dynastically, became two empires in one breast, and explicitly so, although not always fruitfully or peacefully, between 1580 and 1640. These were comparative empires from the start of their expansion against the Moors and their exploration and trade beyond their shores. Portugal and Spain also became the "empires" that other kingdoms would emulate, criticize and seek to displace, sometimes at once, as understood through the accounts that their subjects left along the way.

This study is comparative because it is based on the assumption that, although there have been philosophical discussions about the problems of analogy well before Thomas Aquinas, the urge to compare does yield some suggestive results.[9] Comparative studies in literature, law, ethnology (anthropology), politics, history and other disciplines have been addressed in formal studies for many years. Discussions of comparative literature, for instance, occur in the late nineteenth century and beyond, so this comparative study in culture—which includes examinations of law, literature and history—is a part of a long line of research. Much more needs to be done in comparative studies, but its context was established long ago. The specific use here of "comparing" is a continuing process to which this study contributes. Comparisons, like other kinds of writing, require a selection and order, and with so much ground to cover, over a period of 500 years and more, the choice of topics to compare has to be highly selective. This study could not address this extensive material in any other way. The basis for the shape of this book lies in key moments and themes from many topics rather than a continuous narrative on an array of subjects, balanced in a continuous fashion. The study begins with Portugal, which led the way, and moves in and out of rivals such as Spain, England, France and the Netherlands over the course of many centuries. While providing contexts, the book focuses most on texts that illustrate or embody important aspects of empire, particularly works that say more about one empire. Throughout the volume, the Iberian powers play a central role: they were the first in such an imperial project and were examples, often ambivalent ones, for the countries to their north. England, France, the Netherlands and also the United States played catch-up with Portugal and Spain and even came to prey on the overseas trade possessions of these empires, including their remnants late in their history.

A major rationale for this study is to follow the first great expansion of the western European empires and, while concentrating most on the New World, to place the colonization of the western Atlantic in the wider context of the Atlantic world, including Africa, and the connection with Asia through the Pacific and the Indian Oceans. This extension of context leads beyond my earlier studies, of which this is the third.[10] Affinities and differences in a context define national cultures, literatures, laws and histories more clearly.

Returning to the idea of comparative studies, it is significant that the importance of this method and mode of thought was revisited in the rise of disciplines in the nineteenth century, especially within the universities, and in response to developments in science. For instance, in Dublin, before setting out for New Zealand, Hutcheson Macaulay Posnett, trained as a barrister and as a professor of Classics and English, could in his study of comparative literature in 1886 observe the ancient roots of this methodology: "The comparative method of acquiring or communicating knowledge is in one sense as old as thought itself, in another the peculiar glory of our nineteenth century. All reason, all imagination, operate subjectively, and pass from man to man objectively, by aid of comparisons and differences. The most colourless proposition of the logician is either the assertion of a comparison, A is B, or the denial of a comparison, A is not B."[11] Posnett reminded the reader of how students of Greek thought will remember how mistakes about the nature of the copula produced misleading and confusing "essences" much to the detriment of ancient and modern philosophy. The arts and sciences depend on comparison: "But not only the colourless propositions of logic, even the highest and most brilliant flights of oratorical eloquence or poetic fancy are sustained by this rudimentary structure of comparison and difference, this primary scaffolding, as we may call it, of human thought. If sober experience works out scientific truths in propositions affirming or denying comparison, imagination even in the richest colours works under the same elementary forms."[12] Difference, which Plato, Heidegger, Derrida, De Man all discussed in different forms, is intertwined with likeness through comparison.[13] Another apt point that Posnett made was part of an appreciation of Demogeot's *Histoire des Littératures étrangères* (Paris, 1880)—"each national literature is a centre towards which not only national but also international forces gravitate."[14] This observation is true of any comparative study, that is, a comparative historical approach to the western European empires should shed as much light on each nation as on their international relations. Cultures define themselves but also other cultures.

Although comparative studies are not without disagreements over their definition or object of study, they are able to bring to the table something different from national studies, which have their own important contributions to make. Three reports of the American Comparative Literature Association—the first chaired by Harry Levin in 1965, the second by Thomas Greene in 1975 and the third by Charles Bernheimer in 1993—showed the shift in this one comparative discipline. The third report questioned the traditional standards of the first two reports and widened this field of comparison to television, media, hypertext and other technological representations. The chair, Bernheimer, in an introduction to a volume that grew out of this third report and the response to it, provides as a subtitle for his essay, "The Anxieties of Comparison."[15]

Comparative methods may be viewed with skepticism by those who concentrate on one nation or one field of study alone. For instance, comparative law also faced this resistance, even though it developed in the nineteenth century, when Anselm Feuerbach and others argued for its importance to the legal philosopher, following which chairs of comparative law were set up at the Collège de France in 1832 and at l'Université de Paris in 1846. In Leibnitz's *Nova Methodus discendae docendaeque Jurisprudentiae* (1667), which included an unfulfilled plan for a survey of the laws of various countries, H. C. Gutteridge saw the impetus to the work that was in contradistinction to Grotius's law of nations based on the law of nature that played down or belittled the differences in laws among particular countries, as the foundation of comparative law—Montesquieu's *De l'Esprit des Lois*. However it took a long time for others to follow up his attempt at "a detailed and scientific inquiry into the laws of the world."[16] Despite the study of comparative law for generations, Gutteridge noted a misunderstanding of its nature: "Much of the atmosphere of doubt and suspicion which envelops comparative legal study and has proved, in the past, to be so hostile to its development, would disappear if it were generally recognised that the phrase 'Comparative Law' denotes a method of study and research and not a distinct branch or department of the law."[17] Comparisons could be viewed as a threat to the integrity, originality and importance of a national tradition. Like Posnett, Jerome Hall viewed comparison as going back a long time, but he took it even further—it was "as old as our most primitive ancestors." Further, when discussing theories of comparative law, he asserted that the comparative method was "a nineteenth-century phenomenon—the direct result of the revolutionary progress of philology and biology."[18] The scientific study of the law is a recurrent theme of comparative law into the 1960s. Although this view sees an intensification in the development of the study of comparative law during the nineteenth century, it is also possible for the same scholars to debate about earlier origins, such as Aristotle's Constitution of Athens and the work of Jean Bodin (1530–96) in addition to that of Leibnitz and Montesquieu.[19] What comparative law is and its origins are not matters of consensus.

Comparative studies in the social sciences, such as politics and anthropology, have also created debates within and between those disciplines. Some of these themes and searches for origins also occur in studies of comparative politics. An American textbook in this field during the 1990s began with a quotation from Alexis de Toqueville—"Without comparisons to make, the mind does not know how to proceed"—and it also traces the beginnings of the subject in Aristotle's *Politics,* in which he contrasted the economic and social structures of various Greek city-states to learn about their affect on the political, and defended the comparative method: "Comparing the past and present of our nation and comparing our experience with that of other nations deepen our perspective on our institutions."[20] As in comparative literature and comparative law, comparative politics contained its own strong disagreements over its own nature and the changes within. With the changes of the 1960s, some proclaimed a new comparative politics focused more on non-Western countries and less on traditional law and history.[21]

In comparative anthropology there has also been friction between those studying development in the "Third World" and those focused on the scientific and comparative method.[22] J. D. Y. Peel recognized, as Hall did in his qualification of Gutteridge's view of comparative law as a method and not as a distinct discipline or field, that "At the most general level, comparison is not a special method, or in any way unique to anthropology. Comparison is implicit in any method of deriving understanding through *explanation.*"[23]

Like Posnett, Peel sees the comparison in terms of logic, in this case John Stuart Mill's "Method of Difference," in his *System of Logic* (1843) and interprets this even in terms of textual criticism and history—the methods I use most in this book—which are explanatory even when they are not theoretical, for "All explanations lie open to the challenge of comparison: there is no field of empirical enquiry which does not use comparative analysis."[24] Peel's interpretation of comparison is suggestive partly because it sees the theoretical in close reading and apparently practical criticism as well as the facts and details of history and partly because it places history at the base of culture, which is the main concern of anthropology. He concludes, "What our comparison most importantly teaches is that culture is less a reflexion of society, than a reflexion on history."[25] Another central concern for anthropology is translation, which Mark Hobart sees in relation to comparison: cultures compare themselves to other cultures and translate themselves as they translate others.[26] Ladislav Holy makes a point that is true about many comparative disciplines in the past generation: "with the paradigmatic shift in anthropology, both the objectives and techniques of comparison have diversified to such an extent that there is no longer a 'comparative method' in anthr[o]pology; it has been replaced by varying styles of comparison."[27] The history of anthropology is related to the construction of national, imperial and colonial identity. Anthropologists, as Michael Herzfeld has noted, have been coming to terms with this history and have been developing an ironic awareness of that past and their own social and cultural assumptions, so that, at a time when the end of anthropology has been proclaimed, it can contribute because "there is great value in the destabilization of received ideas both through the inspection of cultural alternatives and through the exposure of the weaknesses that seem to inhere in all our attempts to analyze various cultural worlds including own."[28] Using its own comparisons, anthropology can, as Asad has suggested, break up the narrative of domination and resistance, expansion and reaction, but he asserts that response and resistance to colonialism can be seen in terms of new forms of work, power and knowledge.[29]

The method in this book mixes themes and moments, which seeks out thick descriptions in texts, or even fragments that gesture a greater narrative, sometimes unspoken, beyond themselves. Whereas I have warned of the vulnerabilities of anecdote and analogy, a critique some anthropologists have been subject to and have had to contend with, I have also practiced interpretation in such a way as to make use of these two comparative methods, in which microhistory, anthropology and literature meet, for these story-fragments and likenesses perform disenchantment or what Bertolt Brecht termed an alienation or estrangement effect.[30] This epistemological unsettling helps to enact the means through which cultures try to understand each other through translation and interpretation, skeptical of their own abilities to know the other culture and their own. Through texts, some well known and others not, some literary and others not, some fractured narratives, examples or arguments and others more fully worked out, this study will interpret these interpreters, some away from Europe and others at home reflecting on those who had traveled, and will, recognizing the dangers of ventriloquy, represent these voices as much as possible in their own voice. This process should present some surprises, some unsettling, for those in the past and for this writer and for readers in the present. The story is never quite as we imagine it. The past has a strangeness that can make us strangers to ourselves. Such a bringing together of moments and themes, of how Europeans interacted with each other and with the peoples they encountered, should lead to some unrecognizable recognitions, not all of them comfortable. History and culture are connected in the translation of empire, and in comparing these empires some issues come up quite unexpectedly.

The study opens with a focus on the Iberian powers and the texts they produced in their voyages out of Europe and how they were imitated, opposed and refracted in the works of the French, English and Dutch, all of whom provided examples, negative and positive for the United States. Although this study has a generally chronological movement both in the book and its constituent parts, it also deviates from a rigid chronology. The by-ways and loose ends suggest the roads and sea-lanes not taken and the voices and stories that could not possibly enter a single book.

"After Portugal," chapter 2, begins with Portuguese expansion beyond its peninsular boundaries during the late fourteenth century, which took hold in the second decade of the fifteenth century, and also considers the rivalry between Portugal and Spain during this period and beyond, for instance, in the rediscovery of the Canary Islands. History had bound different parts of the Iberian Peninsula. Only in 1143, when Portugal was placed under the protection of the Holy See in return for annual tribute, did the dependence of Portugal on León begin to wane: in 1179 the Holy See formally recognized Portugal in royal terms. Even after this parting the Spanish and Portuguese provinces were intertwined. From the 1490s Spain would set the pace in the New World, but Portugal pushed forward the early expansion of Europe beyond its limits. Africa, India and East Asia were destinations for the Portuguese. A discussion of Pedro Álvares Cabral arises because his voyage included a journey to the New World, Africa and Asia: chapter 2 includes an account of texts surrounding this voyage, including that by the writer for the fleet, Pedro Vaz de Caminha. There is a view of the Tupinamba in Brazil that goes well with the later account of the French Calvinist, Jean de Léry, who is discussed later in the chapter because Brazil allows for a comparative discussion as well as one of the places in the Portuguese voyages that became connected to Africa and Asia through trade. The examination includes another text, an anonymous narrative of the voyage from Lisbon to Calicut, which was said to have been translated from Portuguese into the Venetian dialect: four manuscripts still exist in differing versions.[31] This is one of a few Italian texts that give various perspectives on Cabral's voyage and thus supplement Caminha's narrative. The Venetians monitored Portuguese voyages because they constituted a challenge to Venice's control of European trade with Asia. Florence, like Venice, had interests in Lisbon and what the Portuguese crown was doing. In 1500, there were in Lisbon more Florentines than any other Italians. Portugal had old dynastic and political connections with France and England, which later became rivals in extra-European expansion. Just as Léry took an interest in the Portuguese, so too did Richard Hakluyt the younger when compiling his collection of travel narratives, especially in *Principall Navigations*. He includes a translation of a Portuguese account for English purposes, to inspire the English to claim land in North America for their empire and to oppose the papal division of the New World into Spanish and Portuguese spheres. The Dutch, who achieved independence from Spain in the seventeenth century, had gained from attacking Portugal, which was, from 1580 to 1640, united with Spain under the Spanish crown. To attack Portugal was to attack Spain. The Dutch were able to insinuate themselves in Portuguese trading posts and strongholds in Africa, India and Asia. They, and later the English, would become the successors to the Portuguese empire. During the Commonwealth and after the Restoration, particularly owing to the alliance through marriage of the crowns of Portugal and England, Richard Fanshawe—an English diplomat on the Iberian Peninsula, whose translation of 1655 of Luís de Camões's epic poem, which was published in 1672—called attention to Portugal. The translation of the poem came about the time of Cromwell's Western Design, his attempt to take colonies from the Spanish in the West Indies, and the publication during the period in which England and Portugal had experienced closer relations. This Portuguese epic was an example of expansion to the English. Even though Hakluyt had made use of English translations of Portuguese writings, Fanshawe became the means by which England was introduced to a literary representation of a turning point in the Portuguese empire. The Dutch became a great challenge to this first great overseas empire, whose history is sometimes occluded because of the lapsed memory of those who came after Portugal.

This book will interlace interpretations and representations of Portugal and Spain, so that the only difference at the end of the book is that their place is reversed: the volume begins and ends with Portugal in different contexts. Chapter 3, "Spain, France and England," amplifies the ghost of this great empire in the works on European expansion overseas. Spain in the New World continued to preoccupy those among their rivals who wrote after the turn of the seventeenth century. When permanent settlements in northern America seemed to be taking hold, the English represented the Spaniards and Natives together. In a translation in 1612 of Peter Martyr's *De nouo orbe*, for example, Michael Lok [Locke] made additions to Richard Eden's translation decades before on the "discovery" of the New World.[32] William Bradford's account of Plymouth Plantation included some representations of Spain, something not emphasized in British and American myths and history of this key moment of colony, nation and empire. Among the French, an example of a work that discusses rivals, more the English than the Spanish, is Gabriel Sagard's *Histoire dv Canada et voyages qve les freres mineurs Recollets y ont faicts pour la conuersion des Infidelles* (1636). In the years just before and after 1600, the English and French, not to mention the Dutch and the Portuguese, all contended in trade and war in the New World. Chapter 3 will discuss texts that represent the pursuit of riches or converts in the Amazon basin, Canada, the Caribbean and elsewhere. During the eighteenth century, the rivalries continued: for instance, some writings suggest that the English still seemed to relish having Spain as an enemy as in the War of Jenkins's Ear (1739–48). In the wake of Spain other rivalries developed, but, as chapter 3 will suggest, the staying power of Spain as a source of fascination and vilification, sometimes at once, well into the eighteenth century is remarkable. Four decades after the independence of the United States, American statesmen responded in different ways to the dissolution of the Spanish empire: for instance, Jefferson worried that one great state might emerge from the Spanish colonies.[33] The presence of Spain in the Americas haunted the western Atlantic long after the wars of independence in the early nineteenth century and after the Spanish-American War of 1898.

"From Portugal to the United States," the fourth and final chapter, will provide some other important contexts, a reason for giving a wider context for the exploration of the New World. The body of this book begins with Portugal and gives Portugal's earlier experience in exploration and trade in the Atlantic and Africa. Although other Europeans could be preoccupied with Spain and its strength in the New World, they could also represent the role of the Portuguese in the seaborne expansion of European trade and colonies. Portugal helped to set the stage. Like the Netherlands, Portugal was a relatively small country with a small population and so its power can be forgotten later. Chapter 4 will serve as a reminder that in the translation of empire and comparison of empires, these key states and their colonies should be considered and represented. The interpretive journey from Portugal to the United States will include an analysis of some British, Dutch and French texts and contexts, leaving Spain aside until a brief discussion of the Spanish-American War at the end of the book. This end of Spanish empire in the Americas and beyond occurred just over 500 years after Columbus's landfall amid the very islands Spain yielded in this war with the United States. Among the texts that will be examined are those by Alvise Cadamosto, Andrew Marvell, Domingo Navarrete and François Valentijn, works that encompass the geography of empire over time and do not rest with Europe or the New World. In comparing empires the Americas need to be viewed in a wider context.

The moments and themes of empire may be spots of time to be visited and revisited. There is no definitive view of this western European expansion. The texts themselves, being such a wide array, like the images produced of lands long unknown to Europeans, bring together various confluences of peoples and cultures. Allusions, stories, opinions, addresses, public pleas all form fragments of the ruin of empire and the construction of new cultures and polities. These are voices overheard, but author and reader, then and now, are part of the history and story. It may be that the interpretation of culture is about history. Rather than comparing the winter of discontent to a summer's day or a hawk to a handsaw, we embody the history that seems so distant from us, each coming together to talk about the angles of refraction or the shifting metaphors and tropes we discover along the way. There are differences in what each of us considers to be comparative and our perceptions of empire, but there is enough common ground for each attempt to uncover and recognize lost, forgotten or unheard voices or familiar documents and accounts placed juxtaposed in a new context. The past reads the present. Portugal reads the United States. But first to Portugal, so crucial to an understanding of western European colonization, and sometimes occluded in the West because its time has passed. The events in Angola during the 1970s and the handing over of Macao in 1999 are histories for another time, but they, too, are part of what follows. The Iberian powers set the stage for European overseas empires, so that France, the Netherlands, England (later Britain) and the United States understood the importance of ships and navies in trade and expansion. What follows is about the meeting and representation of cultures, how people make comparisons in a new framework set out sometimes in old terms. It is the surprises to them and us that mean the most. Cultures and histories throw curves.

Chapter 2 ～

Portugal and After

Portuguese expansion beyond its peninsular boundaries began during the late fourteenth century and took hold in the second decade of the fifteenth century. During the fourteenth and fifteenth centuries, Portugal and Spain were rivals in expansion. The rediscovery of the Canary Islands led to a conflict between Portugal and Castile. Clement VI's bull of 1344 gave Don Luis de la Cerda, great-grandson of Afonso the Wise and admiral of France, the authority to Christianize the islands, but when he failed to take possession, Portugal and Castile, which had supported his claim, continued their disagreement. Later bulls of donation alternately favored the two sides: not until 1479—when, by the treaty of Alcaçovas, Portugal ceded the Canaries to Castile—was the question of ownership settled.[1] Africa was the ground for the second controversy between Portugal and Castile. After the conquest of Ceuta in 1415, Portugal carried out military expeditions in Morocco and voyages to Guinea, thereby making its claim in Africa. In 1434 Gil Eanes helped to lead the way to upper Niger, Guinea and Senegal. There, in the 1440s and 1450s, slaves and gold made for a lucrative trade. In Africa, as in the Canaries, the kings of Castile based their claim to conquest on its possession by their ancestors, the Visigoths, and, by 1454, the two countries were embroiled in this African controversy. Nicholas V issued the bull *Romanus pontifex* on January 8, 1455, giving exclusive rights to King Afonso of Portugal in this African exploration and trade thus extending the bull *Dum diversas* (June 18, 1452), in which Nicholas had given Afonso the right to conquer pagans, enslave them and take their lands and goods. In the bull *Rex regum* (January 5, 1443) Eugenius IV, Nicholas's predecessor, had taken a neutral stance between Castile and Portugal regarding Africa. The Castilians would not accept the authority of the papal letters and continued to claim Guinea until 1479, when, after the War of Succession (in which Afonso invaded Castile in an attempt to annex it), Portugal ceded the Canaries and Castile acknowledged

Portugal's claim to Guinea, the Azores, Madeira and the Cape Verde Islands.[2] The bulls of donation, or papal bulls, were not permanent laws: the parties involved in the disputes did not always accept them as remedies. Portugal and Spain would, however, insist—from the late fifteenth century onwards—that other nations, like France and England, abide by the papal bulls dividing the "undiscovered" world between the Iberian powers. In the Atlantic, during the 1480s and 1490s, the Bristolians may have sought "Brasil" and the Portuguese and Flemings in the Azores might have searched out "Antilia."[3] The desire to seek new and mythical lands was well entrenched amongst various European states before Columbus's proposals and the enterprise of the Indies. From 1435 to 1486, the Portuguese pushed across the Tropic of Cancer past the Equator to the Congo River. In 1488 Bartolomeu Dias rounded the Cape of Good Hope into the Indian Ocean. An undertow of reluctance comprised an aspect of the attitudes of each of the European powers to overseas voyages.

The Portuguese court showed some caution about expansion: it had turned down Toscanelli's proposal for a westward voyage in 1474 and dismissed Columbus ten years later. Christopher Columbus, a Genoese, was in Portugal from 1476 to 1484 where he learned navigation as well as Spanish and Portuguese. He seems to have written principally in Spanish, which he wrote and spoke with a mixture of Portuguese, as well as commercial Latin, which was then used widely in the Atlantic and Mediterranean worlds.[4] Columbus can be seen as someone who was trained as a Portuguese navigator who came to have Portuguese family connections but who, like some other Portuguese mariners, sought out opportunities in Castile when none was forthcoming in Portugal. Shipwrecked in May 1476 while en route to England, Columbus swam ashore to Lagos and then went to Lisbon to see his brother Bartolomeu. In about 1479 or 1480 Columbus, who was well connected with Italian merchants inside and outside Portugal, married Felipa Perestrelo e Monis, daughter of Bartolomeu Perestrelo, an Italian noble and captain of Porto Santo; her maternal grandfather was Gil Aires Monis of Algarve, who had fought at Ceuta. In 1482 Columbus accompanied Diogo de Azambuja on a voyage to the Guinea coast of Africa. Apparently, he was given access to his father-in-law's notes and charts. Columbus had made much of the letter written by Paolo dal Pozzo Toscanelli on June 24, 1474, to Fernão Martins, councillor of King Afonso V of Portugal, but the Portuguese had little faith in Toscanelli's theory that placed Asia closer to the west of Europe than it actually was. In 1483 or 1484 Columbus petitioned João II to finance a western voyage, but he was turned down. It may be that the Portuguese later licked their wounds as the English did considering their lost opportunities once Columbus had returned from the "new-found" lands of the western Atlantic. One Portuguese historian writing in the 1550s—João de Barros—argued that the king considered Columbus to be loquacious and vain (*glorioso*) and that all considered his words to be nonsensical.[5] In Spain a royal council rejected Columbus's petition, so he sought an audience with Ferdinand and Isabella, to whom he was connected through his Portuguese wife.[6] Returning from the first voyage to the western Atlantic, Columbus had to stop in the Azores because of a storm and some of his crew were detained briefly before they were permitted to continue. Columbus reached Lisbon on March 4, 1493, and, despite João II's concern over whether Columbus had been in lands in the Portuguese sphere, the king clothed him and his crew, refitted his ship and let him proceed to Spain and, as Bailie Diffie has noted, this voyage freed Castile from the thin strip of Atlantic coast set out in the Treaty of Alcáçovas.[7] João II ordered that a fleet prepared under the command of Francisco de Almeida seek the lands to which Columbus had sailed. Castile protested this, and Portugal and Spain negotiated and later signed the Treaty of Tordesillas.[8] Columbus, then, trained as a navigator in Portugal but having sailed for Spain to the New World, changed the relations between his two adopted countries. There is, therefore, a Portuguese dimension to Columbus's career. Having contributed a great deal to Columbus's formation, it must have been even more frustrating for the Portuguese than it was for the English, who also wrote that Columbus had considered sailing for them on that first westward voyage, that he altered the lot of Spain and helped to launch it on the way to being the dominant European power and empire in the sixteenth century.

The Atlantic voyages were not as pressing for the Portuguese as the push around Africa to Asia. Although from the 1490s Spain would set the pace in the New World, Portugal was key in the expansion of Europe beyond its bounds. Portuguese landfalls in the Atlantic occurred, before Columbus, in the uninhabited islands of Madeira in about 1419, the Azores in about 1427 and the Cape Verdes in about 1456. In 1497 Vasco da Gama sailed to the Cape Verdes and then sailed to South Africa before proceeding around the Cape of Good Hope and up the coast of East Africa. Although Pedro Álvares Cabral landed in Brazil in 1500, his achievement was, as A. J. R. Russell-Wood has suggested, secondary to the move to consolidate Portuguese presence in India in the first quarter of the sixteenth century.[9] A landfall occurred in St. Helena and Ascension in about 1501. During the early years of the 1500s, the Portuguese may have explored Greenland, Newfoundland and Labrador, and they tried to settle Cape Breton in the 1520s and the rest of Nova Scotia by mid-century.[10] Portugal was well positioned to take advantage of the extension by Columbus, who had sailed for Portugal, of their westward expansion.

Papal rulings were the legal justification for the exploration and settlement of the New World. For instance, the bull *Romanus pontifex* had given the Portuguese the right to reduce the infidels to slavery, so that the inhabitants of these new lands—"so unknown to us westerners that we had no certain knowledge of the peoples of those parts"—had no rights because they were not Christian.[11] The Natives of the New World were considered barbarous and not infidels, so that their potential for conversion saved them, at least theoretically, from slavery. After Columbus's landfall in the New World, the papacy continued to play a role in legitimizing exploration. The gift of the pope, set out in the Bull of May 4, 1493, responded to Columbus's first voyage to the New World: it divided the parts of the world yet unknown to Christians into two spheres, one for Spain and the other for Portugal. The pope, who had Iberian connections, issued a direct threat to those who might not accept his donation "under the penalty of excommunication."[12]

A threat of this type against other Christian princes breaking the exclusive rights of the parties named in the donations occurred in earlier bulls, like *Romanus pontifex*. Although the Portuguese and the Spanish accepted the terms of this bull, they shifted the line of demarcation from 100 leagues to 370 leagues west of the Cape Verde Islands in the Treaty of Tordesillas in 1494. Even though Portugal and Spain claimed the spheres of ownership that the pope had set out, they gave each other rights of passage across each other's territory. Both countries confirmed these terms, including the changes to the bull *Inter caetera* in the Treaty of Madrid in 1495. Issued after Vasco da Gama had rounded the Cape of Good Hope, the bull *Ea quae* of 1506 also made this confirmation. To claim title, the explorers supplemented the bulls by planting crosses with the royal coats of arms on the "new-found" lands.[13]

Portugal lost another opportunity according to one Italian source. The duke of Milan received a dispatch on August 24, 1497 that a Venetian mariner had discovered new islands, including the Seven Cities, and had arrived in England safely and that the English king planned to send him out on a voyage with 15 or 20 ships the following spring.[14] The Milanese ambassador then provided more information for the duke on December 18, 1497 about this "Zoane Caboto," a man "who, seeing that the most serene kings, first of Portugal, then of Spain have occupied unknown islands, meditated the achievement of a similar acquisition for his majesty aforesaid."[15] Portugal and Spain were examples for England, France and, later, the Netherlands in their expansion overseas.

Africa, India and East Asia all became part of the Portuguese colonial sphere. In May 1498 Vasco da Gama arrived in Calicut; in 1512 Portugal developed commerce in the Clove Islands—Bandas and Moluccas; in 1514 Jorge Álvares arrived by sea in Canton; in 1542–43 some Portuguese on a Chinese junk blown by a storm, landed in Japan; some countrymen also visited Korea.[16] For the Portuguese in Africa, knowledge about gold, spices and Prester John was a primary goal.[17] In *Do Preste Joam das indias. Verdadera informa* (1540), Father Francisco Alvares chronicled the search for Prester

John, which Samuel Purchas included in his work, *Hakluytus Posthumous or Purchas His Pilgrimes*, which was a successor to Richard Hakluyt the Younger's *Principall Navigations*, a text to which we shall return later in this study.[18] Portugal explored by land as well as by sea. From the mid-1400s, the Portuguese were in the African interior, and they sometimes put exiles or *lançados* ashore: by the reign of João II (1481–95), the Portuguese had probably reached Timbuktu, Mali and the Congo and by the late 1520s hundreds of *setanejos* or "backwoodsmen" lived in the interior of southeastern Africa where they traded and where some of them had families; across the Atlantic, in 1524, eight years before Francisco Pizzaro, Aleixo Garcia, who had been on the expedition of João Dias de Solis that traveled to the Incan empire, sent back silver samples; a few decades later in Brazil, depending on Native guides, Portuguese settlers moved from the littoral inland to the *sertão*.[19] This simultaneity and comparative context is important because, while my study concentrates on the New World, which was isolated from Europe, it should be remembered that Portugal's experience in Persia, India and China was with countries that already had trade connections with Europe. In these areas from East Africa into Asia the Portuguese often used Native pilots of multifarious backgrounds: Vasco da Gama employed a Gujarati navigator, to lead him across the Indian Ocean and thereby set a precedent in this practice for other European nations.[20] In this expansion to the east sometimes the Portuguese mixed "scientific" precision with marvelous speculation, which, as A. J. R. Russell-Wood has pointed out, is apparent in works like Duarte Pacheco Pereira's *Esmeraldo de Situ Orbis*—probably written in the first decade of the sixteenth century but only published in 1892 to mark, oddly enough, Columbus's landfall—which provides a mixture of accurate information on navigation, allusions to classical and religious authorities and descriptions of monstrosities, such as snakes as long as a quarter league.[21]

The Portuguese sought knowledge, gathered intelligence and left many texts about the lands and peoples they encountered (a great number in manuscript form and a few records by women or Natives about Portuguese expansion and trade): they seem to have written much more about India than about America.[22] The Portuguese moved east and west: in 1488 Dias rounded Africa and arrived in the Indian Ocean; in 1520 Fernão de Magalhães (Ferdinand Magellan), the Portuguese sailing in the service of Spain, rounded the tip of South America into the Pacific Ocean. With that voyage Spain soon became a rival to Portugal in Asia, although the relation between the two Iberian powers was even more complicated at the end of the sixteenth century and in the first half of the seventeenth century. In what follows I would like to focus on the impact of the Portuguese on the exploration and settlement of France, Spain and the Netherlands in the New World, bringing in, particularly in the case of the Dutch, a wider context.

I

The county of Portugal's independence from Leon and Castile occurred in 1128; Pope Alexander III first called the Portuguese leader, Afonso Henriques (1128–85), king in 1179; and it took until 1249 to expel the Moors and have a unified national territory; in 1383, when King Ferdinand, the last of the Afonsina dynasty, died, John I of Castile attempted to seize Portugal but John, prince of Aviz, was victorious; the Aviz dynasty was thrown in crisis on August 4, 1578 when King Sebastian died in battle at Alcazarquiver in North Africa; Sebastian's uncle, Cardinal Henry, lived until 1580; from that time until 1640 the Philippine dynasty reigned: Philip II of Spain was Philip I of Portugal, Philip III (Philip II), Philip IV (Philip III). The Moors and Portuguese took slaves from each other and, after the capture of Ceuta in 1415, slaves were more abundant and the Portuguese practice was sanctioned by the papacy.

Early on April 4, 1418, Pope Martin V issued the bull *Sane Charissumus*, appealing to Christian kings and princes to support João I (John I) of Portugal in his fight against the Saracens and other enemies of Christ.[23] Duarte Pacheco Pereira noted the "holy revelation" that Prince Henry experienced when he learned of the "discovery" and "when the first negroes were brought to these realms," so that "he wrote to all the kings of Christendom inviting them to assist him in this discovery and conquest in the service of Our Lord, each of them to have an equal share of the profits, but they, considering it to be of no account, refused and renounced their rights."[24] This author also goes on to note that Prince Henry, under the authority of his brother, Afonso V, then presented, as part of his case for the right of conquest, the renunciation of the other European kings. On September 8, 1436, Pope Eugene IV published the bull *Rex regum* in which he declared that all newly conquered lands would belong to Portugal. While in the early 1450s Muslim armies attacked Constantinople and Cyprus and Rhodes and Hungary were under siege, Pope Nicholas V issued two important bulls: *Dum diversas* (June 18, 1452) mentioned the Portuguese conquests and gave the king of Portugal power to wage war on infidels and to reduce them to serfdom, all in the name of conversion; *Romanus Pontifex* (January 8, 1454) praised the conquests and discoveries of Portugal and, more specifically, enforced the monopoly of Prince Henry, Afonso V and their successors, whose permission was needed for anyone seeking to fish and trade in these conquered places. With hopes that this offensive would counter the attacks on Europe, the pope was hopeful that the people of India would help Christians fight against Islam. On February 16, 1456, Pope Calixtus III published the bull *Etsi cuncti* in which he no longer addressed the other rulers of Europe but instead appealed directly to Portugal to maintain monasteries in Ceuta. Afonso, on August 31, 1471, published a law that forbade, under pain of death and the confiscation of ships, trade in and about Guinea; the Treaty of Toledo (March 6, 1480) confirmed Africa as Portugal's sphere and the Canary Islands as Spain's; a month later, Afonso V ordered Portuguese captains who found foreigners in the seas in and about Guinea to seize their ships and throw them into the seas.[25] Columbus changed this short-lived monopoly and Pope Alexander VI, a native of Valencia, passed five bulls that curtailed Portuguese power in expansion and discovery, especially in *Dudem siquidem* (September 25, 1493), in which the Spaniards could sail westward and claim any part of India that the Portuguese had not yet discovered. To counter this Portugal signed the Treaty of Tordesilhas (June 7, 1494).[26] These Portuguese attitudes toward monopolies, law and violence would be played out and imitated later on, as we shall see in the discussion of Brazil as described by Jean de Léry.

Portuguese practices at home later became the norm in colonies overseas. For instance, King Ferdinand, on May 26, 1375, published a law by which all rural landowners were to cultivate their lands or rent them for cultivation— *Lei de Sesmaria*—a practice that Portuguese colonies in Africa and Brazil adopted, and in Portugal Black slaves replaced men who were overseas in the fields.[27] Brazil was to be a key colony for the Portuguese, who claimed it during Easter week of 1500 as Pedro Vaz de Caminha, one of the crew of Pedro Álvares Cabral, recorded.[28] This same writer represents themes that Columbus had reported in the New World: the innocence that made it easy to convert the Natives, the nakedness of the inhabitants, the Native signs that indicate gold and other riches, the will of God and salvation. One curious passage in Caminha's account is that he has no doubt that if the *degradados* (banished Portuguese criminals) learnt the Natives' language then these newfound peoples would come into the Christian faith. This cycle of innocence, sin, exile and redemption involves a curious twist. The present discussion of Cabral arises because his voyage was novel: it included a journey to the New World, Africa and Asia and, therefore, allows for an examination of the New World in context.

Apparently, Cabral did not write about his voyage to Brazil and India. Although various sources help to piece together the events of this journey and will be the subject of this discussion, the key source is anonymous written in Portuguese but translated into Italian, included in one of the collections of voyages that were appearing in the first decade of the sixteenth century. In Lisbon in 1502 a volume containing the voyages of Marco Polo, Nicolò de Conti and Hieronimo de San Stefano appeared, and in Vicenza in 1507 *Paesi Nouamente retrouati Et Nouo Mondo da Alberico Vesputio intitulato* was published, providing an example for the collections of Grynaeus and Ramusio and, more indirectly, of Hakluyt and Purchas, which included the narrative that will be discussed here.[29]

The texts surrounding Cabral's voyage to Brazil and India are various, and, as is common in the period, the question of authorship arises as the original manuscripts no longer exist. Not one of the accounts covers the whole of Cabral's voyage, so that, despite some of the problems of authenticity, authorship and transmission, scholars and readers have often consulted an array of accounts and documents. Cabral does not appear to have written a report of his journey: the main documents that survive in Portugal concerning this voyage are Cabral's letter of appointment, parts of his instructions and two letters by Master John and by Pedro Vaz de Caminha sent back from Brazil after its "discovery." The original of the letter from King Manuel to the Spanish monarchs—Ferdinand and Isabella, his cousin and mother-in-law—with whom he got along well, does not seem to be extant but there are copies in Portuguese, Italian and Spanish. There is an anonymous account by someone who sailed with Cabral's fleet, originally written in Portuguese but translated into Italian, of which four editions exist. Along with this account, the letter of Giovanni Francesco de Affaitadi, a prominent merchant, and others related to this period, appeared in a small collection, *Paesi*. The Italians took great interest in this and other Portuguese voyages, while few of the original documents exist they are available in printed form or in manuscript copies and others are to be found in the diaries kept in Venice, such as those by Girolamo Priuli and Marino Sanuto.[30] In what follows there will be a brief discussion of the Portuguese accounts of Brazil and India and the Italian reactions to Cabral's voyage. Before moving on to accounts, letters and diaries concerning Cabral's voyage, it is best to make a few brief observations about some of the surviving official instructions and documents surrounding this expedition.

Even before Cabral's ships left Brazil for India, Caminha, who held the position of writer for the fleet, wrote a letter to King Manuel in which he described the stay in Brazil.[31] Caminha, who seems to have sailed on Cabral's ship, says that he is taking the middle way: "may Your Highness take my ignorance for good intention, and believe that I shall not set down here anything more than I saw and thought, either to beautify or to make it less attractive."[32] He presents himself as a reliable eyewitness, a stance much taken at this time. His letter gave the king his first representation of the new land, Vera Cruz, soon renamed by the king and ecclesiastics as Santa Cruz and later called Brazil after the red wood found there and traded in Flanders for dye.[33] Along the shore the Portuguese saw the Tupi, Natives given various names by the French and Portuguese: "They were dark, and entirely naked, without anything to cover their shame."[34] Although the Portuguese could not understand the Tupi, Caminha provides another reason for the breaking down of communication: when the Tupi approached the boat with boldness, "Nicolao Coelho made a sign to them that they should lay down their bows, and they laid them down. He could not have any speech with them there, nor understanding which might be profitable, because of the breaking of the sea on the shore."[35] The Portuguese and Tupi exchanged hats and, in another locale, Caminha observed once again the nakedness of the people: "They go naked, without any covering; neither do they pay more attention to concealing or exposing their shame than they do to showing their faces, and in this respect they are very innocent."[36] The mixture of innocence and Fall as part of the Edenic interpretation of Natives qualifies the earlier representation of nakedness.

Like Columbus and others before him, Caminha calls attention to the signs of the people they meet and to their willingness to indicate the location of precious metals.[37] When speech was not understandable, signs were interpreted with varying levels of accuracy; when the Tupi came on board Cabral's ship:

> Torches were lighted and they entered, and made no sign of courtesy or of speaking to the captain or to any one, but one of them caught sight of the captain's collar, and began to point with his hand towards the land and then to the collar, as though he were telling us that there was gold in the land. And he also saw a silver candlestick, and in the same manner he made a sign towards the land and then towards the candlestick, as there were silver also.[38]

This letter, like many other early accounts of the New World, dangles before monarchs and investors the riches of the land and often does so in a representational scene that involves willing Natives pointing the way as if to invite the Europeans to find and exploit these resources with their acquiescence and even help. Caminha reports that the Tupi did not like the food and wine offered to them, ignored a sheep and feared a hen. A moment when God and gold come together then appears in the letter: "One of them saw some white rosary beads; he made a motion that they should give them to him, and he played much with them, and put them around his neck; and then he took them off and wrapped them around his arm. He made a sign towards the land and then to the beads and to the collar of the captain, as if to say that they would give gold for that."[39] This kind of interpretation for the purposes of converting God into gold through interpretation—a technique, conscious or not, found in Columbus—is familiar enough, but what is unusual and remarkable is the self-conscious gloss that Caminha adds to this trope: "We interpreted this so, because we wished to, but if he meant that he would take the beads and also the collar, we did not wish to understand because we did not intend to give it to him. And afterwards he returned the beads to the one who gave them to him."[40] Caminha's admission is refreshingly honest: while revealing the intentions of his compatriots and himself, he is not able to guess the true motives of the Tupi involved. Cabral sent Nicolao Coelho and Bartolameu Dias (who had rounded the Cape of Good Hope in 1488) to go ashore and they took with them the two Tupi and let them ashore with new shirts, red hats, two rosaries of white bone beads, rattles and bells. Caminha also says that Cabral sent a young convict, Affonso Ribeiro, to stay with the Natives to learn their customs and way of life and Caminha accompanied Coelho with the implication that the captain wanted some of these events recorded by the fleet's writer. The freed Tupi ran away and quickly stripped off their new garments. In this account these go-betweens had signaled to 200 Tupi to put down their bows, and the scene here described was peaceful and no one, not even the Portuguese convict who was alone with the Tupi, was hurt.

Amidst this hectic yet peaceful scene (in which the potential violence had been diffused), Caminha finds time to describe the shame of females: "There were among them three or four girls, very young and very pretty, with very dark hair, long over the shoulders, and their privy parts so high, so closed, and so free from hair that we felt no shame in looking at them very well."[41] The theme of shame—this time from the Portuguese point of view—recurs, and a coming to terms with their own theological and cultural context of fallenness and guilt combines with a shifting ground between the eyewitness and the voyeur. What Caminha's notion of childhood was and how sexual desire and innocence were related in such a conception is something he does not address. He records to the king that he and his fellow countrymen looked at these girls' genitalia without shame, so he must not have thought this to be unusual or perverse. Concerning a cultural history of childhood in the West, Colin Heywood observes: "Far from 'discovering' the innocence and weakness of childhood at some particular period, people debated these and related issues from the early medieval period to the twentieth century."[42] The minimum age of marriage in canon law for a girl was 12 and for a boy was 14.[43] The time Caminha is writing, the turn of the sixteenth century, is roughly on the long cusp between the Middle Ages and the Renaissance depending on the country in Europe, so that the temporal and cultural factors might affect this view of desire, innocence and childhood. Travel, distance and being away from the mores of home—the very shock of being somewhere among people not yet seen by Europeans—might, because of the very "strangeness" of the situation, cause the writer to represent the exotic and taboo in the guise of other cultures. Caminha is, however, writing to the king to whom he will answer when he arrives at court, so that certain manners, decorum and conventions would constrain him. This moment, then, is "curious" in both senses of the word and it is difficult to resolve any one interpretation of Caminha's report of the watching of the naked girls, on whether this looking is a gaze, leer or observance or some combination of these and other physical reactions and cultural moves.

Before returning to naked females, Caminha revisits speech and signs. The concern of civility and barbarity, which is often observed in texts about the New World at the end of the fourteenth and the beginning of sixteenth centuries and persists beyond, arises in Caminha's account. Of the Tupi, he says, having shifted from beauty to barbarism: "Then for the time there was no more speech or understanding with them, because their barbarity was so great that no one could either be understood or heard. We made signs for them to leave, and they did so, and went to the other side of the river."[44] When the Portuguese filled up their kegs with water, the Tupi "made signs for us to return. We returned and they sent the convict and did not wish him to stay there with them."[45] The Natives did not want the basin and the red caps the convict had intended to give to a chief should he find one, but "then Bertolameu Dias made him return again to give those things to them," which he did to the Tupi who had befriended him: "And then he came away and we took him with us."[46] The intentions of the Portuguese and the assumptions that the Tupi would want the clothing and these articles for washing are here called into question, and it is only the insistence of someone with Dias's prestige and authority that would convince the convict to try again. The cultural premises and insistence of the Portuguese and not the needs or desires of the Tupi make this gift giving happen. Caminha comments that the Tupi friend of the convict was so covered with ornaments and feathers "that he looked pierced with arrows like Saint Sebastian."[47] This Tupinamba practice of covering the body with feathers, something that Jean de Léry later mentions, leads to a comparison, a typology that involves a religious image from Christian iconography, so that the Portuguese see this new people partly in old terms. This stereoscopic view involves one eye on Europe and another on the New World in order to make sense of this topography and those who inhabited it. Never is it actually certain in this stereoscopos or this typology which way is civility and which way barbarism.

After having represented speech, signs, barbarity and gifts, Caminha returns to the topic of girls and women. Speaking about caps of yellow, green or red feathers, he somehow shifts to a young female: "and one of the girls was all painted from head to foot with that paint, and she was so well built and so rounded and her lack of shame was so charming, that many women of our land seeing such attractions, would be ashamed that theirs were not like hers."[48] Like Léry, a French Calvinist who later went among the Tupi, Caminha uses a typology between Tupi women and women from his home country and prefers the Native women to their European counterparts. The Tupi women in Caminha's version are more sexually endowed and lack shame, so much so that the Portuguese women should be ashamed of not having such attractions. The question of whether Caminha should be ashamed for making such a comparison or looking so longingly or at least approvingly at naked girls is something that does not occur to him here. It seems that Caminha has shifted to a comparison between Tupi and Portuguese men when in the next sentence he observes: "None of them were circumcised, but were as we were."[49] There is no Portuguese woman writing to turn the tables on the Portuguese men in such comparing: Caminha is not interested in making the Tupi men sexually attractive and shameless. Instead, they resemble Portuguese men in being uncircumcised.

Caminha's account also shows how careful Cabral was not to expose himself to attack and how eager he was to make religion part of the voyage. A member of the Order of Christ, Cabral ordered all his captains to attend mass and hear a sermon and he carried with him, in addition to the royal standard, the banner of the Order of Christ, an emblem that Prince Henry used in his conflict with the Moors and that da Gama had with him on his first voyage.[50] Father Frei Amrique gave a sermon on "the history of the Gospel" and ended it by dealing "with our coming and with the discovery of this land" and by referring "to the sign of the Cross in obedience to which we came; which was very fitting, and which inspired much devotion."[51] All this was watched by some Tupi on the shore. The mass as it is staged in the letter becomes, then, a spectacle not just for the Portuguese but also for their hosts.

The relation between the king of Portugal and this new land also features as part of the account. Caminha reports that Cabral called together all his captains and asked whether he should send, through a supply ship, the news of finding this place to King Manuel, so that he might order others to reconnoitre it better than Cabral's fleet, which was about to leave for the East.[52] After this decision, which the majority approved, another had to be made. This point in the letter contains a crucial moment in which the Portuguese differ from the Spanish, English, Normans and French, as can be seen in the writings relating to the voyages of Columbus, Cabot and de Gonneville and Cartier.[53] Instead of kidnapping or taking Native hostages, Cabral and his compatriots decide something different. Cabral

asked further whether it would be well to take here by force two of these men to send to Your Highness and to leave here in their place two convicts. In this matter they agreed that it was not necessary to take men by force, since it was the general custom that those taken away by force to another place said that everything about which they are asked was there; and that these two convicts whom we should leave would give better and far better information about the land than would be given by those carried away by us, because they are people whom no one understands nor would they learn [Portuguese] quickly enough to be able to tell it as well as those others when Your Highness sends here, and that consequently we should not attempt to take any one away from here by force nor cause any scandal, but in order to tame and pacify them all the more, we should simply leave here the two convicts when we departed. And thus it was determined, since it appeared better to all.[54]

This passage shows a high degree of self-awareness among the Portuguese and a wisdom not always taken into account by other European explorers in the New World. The Portuguese did not want to "cause any scandal," they wished to "tame and pacify" the Tupi and not inflame them to war and revenge. Columbus left people but also took captives; Cabot brought nameless Natives back to England; Gonneville carried Essomericq to Normandy; and Cartier abducted Donaconna's sons to France. How effective these Portuguese convicts would be at learning the languages and customs of their hosts and how forthcoming were their reports might also be questionable, but that has more to do with class, education, discipline, punishment and the conditions of their embarkation and pardon. Interpreters, go-betweens and mediators often inhabited a liminal space between cultures in which questions of reliability, trust and betrayal were frequently raised.

Like Columbus, Caminha interpreted the gestures of the Natives he encountered. Caminha reported that after this decision not to take Natives against their will was taken, the Natives "all laid down their bows and made signs for us to land."[55] Portuguese and Tupinamba mingled thereafter, exchanging linen caps and bows and other goods for bows and arrows. Caminha also described the uncertain authority of Native "captains" and could not but help describe the attraction of the Tupi women:

> There were among them four or five young women just as naked, who were not displeasing to the eye, among whom was one with her thigh from the knee to the hip and buttock all painted with that black paint and all the rest in her own colour; another had both knees and calves and ankles so painted, and her privy parts so nude and exposed and with such innocence that there was not there any shame.[56]

Here is a mixture of ethnological detail and prurience. The innocence of the Tupi women is part of a representation by someone whose culture expects shame and nakedness to be tied, as it is in the Book of Genesis, but finds a kind of natural or paradisal attitude without guilt. Whether there is a shamelessness in Caminha is another matter.

This letter admits the difficulty of reading signs, particularly between two cultures that have been linguistically and culturally isolated from each other. After this representation of the naked women, Caminha describes an encounter: "When the captain reached him he spoke in our presence, without any one understanding him, nor did he understand us with reference to the things he was asked about, particularly gold, for we wished to know whether they had any in this land." This desire for gold and the chase for knowledge of its whereabouts are aspects this narrative shares with those of the Columbus voyages. (The next move in the text is to describe the old man's lip in ethnological detail.) There is laughter, music and joy in the description of the meeting of peoples, but Caminha says that the Natives "soon became sullen like wild men" and, later, "everything was done to their liking in order to tame them thoroughly."[57] Despite the gift of a red cap, the old man became wary. Even in this Portuguese narrative an embedded resistance, reluctance and distancing sometimes occurs among the Tupinamba, who want to put social or actual space between them and the newcomers. Caminha interprets this reluctant stance as proof that these people are "bestial" and "timid": ("bestial" and "esqujvos") he even accords their beauty to the fact that they are "wild" and not "tamed" ("monteses" and "amansasem").[58] Still, the Portuguese are interested in green and yellow caps and bows of bird feathers to send back to the king: Caminha describes, as part of a description of their bodies and attire, some of the hues as being "colours as in the tapestry of Arras," an example of making sense of life through art and new experience through the familiar.[59] The daily lives of the Tupi form part of the European collection at court and later in museums and galleries. The captain ordered Affonso Ribeiro and two other convicts, as well as Diogo Dias, "because he was a cheerful man," to remain that night among the Tupi. This tradition of using those in penal servitude in the colonies is long-standing. Caminha continues with his description, this time of dwellings and foodstuffs. A sense of realism marks this text. In describing the Tupi's interest in the Portuguese, Caminha speculates on their motives: "Many of them came there to be with the carpenters; and I believe that they did this more to see the iron tools with which they were making it than to see the cross, because they have nothing of iron."[60] Trade and technology, not religion and conversion, were most on the minds of the Tupinamba, an observation made as part of a description of parrots and the ways the Natives cut wood and the bows they produced. The Tupi ate with the Portuguese, but Sancho de Toar did not give ship wine to the two guests he took aboard because he "said that they did not drink it well."[61] This prudence is admirable and was not always followed later in colonization. The captain wanted the Portuguese to kiss the cross so the Tupi would follow suit. At once, ten or twelve did, which leads Caminha to make a statement reminiscent of Columbus: "They seem to me people of such innocence that, if we could understand them and they us, they would soon be Christians, because they do not have or understand any belief, as it appears."[62] More than Columbus, Caminha comprehends the lack of understanding between the two groups and speaks with less certainty and more with the qualification of appearance. The Portuguese phrase, "seg° pareçe" (as it appears), suggests the admission of the difficulty of knowing the reality of situation amid the hope for conversion.[63]

Nonetheless, a passage of more certitude follows on this speculation that involves the understanding of misunderstanding and the hermeneutics of the apparent. From this hope and doubt, Caminha turns to the king and his certain desire to increase the faith:

> And therefore, if the convicts who are to remain here will learn their language well and understand them, I do not doubt that they will become Christians, in accordance with the pious intent of Your Highness, and that they will believe in our Holy Faith, to which may it please Our Lord to bring them. For it is certain this people is good and of pure simplicity, and there can easily be stamped upon them whatever belief we wish to give them; and furthermore, Our Lord gave them fine bodies and faces as to good men; and He who brought us here, I believe, did not do so without purpose. And consequently, Your Highness, since you so much desire to increase the Holy Catholic Faith, ought to look after their salvation, and it will please God that, with little effort, this will be accomplished.[64]

The hope for cultural understanding and religious conversion is anchored in Portuguese convicts learning the Tupi language and becoming interpreters, mediators or go-betweens. Why is it that these outcasts get a second chance on which the spread of Portuguese Christianity depends? Would it be more of a priority if priests, scholars or administrators were chosen in their stead for this task or at least as a complementary group? The convicts are the "if" in the logical therefore clause in search of the "then" of the conversion of the Natives. Caminha, after just having expressed his doubts and his acknowledgment of the difficulties of knowing and appearances, says "I have no doubt" and "I believe" to confirm the strong possibility of conversion of the Tupi. Still, this certainty is based on what preceded and the "if" of the convicts' ability to learn the language of the Tupinamba and to come to understand them. Caminha appeals to divine providence as the reason for Cabral's coming upon this people and land new to the Portuguese and for their task of converting the Tupi to Christianity. This is the purpose in this chapter in history. There is, in this part of Caminha's work, opposite but simultaneous semantic forces, so that textual undertow pulls the reader in various directions. It may be that Caminha, like Columbus before him and Léry after him in the New World, is being realistic but also wants to protect the Tupi from being treated as heathens and suffering the terrible consequences. The Native as *tabula rasa* promises hope and can be controlled and protected. Docility means obedience. The Tupi have good bodies and faces and, for Caminha, therefore good souls.

This theology of equating outward and inward goodness leads Caminha from salvation to the production of food, of why, without tilling the soil, the Tupi "are stronger and better fed than we are with all the wheat and vegetables which we eat."[65] Still, there is talk of taming the Tupi with clothes, mattresses and sheets. The Portuguese plant the cross, "so that it might be better seen," but the unspoken corollary might be that it was also to help take possession of the land.[66] The Portuguese set up an altar beside the cross, which had the king's arms and device, and when Frei Amrique said mass, "when it came to the Gospel and we all rose to our feet with hands lifted, they [the 50 or 60 Tupi] rose with us and lifted their hands, remaining thus until it was over."[67] The same imitation also occurs with the elevation of the Host and remained there with the Portuguese until the friars, priests, the captain and the rest of the men took communion, but Caminha becomes more specific in reading the signs of possible conversion: a Tupi of about 50 or 55-years old remained behind, collecting the other of his people who had stayed and calling others: "He went about among them and talked to them, pointing with his finger to the altar, and afterwards he lifted his finger towards Heaven as though he were telling them something good, and thus we understood it." Caminha's skeptical hermeneutics is here held in abeyance as he represents the understanding of his fellow Portuguese in interpreting this gesture and as part of a parallel scene of Portuguese and Tupi religious practice during the mass, a parallelism built on a series of doublings of actions. The Portuguese priest's sermon on "this your holy and virtuous undertaking" follows on this Tupi man's gesture to altar and heaven.[68]

The next move in this text suggests that the Portuguese took with them, as would be expected, their earlier experiences in expansion and meeting with other cultures. This translation of their own experience to the New World would be intensified because it seems that Cabral went to the New World by accident on his way to India. The preparations the Portuguese had made for the journey to Asia, as in the case of the first journey of Columbus, would be applied to the peoples they found in the western Atlantic. This transference is apparent in the religious paraphernalia that the Portuguese had at hand. Caminha notes "when the sermon was over, Nicolao Coelho brought many tin crosses with crucifixes, which he still had from another voyage, and we thought it well to put one around the neck of each; for which purpose the father, Frei Amrique, seated himself at the foot of the cross, and there, one by one, he put around the neck of each his own [cross] tied to a string, first making him kiss it and raise his hands."[69] Here, then, is a ready practice from earlier Portuguese encounters with other cultures in Africa and beyond. The captain seems to have been happy with the Tupi man who pointed to the altar and the sky, so he took him, along with his brother, to the ship to eat: "And he gave him a Moorish shirt, and to the other one a shirt such as the rest of us wore."[70] This gift of a garment in the style of the Moors, a group the Portuguese had expelled and the Spaniards had recently engaged in a final defeat, shows the vagaries of trade and cultural exchange.

To the New World the Portuguese brought traces of, and contacts with, other worlds.

Caminha derived recommendations and conclusions from this meeting between the Tupi and the Portuguese. What he reports to the king is based on a consensus, a rhetorical coming together of Portuguese opinion: "And as it appears to me and to everyone, these people in order to be wholly Christian lack nothing except to understand us, for whatever they saw us do, they did likewise; wherefore it appeared to all that they have no idolatry and no worship."[71] The blank slate of the Tupi means that they will not suffer for being idolaters and need only understanding to be complete Christians, something, he implies, the Portuguese can furnish. Caminha is supporting the plan Cabral had put in place, which Caminha has already reported, for he recommends the following action to the king: "And I well believe that, if Your Highness should send here some one who would go about more at leisure among them, that all will be turned to the desire of your Highness. And if some one should come for this purpose, a priest should not fail to come also at once to baptize them, for by that time they will already have a greater knowledge of our faith through the two convicts who are remaining here among them. Both of these also partook of communion to-day."[72] This strategy rests on the religious knowledge of the two convicts as well as on their abilities to come to understand the Tupi language and culture—a surprising tactic, at least to the modern reader. Caminha shifts to a description of a young naked woman who was given a cloth to cover herself at mass, which gives the writer another pretext to expound on the pliable and prelapsarian nature of the Tupinamba: "the innocence of this people is such, that that of Adam could not have been greater in respect to shame. Now Your Highness may see whether people who live in such innocence will be converted or not if they are taught what pertains to their salvation."[73] Innocence and experience, God and gold also exist side-by-side as they do in Columbus's narratives.

In the description of the land and climate Caminha gives the king an idea of the nature and extent of this territory, whose riches are as yet unrevealed— "Up to now we are unable to learn that there is gold or silver in it, or anything of metal or iron"—and whose temperate climate is like "that of Entre Doiro e Minho."[74] Amid this standard part of European narratives about the New World (and probably any lands they come upon outside Europe), which is the report on actual and potential resources, Caminha catches himself: "So pleasing it is that if one cares to profit by it, everything will grow in it because of its waters. But the best profit which can be derived from it, it seems to me, will be to save this people, and this should be the chief seed which Your Highness should sow there."[75] The greatest goal is conversion and salvation but at the very least this new land could be a stop on the way to Calicut. Commerce and religion are closely intertwined in this text.

II

There is in Cabral's voyage, as in many in the first decades of exploration of the New World, an Italian dimension. Some of the documents surrounding this voyage are of uncertain authorship or textual status, such as the letter of Master John to King Manuel (May 1, 1500) and the letter from King Manuel to Ferdinand and Isabella (July 29, 1501). Another text, an anonymous narrative of the voyage from Lisbon to Calicut, is said to have been translated from Portuguese into the Venetian dialect—four manuscripts of which still exist in differing versions, including the first edition of *Paesi nouamente retrovati*—although no contemporary copy in Portuguese is extant in Portugal.[76] This and other Italian texts provide some other points of view on Cabral's voyage in addition to Caminha's account. The Venetians were interested in the Portuguese voyages because of their challenge to Venice's control of European trade with Asia.

A few details of this anonymous narrative should suffice to observe some of the ways that it complements and differs from Caminha's account. The anonymous report records how the captain sent some of his crew ashore to observe the people who were there. This account also stresses nudity and the linguistic divide: "And they found that there were people of dark colour, between white and black, and well built, with long hair. And they go nude as they were born, without any shame whatever, and each one of them carried his bow with arrows, as men who were in defence of the said river. On the aforesaid armada there was no one who understood their language. And having seen this, those in the boat returned to the captain."[77] These people do not feel shame in their nakedness, but they also seem to understand defending territory. This account does not have the same almost exclusive emphasis on the innocence of the Natives that Caminha's narrative does. One of the boats brought two of the Natives to the captain, but in this exchange "they did not understand one another either in speech or by signs."[78] This lack of understanding at any level still permitted the captain to have the two stay overnight and to have them dressed in shirt, coats and red caps (*berettas*) before putting them ashore. Thus far, no kidnapping has marked the Portuguese landing in the New World.

This anonymous account also takes a different view of the convicts than Caminha's narrative does. Here, the captain determined to leave in this land "two men, exiles [*banditi*], condemned to death, who were in the said armada for this purpose"; the convicts, after they were left, followed the captain's orders and erected a cross, "They began to weep and the men of the land comforted them and showed that they pitied them."[79] The emotional dimension of this abandonment and the planned and apparently conventional nature of this practice are represented here, whereas in Caminha these convicts are regarded idealistically as those who would learn the language and customs of the Tupi for the greater glory of the king and the Christian faith. Although there is ethnographic detail in this account, it is much less elaborate than the descriptions in Caminha's text.

In this anonymous narrative the representation of the New World is a prologue to the rest of the voyage. Before we return to Brazil, it is worth mentioning a few instances that place the Portuguese in the western Atlantic in context. In focusing on Cabral's "discovery" of Brazil, it is easy to forget the rest of his voyage to his original destination. Cabral's armada made its way around the Cape of Good Hope and sailed toward Arabia in a terrible storm. The Portuguese came across two Moorish ships whose captain was a friend of Portugal's and an uncle to the king of Malindi, but in the unfortunate skirmish, this captain lost his wife and child who drowned trying to escape the Portuguese and the Moors threw their gold overboard. After Cabral apologized, the Portuguese set out in search of Zaffalle, a land of gold and other riches. The Portuguese fired bombards or breech-loading cannon, which, in a meeting of Cabral and the king on ships at sea, metaphorically backfired because this show scared the king of Chilloa, a Moor, who came to see the Portuguese as corsairs rather than the trading partners they had presented themselves as and he had accepted them as. Cabral had better luck with the king of Melinde: the Portuguese presented gifts and letters from their king in their own language and in Arabic, something that led to rich gifts in turn from the king of Melinde. Despite the apparent friendliness of this exchange, the parties were not without arms at the ready. Cabral asked the king for a pilot and was given "a Guzerati pilot from the ships of Chombaia which were in the port. The captain also left two Portuguese convicts, one of them to remain in Melinde, and the other to go with the ships to Chombaia."[80] This exchange, not unlike the use of hostages, suggests a wary but amiable arrangement and shows that the use of convicts by the Portuguese was nothing particular to their relations with the Natives of America. Rather, an earlier practice seems to have been translated to the New World.

The area of the Persian Gulf and Red Sea held great attraction to the Portuguese, much to the dismay of the Venetians. The anonymous writer notes "a very rich and beautiful Moorish city which is called Magadasio [Mogadishu]" and observes that there is a great and powerful king in Combaia, a land that "is the most productive and rich in the world."[81] The text notes the riches and that many there are Moors and "idolaters." This land was part of the trade with Arabia and India. At Calichut (Calicut), the Portuguese once more fired their artillery, "at which the Indians marvelled greatly, saying no one had power against us except God."[82] Interpreters or go-betweens were a significant part of the negotiations. Cabral and the king of

Calichut make use of hostages in their negotiations, exchanges and trade. The ethnographical descriptions occur here and are similar in detail to those made in the cultural encounters in the New World, which, after all, follow on earlier contacts with other cultures adjacent to Europe. This narrative describes the king—"And he was nude above and below the waist."[83] Nudity seems to have interested the Portuguese when they came across others in distant lands. In this meeting, however, his apparel included jewels and precious metals, probably as a measure of the opulence of the king and his land, and his litter prompted the comment: "It was rich beyond description."[84] After describing many other accoutrements of the king and before more accounts of the splendors of the court, the anonymous author uses the topos of inexpressibility to express the richness of the litter. Various rhetorical strategies amplify the elaborate wealth of king and country. Cabral is not allowed to approach the king, but he was still able to present the king with a letter from the king of Portugal in Arabic. The narrative does not report the contents, something to which we shall return in due course. After a description of the gifts presented to the king, the account chronicles how the king and Cabral agreed that he should return to his ship and that the hostages would return to the ship the next day so Cabral could come ashore. A zambuco with some men of Calichut went ahead and told the hostages of Cabral's return to the ship, which prompted them to jump into the seas, although the Portuguese were able to capture two as protection for the Portuguese men and property ashore, and send word to the king about the incident that one of his clerks had instigated. The complex exchanges after this incident led to tense negotiations and mediations involving the family of a rich merchant from Guzerat; Areschorea, the chief factor; the king; and others. The author shows his own suspicions in this situation: "The language which our men spoke was Arabic, so that no one could converse with the king except through Moors as intermediaries. These are bad people and were much opposed to us, so that they were at all times deceitful and prevented us from sending anyone to the ships."[85] As we shall see from the letter that Cabral had carried from the king of Portugal in Arabic, which the Arabs would have interpreted for the king of Calichut, these "Moors" would not be amused by the Portuguese attitude toward them or from their attempt to cut them out of a trade they had been involved with for a long time. Cabral's instructions on how to conduct himself in India were founded on the premise that the Zamorin of Calichut was a Christian who would thus be friendly.[86] This assumption proved to be false. The problem of interpretation and translation was apparent to the anonymous author, so the Arabs could not be an excluded third party as much as the Portuguese might have desired that situation.

The anonymous narrative describes that the treaty took more than two months to complete, how a Portuguese caravel captured a large Arab ship with 300 men at arms and the customs and manners of Calichut. One of the striking observations is an indirect correction to the king's instructions based on the ideas of Vasco da Gama and the members of his fleet concerning the monarch: "The king is an idolater, although others have believed that they are Christians."[87] Descriptions of nakedness and relations with women were not confined to cultural encounters in the New World. The men at court are notable because of their color, class and degrees of nudity: "Almost all his nobles and the people who serve him are men dark as Moors. And they are well-built men, and go nude above and below the waist."[88] It is not only in the New World that men have lives less informed by shame and more involved with sex than their Portuguese counterparts. These men at the court of Calichut experience sex and marriage differently from the Portuguese:

> They marry one wife or five or six women, and those who are their best friends gratify them by sleeping with their wives, so that among them there is neither chastity nor shame. And when the girls are eight years old they begin to secure gain by this means. These women go nude almost like the men and wear great riches. They have their hair marvellously arranged and are very beautiful, and they entreat the men to deprive them of their virginity, for as long as they are virgins they cannot procure a husband.[89]

These sexual practices, which differed from those encouraged in Europe, including what would probably stretch the age limits for the involvement of children even for the Portuguese of that time, are neither praised nor criticized. It is different if not opposite to what is lauded at least textually and ideally in Christianity, where monogamy, virginity and the covering of the shame of nakedness are all prized. The author leads next to the sex life of the monarch and his spouses: "The king has two wives, and each one of them is attended by ten priests and each one of them sleeps with her carnally to honour the king, and for this reason the sons do not inherit the kingdom, but only the nephews, sons of the sister of the king."[90] Beyond sex and succession, the author records burial and cremation practices and the sacredness of cows, but he also describes the Guzerate merchants, vegetarians who do not drink alcohol, who "are whiter men than the natives of Calichut," who "woo and marry one woman as we do" and who "are very jealous and hold to their wives, who are very beautiful and chaste."[91] This author distinguishes between the peoples he meets, so that there is a multiple otherness and a sense of difference.

One group the narrative describes is the "Zetieties," or Chettys, Tamil merchants in south India who were considered to be foreigners because they came from the Coromandel coast, who are idolaters who buy and sell jewels, pearls, gold and silver and "who are blacker men" and "go nude" and talk each day "with the devil invisibly."[92] Even though much of the description signals what the Arabs are trading with this people and how wealthy they are, including the spice trade to Cairo and Alexandria, the author notes the sexual practices among the Tamils and the local population in this area: "The wives of these men are very corrupt in wantonness, like the Natives of the land."[93] In the mountains a certain King Naremega [Narasimha], an idolater, is said to have 200 or 300 wives and "The day he dies they will burn him and all his wives with him."[94] Culture and religion, and not trade alone, interest the Portuguese in their travels. The multiplicity of the region is not lost on this Portuguese participant, ethnological observer and writer: Cabral's fleet came across cultures of vast difference in America, Africa and Asia and had to come to terms with this otherness in a brief period.

Not all the cultural encounters went smoothly. This anonymous author reports the slaughter of Moors and Christians in Calichut about three months after the Portuguese had been there, when they had signed a treaty with the king. The Portuguese thought the king of Calichut, "a seditious man," was breaking the treaty by not filling the Portuguese ships first with merchandise and that the treaty allowed the Portuguese to take Arab ships that loaded before the Portuguese vessels. The seizure of such a ship led the Moors to complain to the king that the Portuguese "were the worst robbers and thieves in the world" and, because their ship had been so taken, said "that they were obliged to kill all and that His Highness should rob the house of the factor."[95] This the king did. Many died. With seven or eight crossbows, "we killed a mountain of people," but ultimately, many Portuguese died and because the ships dared not approach the shore, the factor "Areschorea was slain and with him fifty and more men," although 20 people, including his 11-year-old son and the author of this narrative, escaped by swimming.[96] In retribution Cabral ordered that ten Arab ships be taken: and the Portuguese killed those on board numbering 500 or 600 while capturing 20 or 30 more and killing and eating 3 elephants and stealing the cargo and burning what could not be taken. The next day they bombarded the city and "slew an endless number of people" before the Portuguese moved on to Cochin [Chochino, Cucchino].[97] This was a bloody end to what was supposed to be a treaty with a sympathetic Christian king. The consequences of cultural misunderstanding and clashing trade practices were terrible.

In Cochin, the king and Cabral exchanged hostages through the offices of "a poor man of the Guzerate nation who voluntarily left Calichut to come to Portugal."[98] At Carangallo [Crangamore] the Portuguese came upon "Christians, Jews, and infidels [*Zafaras*]. Here we found a Jewess of Seville who came by way of Cairo and Mecca, and from there two other Christians came with us; they said that they wished to go to Rome and to Jerusalem. The captain had great pleasure with these men."[99] The encounter here, then, is not one of a group and another culture but a mixture, a Guzerate who wanted to leave for Portugal and who acted as a go-between and a Jewess from Spain who had left her home with no explanation given in the text (perhaps she had been expelled in 1492). When an armada from Calichut came upon the Portuguese, Cabral left his hostages with his factor and decided to continue to Portugal, "taking the two men of Chochino with us. He began to cajole them, begging them to consent to eat, for now they had not eaten for three days and then they ate with great grief and sorrow, and we continued on our way."[100] The king of Cochin wrote three letters in which he names the writers and gives his version of this event and tells Dom Manuel that he had fought for the Portuguese against the Zamorin of Calecut [Calechut] under difficult circumstances and despite the odds. Of Cabral and the Portuguese, the king of Cochin said: "When their ships were loaded an armada from Calecut came to fight with them, and two of my writers named Ytalaca and Parangova were in the ships as hostages. And they made sail and carried them to Portugal. And thus the Portuguese remained on shore with me."[101] Later, when the Portuguese were in Chanonon [Cananore], the men of Cochin (or Chochino) sent in letter to their king to say that they were sailing to Portugal and Cabral wrote to his factor, who had the Portuguese hostages with him, about what had happened; here the king of Chanonon had invited the Portuguese to fill their ships and said that even though the Portuguese captain offered to trade in cruzados, he could do so on a return voyage, "for he had well learned how the King of Calichut had robbed us and what good and truthful people we were."[102] The king's largess did not stop there, for when he asked whether Cabral desired anything more, "The captain told him no, except that His Highness might send a man to visit Portugal. The king immediately sent a gentleman who was to come to Portugal with us."[103] This king belonged to a place whose language was like that of Calichut and belonged to the "Caferis," or Kāfirs, people who do not have faith in Islam, a term applied to Black Africans who were nonbelievers and to the Portuguese.[104] Cabral, who used Guzerate interpreters, let a ship pass from Mecca, except for taking a pilot, because it was from Combaia. Religious and racial difference have much less weight here than who helps each other economically and politically. Cabral was obviously interested in knowledge of languages and the sea in his quest to set up Portugal as the leading force in trade in the Indian Ocean. He would profit from go-betweens in this cultural exchange informed by trade.[105] Where persons or ships are from and whether they are allied or not means a great deal in this critical time of flux in the Indian trade.

There were many dangers on these trips. A shipwreck in the Gulf of Melindi, which this anonymous narrative described, illustrates this point. The Portuguese, who lost a ship of 200 tons ("tonelli") laden with spices, burned the ship so the Arabs would not get a hold of the cargo, but, according to

João de Barros in *Da Asia* (Lisbon, 1777), apparently the "Moors" of Mombasa sent out divers and retrieved cannon they later used against the Portuguese.[106] The narrative rounds off with a description of the ships that returned to Lisbon; the arrival at the Cape of Good Hope; gold, whose trade seems controlled by Moors, but that comes from a mountain in a region where the people are not Islamic; the prices that drugs and spices are worth in Calichut; the places of origin for the spices and their distance from Calichut.[107] Trade and intelligence were important aspects of the writing about this voyage. Writers seemed to be as important for the king of Portugal as for the king of Cochin.

As the Cabral voyage has illustrated, a typology came to exist between the Portuguese interests in the New World and in the East. The Portuguese expansion or incursions into the Indian Ocean had implications for Venice as well as for Africa, India and beyond. As Spain had expelled the Moors and Venice feared that the Muslims would affect its control of the lucrative trade of drugs and spices into Europe, the two states shared a common interest. The Italians are never far from any early history of overseas exploration in western Europe—Colombo and Vespucci for Spain, Caboto for England, Verrazzano for France, not to mention the Italian bankers and merchants in Italy and various countries—so that it is no surprise that the correspondence of ambassadors or the excogitations of diarists, from states like Venice, can yield important views on this expansion and exploration. Among Venetians, Domenico Pisani, Marino Sanuto and Giovanni Camerino, also known as Giovanni Matteo Cretico or Il Cretico, are writers whose works have particular implications for a comparative history of empire. Pisani, appointed Venetian ambassador to Spain on September 7, 1500 and also ambassador to Portugal, reminded Ferdinand and Isabella of the aid they had promised Venice and sought the support of the Portuguese fleet against the Turks. In March 1501 Dom Manuel did send an armada to help Venice against the Turks. Il Cretico acted as secretary to Pisani, so one would usually be in the opposite Iberian court and thus both would cover Portugal and Spain. When on June 23, 1501 the first of Cabral's ships arrived from India, Il Cretico wrote a letter to Venice about the voyage, a report that described the participation of Bartolomeo Marchioni in the enterprise and that caused dismay about the Portuguese incursion in the trade with the East. Girolamo Priuli, a diarist, also reported the dismay in Venice over the Portuguese expedition to India.[108] Other letters are of importance, such as those by Angelo Trevisan di Bernardino, another secretary who accompanied Pisani to Spain, and by Giovanni Francesco de Affaitadi. Trevisan knew Columbus, Il Cretico and Peter Martyr, whose papers he had been given access to. Affaitadi was from the prominent banking and mercantile family in Cremona who, before Columbus's landfall in the New World, had, with other Italian families, established a branch in Lisbon in hopes of gaining a portion of the Portuguese trade in Madeira, Cape Verde and Africa. The Affaitadi, some of whose accounting books were preserved in Antwerp, had gained, for a time, exclusive trade in spices with Flanders, in exchange for copper and silver, and were later joined in this by other Italian merchants and by the Welzers and Fuggers of Germany. The agents of the Affaitadi later extended to Seville, London, Lyons and beyond. In some ways, although my study makes distinctions between Europeans, often involved in rivalries, it also notes some of the affinities and the cooperation among states and individuals in trade and war.[109]

The letters themselves provide a Venetian point of view and supplement the Portuguese documents we have already discussed. In a letter of June 27, 1501 (one of the versions says July 27), Il Cretico addressed the doge of Venice and sent him the letter through Pietro Pasqualigo. He announces "they have discovered a new land" that "is inhabited by nude and handsome men."[110] Il Cretico provides another point of view on the conflict at Calichut (Calicut but Colochut in this text), not necessarily of an eyewitness but a third party reporting who is not a Portuguese or a Muslim participating in the events there. Although the Portuguese were at first well received, soon the Sultan's merchants became angry because the Portuguese "had interfered with them and wanted to load first" and the factor of the king of Portugal "complained to the lord (of Colochut), who was of the opinion that he should come to an understanding with the Moors, and said that if they took on a cargo he should take the spices away from them. As a result of this they came to blows, and all the land favoured the Moors"[111] Nor does Il Cretico, even as he is balanced about the causes of why the Muslim merchants were upset, avoid the description of the massacres that each side inflicted on the other. First, the people of Colochut "ran to the house assigned to the Portuguese, and they cut to pieces all who were (within and) on the land. Those were about forty."[112] The Portuguese retaliation shows up in Il Cretico's account, for when they learned of this attack, the Portuguese ships "came and destroyed the people of the Sultan, and with their artillery they did great damage to the land and burned a number of houses, because they were covered with straw."[113] Il Cretico does not go into the actual horrors of the violence on both sides. He adds that "a baptized Jew," apparently Gaspar da Gama, acted as a guide and conducted the Portuguese to Cuzin [Cochin] and mentions the exchange of hostages with the king of that land, the reasons they averted a battle with the Moors and people of Colochut— they had cargo—and the kindness of the king of Cananore: "In coming they reached an island where is the body of Saint Thomas, the apostle. The lord of this treated them very kindly, and, having given them relics of the afore- said saint, asked them to take spices from him on credit until the return voyage. They were laden and could not take more."[114] This version, although it makes mistakes as in the reference to Saint Thomas, supplements the extant Portuguese accounts, sometimes reconstructing motives, particularly of those of the other cultures the Portuguese encountered.

Writing to Domenico Pisani on June 26, 1501 in a letter that arrived in Venice in the middle of July, Giovanni Francesco de Affaitadi described the Portuguese aid to Venice against the Turks and the arrival of the Portuguese ships from "Colocut," an expedition that he described, noting that ten of the ships were the king's, another of Dom Diogo da Siva de Menezes and yet another of Dom Álvaro, a son of Dom Fernando, duke of Bragança, in partnership with Bartolomeo Marchioni, a Florentine merchant and banker living in Lisbon, Girolamo, a Florentine whom Dom Manuel had made a citizen of Lisbon, and a Genoese (perhaps Antonio Salvago).[115] This account gives another point of view on the disagreement between the Portuguese and "Moors of Mecha" at "Coloqut": "One day the Moors and the factor of the king [of Portugal] came to a misunderstanding, one saying that he wished to load before the other, and the Moors killed twenty-five or thirty of the principal Portuguese, among whom were the chief factor and writers and certain *frati de observantia* whom the king sent in the said armada."[116] There do not seem to be precise details about these Franciscans, apparently fallen at the hands of the Moors of Mecca, whose ships sailed from the port of Mecca—Jidda, but Cabral had carried with him an image of Our Lady of Hope (*Nossa Senhora de Esperança*), placed, upon his return, in the care of the Franciscans in a chapel near Belmonte, so that there might have been a connection not just between the king and that order but between the captain and them as well.[117] Trevisan's account shows the terrible retribution that Cabral exacted for these killings: the survivors swam to the Portuguese ships and told what happened, so Cabral "began to bombard the Moorish ships" and thus sent "twelve ships to the bottom" and killed "more than three hundred Moors. This done, he began to fire the bombards toward the shore and killed many people, burning many houses. And the next day they captured many of the men of Coloqut and took them to their ships."[118] The capture is something this account adds to previous renditions, and here the person who dissuades the captain from returning to the site of this violent encounter is a "Jew," not baptized as in Il Cretico's description, but the wise figure who knew where the spices grew, so that "The captain, after considering the proposal of the Jew, determined to do what he said," that is to sail to Chuchi [Cochin], whose king, an enemy to the king of Coloqut [Calicut], is also generous in this narrative.[119] In this account, the action between the king of Chuchi, including an exchange of hostages, was done "with great friendship."[120] This account also explains clearly that the armada of Coloqut was left behind "because those ships did not sail unless they had the wind behind them": technical matters mattered.[121] After gesturing toward "the fame of the riches" of the king of Coloqut, Affaitadi tells Pisani about Lichinocho [Cananore], whose rich king sent presents to Cabral and two ambassadors to visit the king of Portugal, and about Zofala, where a great trade in gold occurred.[122] While also recounting the storms and losses of ships, Affaitadi said that the ship that had just arrived, which belonged to Signor Alvaro and which was the smallest in the fleet, was sent ahead because it was the best and would gives news to the king first. Having briefly described the cargo, Affaitadi passes judgment on the outcome of the voyage and names his source without being too specific: "This discourse I have made to advise Your Magnificence of the success of this matter of Coloqut. The above news was obtained from a mariner of the small ship which has arrived, which ship is still at Restello and is daily expected here. It is understood that another is expected who is advised of everything in particular."[123] This further source is a matter of speculation, but what is certain is that Affaitadi considered the expedition a success and was attempting to find out more in order to send it on to Venice.

In a letter of December 3, 1501, Trevisan, showing more faith in the checking of facts about Cabral's voyage, wrote that Il Cretico "comes from Portugal at the end of this September, well informed concerning the voyage to Calicut, and is continually working on a treatise [*tractato*]."[124] The Italians had also gathered intelligence about earlier voyages: for instance, the expedition of Giovanni Caboto, a citizen of Venice. From London in August 1497, Lorenzo Pasqualigo had written his brothers about "that Venetian of ours" who had sailed from Bristol to new lands and the duke of Milan received a dispatch to the same effect; in December 1497, the Milanese ambassador amplified this "discovery" by noting that Caboto had followed the example of Portugal and Spain in exploring and acquiring new lands for England.[125]

Other forms of writing among the Venetians were used in representing Cabral's expedition to Brazil and India. The diaries of Girolamo Priuli (1476–1547), a member of a prominent mercantile family, and of Marino Sanuto the younger (1466–1533), a statesman, also contain material on the Portuguese and, in particular, about Cabral's voyage. Priuli emphasized the epochal importance of Cabral's accomplishment: this voyage to India "was of greater importance to the Venetian state than the Turkish war, or any other wars which might have affected her."[126] Then Il Cretico's letter appeared in the diary as it did in Sanuto's and in *Paesi*. Priuli shows skepticism and hope as "in this letter are many things of great wonder in our times and almost incredible, which give me something very instructive to consider; but time will better enable us to understand the truth."[127] In this pursuit of the true, which Priuli understands to be provisional and unfolding, he is not afraid to do his best under the circumstances: "But if God will lend me life, I shall

endeavour to note the result so far as it can be understood, for already so
much has been found out that nothing more can be learned now that infinite time desires should be known."[128] Priuli built in possible reactions to the
news, interpretations of this momentous event, into his own hermeneutics of
discovery. Judging the profits of this voyage was part of this interpretive
project. Priuli did not agree with those who thought that Portugal would be
dissuaded by the hardships and losses: "And if this voyage should continue,
since it now seems to me easy to accomplish, the King of Portugal could call
himself the King of Money because all would convene to that country to
obtain spices, and the money would accumulate greatly in Portugal with
such profit as would follow each year from similar voyages."[129] Nor does
Priuli wish to mask the great sea change Cabral's voyage will have on Venice.
He sets a dramatic scene of the reaction of Venetians to this event and moves
toward a personal note:

> When this news was truly learned in Venice, the whole city was much stirred
> by it, and every one was stupefied that in this our time there should have been
> found a new voyage which was never heard of or seen in the times of the
> ancients or of our ancestors. And this news was held by the learned to be the
> worst news which the Venetian Republic could have had, to lose the liberty
> abroad. And the wars and the travails which we now have and for some time
> may have, are of the smallest moment in comparison with this news. And for
> this reason I wish to tell the truth and not to deceive.[130]

This voyage marks, for Priuli, the shift in the spice trade, and therefore in
economic power, from Venice to Portugal, so that this event, for the Venetian
Republic, had more immediate and deleterious effects than Columbus's
voyage to the New World. Venice, who has maintained supremacy at sea, will
not be able to compete with a sea route and the foreigners will take their business elsewhere: "Therefore, now that this new voyage of Portugal is found,
this King of Portugal will bring all the spices to Lisbon. And there is no doubt
that the Hungarians, Germans, Flemish and French, and those beyond the
mountains, who formerly came to Venice to buy spices with their money, will
all turn towards Lisbon, for it is nearer to all the countries, and easier to
reach."[131] Although Priuli's geography seems a little uncertain in places in this
comment, his point is clear: others will do business with the Portuguese
because of the superiority of a sea route to and from India. The foreigners
will ebb because the sea route does not have all the disadvantages, including
presents, duties and excises [*gabelle*] paid along the way, through the countries that the Sultan controls, all of which multiply something worth
a ducat to the cost of 60 or 100 ducats.[132] Priuli reiterated his point about
the vast cost advantage to Portugal in the Indian trade and its proximity
to Flanders, Hungary, England, France and elsewhere. Priuli uses further

amplification to trumpet the doom of Venice. When, as a result of the new Portuguese trade with Calicut, the spices in the Venetian galleys lessen and thus too the merchants, the consequences will be dire: "And when this traffic in merchandise is lessened in Venice, it can be considered that the milk and nutriment of Venice are lessened to a *putino*. And because of this I see clearly the ruin of the Venetian city, because as the traffic lessens, so lessens the money which has produced the Venetian glory and reputation."[133] Priuli then proceeded to report what unnamed others have more optimistically said about Cabral's voyage and its consequences, but he did not find himself swayed and apologized to "the reader" of his diary about his style and confused manner.[134] This diary seems to have been meant for some kind of readerly consumption: how public and extensive is hard to say. In the entry of August 1501, Priuli repeats his view that the king of Portugal will send out annual voyages to Calicut that will "cause the ruin of the Venetian state."[135] The entry of September 1501, concerning a report of the ninth day of that month, reiterated the importance of this new voyage for Portugal, bringing gold and spices, and its ill effects on Venice, but this time although considering that the wise predict the ruin of Venice through Portugal's trade with India, Priuli added the caveat: "Still, this is a presumptuous prognostication, since the heavens may dispose otherwise."[136] That being said, Priuli returned to the subject of the bad way in which Venetian merchants find themselves and the prediction that the German merchants will go to Portugal for cheaper and better merchandise.[137] The next entry, about September 14, repeated the many iterations of the king of Portugal being "a great lord of money" and Lisbon becoming the new European center for trade with India, and Priuli mentioned that the king of Portugal, owing to the losses from the past voyage, would tax ships returning from India 29 percent.[138] In the entry concerning September 19, 1501, Priuli continued to describe the cargo of the Portuguese ships, mentioning letters from Bruges in Flanders that two caravels had arrived from Portugal with spices from Calicut, "So that this can be considered the beginning of the damage which the Venetian state can receive from the voyage found by the King of Portugal."[139]

This Portuguese breakthrough in seafaring and trade caught the Venetians by surprise: the shock of Portugal shook Venice. Sanuto's diary also chronicled the growth of Portuguese power. When Dom Manuel wrote the doge of Venice, Agostino Barbarigo, on February 22, 1501, offering an armada to help the Venetians against the Turks, he used his new title, confirmed by the pope in 1502, "King of Portugal and of the Algarves on this side and beyond the sea in Africa, Lord of Guinea, and the Conquest, Navigation and Commerce of Ethiopia, Arabia and India."[140] In his diary, Marino Sanuto noted the discovery of "2,500 miles of new coast" from whence caravels "laden with brazil-wood and cassia" returned: he also reported the arrival in Lisbon of caravels with a cargo of spices coming back from Calicut.[141]

Florence, like Venice, had interests in Lisbon and what the Portuguese crown was doing. In 1500, there were more Florentines in Lisbon than any other Italians. In 1494 the Pisans had destroyed the Florentine marine and disrupted the profitable maritime trade between Florence and Portugal, but when Portugal expelled the Jews, the Florentines filled the gap and benefited most among the Italians from the sea route from India because the Venetians were not entirely trusted in Portugal. Of the Florentines, the Marchioni was the most prominent family: in 1487 João II secured from its head, Bartolomeo Marchioni, credit for 400 cruzados for Pedro de Covilhan and Afonso de Paiva, which led to a letter of credit to the banking house in Naples of Cosimo de' Medici. Marchioni also had connections with the Florentine banker in Seville, Juanoto Beradi, who died in 1495 and whose successor then was Amerigo Vespucci.

Marchioni, probably the richest person in Lisbon, was one of the key financiers of the Portuguese voyages to India, including the second voyage of Vasco da Gama.[142] A vast web of connections shows the comparative and cooperative nature of European expansion and empires, so that although each country was distinct in its exploration, trade and settlement, each was related to the other. Early on, the Italians were the clearinghouse of money, navigators and ideas. Providing another point of view of the Portuguese at Calicut, Bartolomeo Marchioni remarked: "Great honour and good reception were given them; and they held mass on shore. Their merchants and factor then began to trade [*s'abazarare*]."[143] The cause of the ensuing conflict seems to have been, as accounted elsewhere, the Portuguese desire for priority: "And wishing to load first, the Portuguese came to such a difference that the Moors raised a great tumult and killed all the Portuguese who were on land, including their factor."[144] The Portuguese reaction appears to have been similar to that given in other narratives: "And when those in the Portuguese ships saw this, they withdrew the ships and began to burn the Moorish ships and to bombard the land; and they destroyed thus many houses and killed many people and burned fifteen of those Moorish ships."[145] Marchioni gave his own version, including some variations on details like those in the other accounts of this voyage—the friendly king, enemy to Calicut, who would trade on credit and the honor of their word and who sent an ambassador to the king of Portugal with "infinite presents"; the 15,000 Moors of Calicut pursuing the Portuguese with 150 sail and being eluded because the Portuguese did not want to engage as their ships were full of valuable cargo; the finding of the body of Saint Thomas, the apostle, and the relics brought to the king in Lisbon; four ambassadors and two Christians returning with the fleet; the rich cargo brought home to Portugal; the two "marvellous" parrots of different colors that are "an arm [*gomito*] and half long."[146] The conclusion Marchioni reached is also instructive: "And they gave notice of many other and various birds and animals, so that where Pliny told untruths, these prove his history."[147] The right and wrong of an ancient authority is as much a function of the assessment of Cabral's expedition as of earlier Portuguese and Spanish voyages. In a letter of July 1501, the Florentine, Marchioni, came to the same conclusion as the Venetian, Priuli: given the rich cargo of pepper, cinnamon, ginger, cloves and other spicery brought back from India, the Portuguese will "be able to furnish from this route all the West, and also Italy, in time. They must give great trouble to the Venetians, and on the route more to the Sultan who enjoys the traffic from there, because by this route they come at rather small expense and more easily."[148] In this letter Marchioni also mentioned the gold mines the Portuguese visited, the birds and animals that proved Pliny right; the silk supply in Strava and Zanzura [Zanzibar]; and the Paternoster beads sold by the Moors, who "are white and resemble men of the Sultan of Babylonia."[149] Color, although not as much a preoccupation as it would become in the later phases of European colonization, is something that does recur, however briefly, in passing in letters, diaries and narratives in the early periods of imperial expansion.

When Gaspar de Lemos returned from Brazil to Portugal during the summer of 1500, carrying with him letters to the king from various members of Cabral's fleet and especially the one from Pedro Vaz de Caminha, and after news had also been received from Spain in Lisbon that in September 1500 Vicente Yañez Pinzon had reached Palos and had reported that he had visited South America and had returned with a cargo of brazil-wood, the Portuguese decided to send out an expedition to claim the land for Portugal. A Florentine, Vespucci, perhaps at the suggestion of Bartolomeo Marchioni, was chosen for this task but, probably because Dom Manuel was not sure whether the new lands were in the Spanish or Portuguese sphere, he was sent as a representative of both Portugal and Spain. Vespucci, who was interested in cartography, had been to the New World twice. Departing in May 1501, Vespucci stopped along the African coast and came across the ships from Cabral's fleet.

Before leaving for Brazil, Vespucci, or someone in his fleet, sent a letter, addressed to Lorenzo de'Medici, to Lisbon that was to be transmitted to Florence and one based on the views of Gaspar de India, the interpreter. The authenticity of the letter is disputed by some historians because it is not in Vespucci's hand and does not seem to have been the kind of letter he would write.[150] Whatever the provenance and the author, this letter of June 4, 1501 reiterated themes from other accounts of the Cabral voyage. Vespucci, or the author of this letter if it is not his, told Lorenzo that the report from Cabral's fleet was given in a "disconnected manner" because there were no mathematicians or cosmographers in that expedition and that although "Vespucci" was reproducing the disconnectedness of the telling, he had "somewhat corrected it with the cosmography of Ptolemy."[151] The ancients still held authority in the matter of natural philosophy, cartography and navigation. This letter, unintentionally or not, qualifies the boldness of Cabral's "discovery" in the New World: "they went ashore in a land where they found white and nude people of the same land which I discovered for the King of Castile, except that it is further to the east."[152] Color, nudity, priority for Spain or Portugal and geographical position were all key themes in this observation. The letter, which barely mentions the western Atlantic, was especially concerned with spices, gold and other riches and where they were located and what was a fairly detailed itinerary of Cabral's voyage on the other side. This report was interested in many ships laden with drugs, spices and precious jewels. Particularly in describing ships called *giunchi*, it attempted to describe these riches with some care and precision, told of the great riches of the king of Portugal and assumed that the spices that go to Italy through Alexandria were also from the places the Portuguese had just explored.[153] Implicitly, then, Vespucci was saying that Cabral's voyage into the Indian Ocean would bring about great changes for Italy—his phrase "Thus goes the world" after stating his belief that the spices in Italy have such provenance leads me to this conclusion. At such a time of great change, Vespucci hung on to his old authorities: "And if the provinces and kingdoms and names of cities and islands do not agree with the ancient writers, it is a sign that they are changed, as we find in our Europe when, through a marvel, one is known by an old name."[154] Trying to see the new through the familiar and the miraculousness of the old surviving in the new are two marvels that Vespucci holds to as he is about to sail to the southern parts of the New World. The letter ends with a religious hope about this voyage on which he is about to embark, something he recognizes "is dangerous as to the frailty of this our human life. Nonetheless I make it with a free mind, for the service of God and for the world. And if God is served through me, He will give me virtue to such an extent that I may be directed to His every wish, if only to give me eternal repose for my soul."[155] This is an indirect prayer of a man caught between God and the world, trying to know what he can before the unknown. When the French and, later the Dutch, reached Brazil, the scene had already been set by the Portuguese and the Spaniards, so that Cabral's voyage, and the debate surrounding it as well as its African and Asian dimensions, extends the context usually extended to the suggestive narrative of Jean de Léry concerning Brazil in the mid-sixteenth century.

III

It was not for the Portuguese alone to bring conversion to the inhabitants of Brazil. From 1580 to 1640, Portugal was joined to Spain and together they drove the French out of Brazil, where they had been since the first decade of the sixteenth century: the rivalry and conflict between France and Portugal in Brazil is something Jean de Léry had noted during his time there in the 1560s. Although Binot Paulmier de Gonneville, a Norman, voyaged to Brazil in his ship "L'Espoir" three to five years after Cabral, the French did not develop as many posts as the Portuguese. Of Nicholas Durand de Villegagnon, who sailed in 1555 for Brazil, Léry said: "Once he had unloaded his artillery and his other gear, so as to enjoy greater security against both the savages and the Portuguese, who already have so many fortresses in that country, he began to build a fort."[156] The precedence of the Portuguese is already on the minds of Villegagnon and Léry, who was also on this expedition. France, as Max Savelle noted, was interested and participated in overseas expansion well before Columbus's landfall, so it challenged the monopoly that the pope had granted them in exploration and dominion of unexplored lands.[157] The French had been in the Grand Banks since the first decade of the sixteenth century; in 1524 Lyon merchants had provided for Giovanni da Verrazzano, whose voyage brought him to North America and not the promised land of Asia; French corsairs, like Jean Ango, raided the Spanish and Portuguese fleets in the waters off Europe, America, Africa and Asia; in 1536 François Ier entered into a treaty of friendship with Portugal and used its ports as bases to attack Spanish shipping; in the 1530s and 1540s, amid these hostilities with Spain, the king of France sent Cartier and Roberval into North America in areas that the papal bulls had designated as Spanish and Portuguese; in one of the wars, from 1542 to 1544, the French fared badly and signed a peace treaty following which François Ier banned his subjects from voyaging to the Spanish colonies.[158] The Portuguese were involved in the Black African slave trade in the fifteenth and sixteenth centuries and beyond. According to André Thevet, the Portuguese altered their tactics when French corsairs and English privateers attacked a caravel, which had slaves as a crew.[159] This is the context for Villegagnon's voyage to Brazil in 1555, and Léry comments on the monopoly that Portugal and Spain held so dear:

I will add this, by way of preface to some episodes that we will see further on: the Spaniards boast, and even more do the Portuguese, of having been the first to discover the land of Brazil and, indeed everything from the Straits of Magellan, fifty degrees on the side of the Antarctic Pole, to Peru, and on through to this side of the Equator; they consequently maintain that they are the lords of all those countries. They claim that the French who travel in those parts are usurpers, and if they find them on the sea and at their mercy, they wage such war on them that they have even flayed some of them alive, or put them to some other kind of cruel death. The French, who maintain the contrary—that they have their due share in these new-found countries—, not only refuse to be beaten by the Spaniards (and even less by the Portuguese) but defend themselves valiantly, and often render blow for blow to their enemies who (to speak of them dispassionately) would not dare to accost or attack them if they did not see themselves to be stronger and to outnumber them in vessels.[160]

In this prefatorial aside Léry encapsulates a French view of the conflict between the French on one side and the Spanish and Portuguese on the other. While he chides the Spaniards, something that is part of the Black Legend of Spain (which we will come across again in this study), he renders the Portuguese as insisting more on their priority and precedence and as being more pusillanimous than even the Spaniards. Léry, who is often quite balanced in his representations of the Tupinamba, is harsh on the rivals of France. He is also frequently a tough critic of France, especially in using a satirical or critical typology in which the Natives of the New World, after putting aside surface criticism, are portrayed as having better behavior and customs than those of the French, who have long tolerated abuses. Portugal, the chief contender with France for the riches of Brazil, does not always come out well in Léry even if the latter also provides critiques of his native country and the excesses and madness of its civil war: this author is looking back from about 1578 through the internecine strife to Villegagnon's expedition to Brazil in 1555.

Spain and France had been at war in 1552: Spanish privateers raided the French fisheries in Newfoundland while the French corsairs attacked Spanish fleets and colonies in the Caribbean and, under the command of Jacques de Sores, took Havana in 1555. A truce that gave up the right of the French to trade in the West Indies occurred in 1556 and lasted not even a year until a new conflict began. The Spanish negotiators wanted their monopoly, set out in the papal donations and its treaties with Portugal, whereas the French desired an open-seas policy: instead, a compromise was reached in which the Indies were not mentioned in the Treaty of Cateau-Cambrésis (April 3, 1559), so the French might operate there freely, except in areas that Spain controlled and in which it meted out its own punishment. The treaty also seemed to imply in this informal understanding that such events in the New World were not a cause of war (*casus belli*) in Europe, so that there were two spheres for laws and conventions.[161] This implied an informal agreement that would allow a challenge to the Iberian monopoly: however, the effort by Jean Ribaud (Ribaut) and René Laudonnière to found a colony in Florida in 1562 failed in the face of Spanish force in 1565. Although civil wars had weakened France, the French made progress in the last decades of the sixteenth century and were able, partly owing to Samuel de Champlain, to found Acadia and Québec in the first decade of the seventeenth century.

At a time when Portugal was joined to Spain, the French established these colonies in lands that belonged to the Iberian powers according to the donations and their treaties of the 1490s and thereby challenged successfully the Spanish monopoly. Philip II of Spain would not put into the Treaty of Vervins (1598) a provision to prosecute French ships in American waters because that would acknowledge their existence there, so such prosecution was avoidable for offending ships from both sides.[162] Like France, England, too, challenged this Iberian monopoly.

Who was the pirate depended on which point of view was being recorded. Léry's judgment of a captured Portuguese caravel and its captain, who decided to yield because he was downwind, rebounds on the French:

> Our captains had decided long before to "equip themselves" (as we say today) with a ship of this kind, which they had always vowed to take from either the Spanish or from the Portuguese; the more surely to take possession of it, they immediately put some of our people in it. However, because of certain considerations regarding the master of this ship, they told him that if he could speedily find and seize another caravel nearby, they would give him back his own. For his part, he preferred to have the loss fall rather on his neighbor than on himself; so he was given, according to his request, one of our barks armed with muskets and filled with twenty of our soldiers and some of his men, and like the true pirate that I think he was, the better to play the part and not get caught, he sailed well out in front of our ships.[163]

The description might well reveal the apparent willingness to sacrifice common cause for self-interest among the Portuguese, but it also reveals the sly tactics of the French, which become the subject of the witty euphemism "equip themselves" ("s'accommoder") for seizing ships. Although this incident could have been worse, it is not as if the French took such a high ground that they renounced piracy. Léry has a gift for exposing short-comings, even, and sometimes particularly, those of his compatriots. On Christmas day the Portuguese "sea-rovers" shot at a caravel of Spaniards and seized them and the cargo of white salt; of caravels, Léry says:

> Since, as I have said, they had decided long before to "equip themselves" with one of these, they took it with us to Villegagnon's settlement in Brazil. It is true that they kept their promise to the Portuguese, who had seized this ship, to return his caravel; but our seamen (cruel in this respect), who had put all the Spaniards, dispossessed of their goods, pell-mell in with the Portuguese, not only left no morsel of biscuit or of other supplies with these poor people, but what was worse, they tore their sails, and even took away their ship's boat, without which they could not approach land. I think that it would have been better to send them to the bottom than to leave them in such a state. And indeed, abandoned thus to the mercy of the water, if some ship did not come to their rescue, they must have either drowned or died of hunger.[164]

Curiously, even though Léry denounces French cruelty here, which certainly is a counterbalance to the Black Legend of Spain and to the Spanish mistreatment of the French as set out by Nicolas Le Challeux, he prefers putting the Spanish crew out of their misery rather than explicitly saying none of this should have been done. Yes, implicitly, the Spaniards should have had use of their boat, but they do not receive a defense that includes an explicit denunciation of the French captains who authorized these cruel measures. The Spaniards suffer abuse from the French with the help of the self-interested Portuguese.

When this French expedition arrived in Brazil, they came first among "the nation called *Margaia*, allies of the Portuguese, and therefore such enemies of the French that if they had had us at their mercy, we would have paid no other ransom except being slain and cut to pieces, and serving as a meal for them."[165] The French kept their distance for safety but traded: there was already tension between Portugal and France and their different Native allies in Brazil. The French were hungry and, despite their wariness, ate the food that the Margaia had given them and the next day, a Sunday (there seem to have been no holidays from war), they came upon

> a Portuguese fort, called by them *Espirito santo* (and by the savages *Moab*). Recognizing both our equipage and that of the caravel that we had in tow (which they judged correctly that we had taken from their countrymen), they fired three cannon shots at us, and we fired three or four at them in reply. But because we were too far for the reach of their shot, they did us no harm, and I think we did none to them, either.[166]

The places have split identities between the earlier names given by the Natives and the new names the Europeans have used. Even at a place the Portuguese have called the Holy Spirit there is armed conflict. The French, identified by the Portuguese as carrying plunder from their countrymen, evaded the attack.

Warfare becomes more complex when the Europeans enter into alliances with rival Native nations. Of the Tupinikin Tupinamba, Léry, in his chapter on war, notes: "their closest and principal enemies are those whom they call *Margaia*, and their allies the Portuguese, whom they call *Pero*; reciprocally, the Margaia are hostile not only to the Tupinamba, but also to the French, their confederates."[167] This is the kind warfare that later occurred in North America when the English and French contended for the northern part of the continent. Léry places the conflict in the context of the chapter on drinking and eating (roots and grains) because of some of the practices of the Tupinamba. In a village Léry spoke with a *moussacat*, a Tupinamba father who offers hospitality to people passing through, who recounted "we surprised a caravel of Peros" and added "After we had slain and eaten the men who were in it, as we were taking possession of their merchandise, we found some big wooden *caramemos* (that is what they call barrels and other vessels) full of drink."[168] Léry mentions that the three days of stupefaction or "bacchanalian celebration" was owing to Spanish wine.[169] The theme of cannibalism returns to Léry's text, which shows the ceremonial and cultural intricacies of this practice. The conflict had terrible consequences for the Europeans as well as for the Natives. In the chapter on law and civil order, Léry, recounting an incident in which an old man wanted to kill him because Léry had killed a duck that belonged to one of his friends, listened to his interpreter and, after the man had slept off his strong drink—*caouin*, he took a different view:

> However, as it turned out, the Tupinamba knew perfectly well that, already having the Portuguese for enemies, if they had killed a Frenchman an irreconcilable war would have been declared between them and that they would be forever deprived of our merchandise; so everything that my man had done was in jest. And in fact, when he woke up about three hours later, he sent a message to me saying that I was his son, and that what he had done to me was only to test me, and to see by my countenance whether I would be valiant in war against the Portuguese and the Margaia, our common enemies.[170]

Léry tries to teach the old man a lesson, but concludes that the Tupinamba are loyal friends and that their elders urge their young to treat the French well, particularly because they value the knives, axes and pruning hooks they once lacked. This anecdote, or narrative within a narrative, relates the personal to the public, an event in Léry's experience of the greater political and economic framework. In the relation between Léry and the old man, the French and the Tupinamba, the Portuguese and their allies enter into the equation.

To return to the arrival of Léry's group, we can observe how Portuguese names qualify their claims to the new lands. Despite the fact that the Native name of Guanabara and the Portuguese one of Janeiro meant that the French were not the first in Rio, the French had claimed this place: Villegagnon had been there since the year before when Léry's ship arrived and Léry comes to reiterate the Portuguese "discovery" of this spot, to say that the French frequent this port often and to describe its physical situation in detail.[171] Rio de Janeiro or Fort Coligny (as the French called it) is, according to Léry, a natural fortress and it is only French incompetence that allowed the Portuguese to take it in a surprise attack in 1560. After Léry returned to France, Brazil was a contested land. More specifically, Léry blames Villegagnon for dishonoring the name of Gaspard de Coligny and of Antarctic France because he rebelled against the pure religion (Calvinism) and abandoned the fortress to the Portuguese.[172]

The traces and claims of the Portuguese are without erasure in Léry's text. For instance, even in ethnological descriptions of everyday life, he remarks on cross-cultural change and adaptation and cannot avoid the mark of Portugal: "Our Americans have a great many ordinary hens, which the Portuguese introduced among them."[173] The Portuguese hens may have helped to modify how the Tupinamba, who were supposed to be French allies and hostile to the people who introduced them to these animals, adorned their own bodies, for they dyed red the feathers of these white hens with brazil-wood, which they cut up more finely than mincemeat with the iron tools—replacements for their sharp stones—acquired from Europeans, and applied these feathers to a gum smeared all over their bodies. Léry wryly observes: "It is likely that some observers, who upon their arrival saw these people thus adorned, went back home without any further acquaintance with them, and proceeded to spread the rumor that the savages were covered with hair. But, as I have said above, they are not so in their natural state; that rumor has been based on ignorance and too easily accepted."[174] Here is a wonderful example of cultural modification and circulation: cultural and material exchange begets unexpected results. The European iron tools and hens seem to have modified the way the Tupinamba prepared the feathers and the manner in which they adorned themselves, but some of those same Europeans, ignorant of this trade and cultural exchange, misinterpreted the very process they helped to enact. These new mixed cultural practices could baffle the very Europeans whose own culture influenced that of the Natives. Léry shares with the reader his position of being in the know, the kind of superior knowledge the satirist uses and the playwright employs in dramatic irony. This satiric edge and typological approach, in which Léry uses America and Europe to read each other, is something Montaigne also employs with great effect. "Travel writers," long before Columbus, represented the "away" of other lands to appeal to or speak about the "presence" of home. Like Erasmus and Thomas More, and perhaps in the spirit of Herodotus and Lucian, Léry and Montaigne mix the ethnographical and satirical.

These hens, then, become part of a preexisting framework for hens among the Tupinamba, which become a focus for cultural and agricultural differences between the Europeans and the Natives:

> I will also begin this chapter on birds (which in general our Tupinamba call *oura*) with those that are good to eat. First, there are a great many of those big hens that we call "guinea hens," which they call *arignannoussou*.

The Portuguese have introduced among them a breed of ordinary little hens that they did not have before, which they call *arignanmiri*. Although they set great store by the white ones for their feathers, which they dye red and use to adorn their bodies, they seldom eat any of either breed.[175]

Even the relation between the "Americans" and French, who have brought "wheat-seed and wine-stock," and others who have followed them, seems to be placed in the context of the Iberian powers because Léry begins his descriptions of breads in Brazil with "The Spanish and Portuguese, at present settled in several places of the West Indies, now have a great deal of wheat and wine that Brazil produces for them, so they have proved that it is not for lack of the right soil that the savages have none."[176] Even while Léry sets out French precedence and innovation in the cultivation of wheat and wine, he modifies the French contribution in terms of apparently earlier Portuguese and Spanish practices. Origins and influences, as in many French and English texts about the New World, become a recurring theme in what might be called a textual dance of complementary rivalry. These oxymoronic urges are not unusual in the representations of the New World. Portugal, as well as Spain, can beget colony envy because they developed the first seaborne empires with the support of the papacy at a time when western Europe was Catholic and based its religious authority in Rome.

Another example of Portuguese traces and cultural modifications is citrus fruit. Léry notes: "so I have heard" America did not have lemon or orange trees, yet "the Portuguese have planted and raised some, on or near the seashores that they frequented, which have not only greatly multiplied but also bear sweet oranges (which the savages call *morgou-ia*) as big as two fists, and lemons, which are still bigger and in even greater abundance."[177] The priority and influence of the Portuguese on the Natives are themes Léry admits. He even allows that the Portuguese have had success with sugarcane "in the places that they possess over there," whereas the French have not yet done so.[178] Names, crops, lands are not simply a French domain, so that even in the rivalry, Léry gives compass to the Portuguese.

A certain sympathy existed between Léry and the Portuguese or fellow Christians he describes. In the first instance a member of the Margaia nation, who had been to Portugal and baptized Antoni, asked to be delivered from the Tupinamba and was understood because one of the French, a locksmith, knew Spanish and understood Portuguese. The French set out to bring this prisoner, Antoni, a file the next day, but the Tupinamba suspected something and showed the French the body of Antoni on the boucan and his head, which caused in them "great peals of laughter."[179] Although he is careful to give the Tupinamba their due, he can also be critical, as Léry demonstrates when he talks about the "cruelty of the savages."[180] Léry's long description concentrates on the cultural difference in this encounter:

> one of our savages surprised two Portuguese, in a little house made of earth in
> the woods, near the fort called *Morpion*. The Portuguese defended themselves
> valiantly from morning to night; after their supply of harquebuses and cross-
> bow arrows was exhausted, they came out with two-handed swords, with
> which they countered the blows of their assailants so well that many were killed
> and others wounded. However, the savages, attacking more and more relent-
> lessly, resolved to be cut into pieces rather than withdraw without victory.
> Finally they laid hold of the two Portuguese and took them prisoner.[181]

What the French were doing to prevent this conflict is a matter of debate.
We have seen earlier in the case of Antoni that their interventions did not
always have the intended effects. Sometimes, they seem to profit from the
Native plunder of Portuguese goods:

> Of their spoils, a savage sold me some ox-skin garments, and one of our
> interpreters obtained a silver plate that they had pillaged, along with some
> other things from the house that they had broken into; since they were
> unaware of its value, it only cost him two knives.[182]

The go-betweens, and Léry himself, profited from the war and spoils.
The Natives had something prepared for the Portuguese twosome:

> When they returned to their villages, they tore the beards out of these two
> Portuguese merely to humiliate them, and then put them cruelly to death.
> What is more, because these poor tortured men cried out in their pain, the
> savages mocked them, saying "What is this? Can it be that you have so bravely
> defended yourselves, and now, when it is the moment to die with honor, you
> show that you have not even as much courage as women?" And thus they were
> killed and eaten in the savage style.[183]

Even though Léry shows a kind of balance and an ethnological urge, he is not
impressed with this cruelty and brings out the typology with French
barbarism in its civil wars: he outlines the lamentable record in France,
"so that those who read these horrible things, practiced daily among these
barbarous nations of the land of Brazil, may also think more carefully about
the things that go on every day over here, among us."[184] Cruelty, then,
despite the Black Legend of Spain, is not something that any one group has
a monopoly on, so that the Tupinamba and the French are also implicated
by Léry, who himself enjoyed the spoils of the two poor Portuguese. This
complication suggests, even through a French text, that no one, not even the
Portuguese, escaped the mixed and problematic motives and actions of trade,
colonization and armed conflict.

IV

The independence of Portugal occurred as a result of the dynasty of Afonso VI of León (1072–1109): he married as his second wife Constance of Burgundy, which marked the beginning of "French influence" in the Iberian Peninsula. Constance's nephew, Duke Eudes of Burgundy, and his cousin Raimundo—who married Afonso's legitimate daughter, Urraca, and became count of Galacia—became influential in the Peninsula. The Burgundian and French knights helped to fight the Muslims. Henry of Burgundy married Afonso's bastard daughter, Teresa, in 1095 and a year or two later became the count of Portugal. Not until 1143, when Portugal was placed under the protection of the Holy See in return for annual tribute, did the dependence of Portugal on León begin to wane. Only in 1179 did the Holy See formally recognize Portugal in royal terms. As part of the Reconquest, in 1147, French, English, German and Flemish crusaders en route to Palestine helped take Lisbon from the Moors. During his reign Sancho I peopled newly conquered lands in Portugal and organized them into *concelhos* or municipalities, a system that was to be the basic means of organizing Portuguese settlements overseas.[185]

The Burgundian dynasty in Portugal was embroiled, along with other European powers, in the Castilian succession in 1373: Fernando allied himself with John of Gaunt, a member of the English royal family, in the hopes of a joint invasion of Castile. In 1380 Fernando entered into an alliance with Gaunt and with the English crown, but, perhaps disappointed with the English army that Gaunt's brother, the earl of Cambridge, brought to Portugal, Fernando married his only daughter to John I of Castile. When Fernando died, his bastard brother, John of Avis, challenged his niece the queen and her husband, John I, because they had proclaimed themselves sovereigns in Portugal. In 1385, John of Avis defeated John I of Castile and secured a formal alliance with England (Treaty of Westminster, May 9, 1386), aspects of which persisted six centuries and beyond despite the vicissitudes in the relations between the two countries. The Burgundians and English had had much to do with the early formation of the Portuguese royal house, but the marriages into the royal house of Castile created dynastic tensions between Portugal and Castile. Prince Henry the Navigator (d. 1460), a great force in Portuguese exploration and expansion in Africa, was the third son from this marriage between John and Philippa.

Portugal was on the main route between Flanders and Italy: the Italians had opened trade with the Portuguese in the early fourteenth century and English merchants had privileges there as well; Antwerp and Bruges became the principal markets for the Portuguese and Flemish capital and shipping grew in significance. Portugal also became an important center in the slave trade—in the 1430s the first African slaves were brought to Lisbon.[186] Slavery was to become a key factor in the Portuguese role in the colonization of the New World. Madeira and the Azores in the fifteenth century produced wine and sugar, providing exports for Lisbon and a valuable example for those who would later colonize Brazil. Many of the old Portuguese nobility had sided with the Castilians and, no longer a force in Portugal after 1385, were replaced with a new nobility from John of Avis' supporters. The connection to Castile and, later, Spain was something that could not be avoided so readily. Although Portugal had long disputed the Castilian claim to the Canaries, it acknowledged it in 1479. "Spain" was a rival in expansion and colonization: whereas in 1488 Dias rounded the Cape of Good Hope, in 1492, Columbus set sail to the western Atlantic. The Portuguese, as we have seen, entered with Spain into the Treaty of Tordesillas in 1494: Vasco da Gama reached India in 1498 and Cabral, Brazil in 1500. Portugal was making breakthroughs, but its exploration was in relation to that of Spain and subject to the authority of the pope. In 1529, after the question of the Moluccas was settled, Portugal and Spain agreed to set out another line of demarcation in the Pacific.

For the Iberian powers, the sea was closed and the world was effectively divided between them. For the first time since independence, Portugal now saw its national interest as coinciding with Castile. Owing to Portugal's imperial interests and to the Reformation, it loosened its ties with England. Whereas João II (John II) had admitted Spanish Jews, Manuel expelled them and thus kept in line with the policy of Isabella and Ferdinand. Dynastic marriages yoked the two nations: João III and Sebastião (John III and Sebastian) were half Spanish and Philip II was half Portuguese. Other institutions drew them together: for instance, the Jesuits, who began in Spain, gathered great power in Portugal and were key to education there. Castilian became one of the languages of the Portuguese court and writers, like Camões (Camoens), also wrote copiously in that language. John III, married to the sister of Emperor Charles V, had as his heir a grandson, Sebastian, who ascended the throne when he was three-years old and who, unmarried and without a clear heir, died in 1578 when his army was soundly defeated at Alcazar-Kebir in Africa. After his aged great-uncle, a cardinal, King Henry died, having ruled from 1578 to 1580, his kinsman, Philip II of Spain, ascended the throne. This Iberian union, a kind of greater modern version of pagan, Visigoth and Christian Hispania in which the Portuguese and Spanish empires complemented each other in trade, is something that was, according to Vitorino Magalhães Godinho and A. H. Oliveira Marques, attractive to more than a few in Portugal, so that in the last half of the sixteenth-century Seville, and not Antwerp, was the main connection for Portuguese trade.[187] Despite Philip II's attempts to separate the administration of the two kingdoms, warfare brought them closer together. The great armada of 1588 was formed in Lisbon; Portugal lost its English and Flemish trade, and the Dutch, excluded from the emporium, sought the products at the source itself. Philip III and Philip IV were less concerned about Portuguese interests than Philip II. Soon the Dutch had a presence in the Portuguese sphere in Asia, Africa and America. Taxation and wartime levies on troops, imposed by the Spanish, were two aggravations for the Portuguese. The French tried to foment rebellion among them and when Catalonia rebelled in 1640 so too did Portugal—and successfully.[188]

This period, between 1580 and 1640, of Iberian unity certainly seemed threatening to countries like England. When Richard Hakluyt the younger was helping to write, translate, collect and edit works that would construct an English nation on the verge of empire, he selected one text from this period that was both Portuguese and Spanish and that represented Spanish interests in North America, the place Hakluyt thought most suitable for English expansion and colonization. Having set out the legal, cultural and political background of the relation between Portugal and Spain, I think that this text suggests more than is apparent at first.

It is not surprising that Richard Hakluyt the younger would take an interest in Portugal when compiling his collection of travel narratives, especially in *Principall Navigations*, which has been called the prose epic of the English nation. It is well known that the papal bulls of 1493, which divided the world into eastern and western spheres between Portugal and Spain, and the Treaty of Tordesillas (June 7, 1494) were designed to give the Iberian powers a monopoly on exploration, so from that time forward England and France had to look to Portugal and Spain as imperial *exempla* and had to seek ways to circumvent the papal decree and the treaty by other legal maneuvers, such as legal fictions like *terra nullius*.[189]

But before discussing a specific instance of the English debt to Portugal, I will return to the context of Iberian history and the role of England in it. Portugal and Spain both expanded south against the Moors who held much of the Iberian Peninsula for centuries. The kingdom of Portugal was centered on Oporto and achieved independence in 1140. In 1147 English crusaders helped to capture Lisbon. In 1267, two centuries before the Spaniards won Granada, the Portuguese defeated the Moors. With the help of John of Gaunt's archers, the Portuguese beat back the Spaniards at the battle of Aljubarrota in 1385. The next year Portugal and England signed a treaty of friendship. In 1387 Gaunt's daughter, Phillipa, was married to King João I (John I). The Portuguese had two great ambitions. First, they wanted to wrest North Africa from the Muslims. Second, they wished to explore the coast of Africa as a means of finding passage to Asia.[190]

The first ambition, though costly, changed European history because it helped shift the balance of power from the Mediterranean (especially Venice) to the Atlantic (particularly Portugal and Spain), because it allowed for direct contact and trade with the East (which had lessened after Marco Polo) and because it served as a prelude to the exploration and settlement of the New World. In his great epic *Os Lusiadas* (*The Lusiads* in English) (pub. 1572), Luis de Camões represents Vasco da Gama's journey beyond the Cape of Africa to India, so that he begins the poem *in medias res*. Camões is thereby able to take up da Gama's achievement beyond Bartolomeu Dias's furthest point. How well Hakluyt knew *The Lusiads* is uncertain, but as he was collecting prose works for his collection, he does not include any of it. The first *Index* of banned books developed in Italy in 1543; a Spanish version appeared in 1546; and in Portugal in 1547: the censorship increased in the "Indices" such as those of 1551, 1561, 1581 and 1624, and eventually, although not in the first instance, Camões was among those mutilated or proscribed as being against "our holy Faith and good customs."[191] Whereas João III had attracted foreign figures, such as James Buchanan and Nicholas Claenarts, to the University of Coimbra—which he had reestablished and whose chancellor was Bento de Camões, the poet's uncle—his successors had allowed the the Holy Office to prosecute and scatter the humanists at Coimbra and Buchanan himself had gone to Edinburgh.[192] While Gil Vincente, the Portuguese playwright, wrote about a quarter of his plays in Castilian only and about another third were in both languages, Camões, and many of the finest Portuguese contemporary authors, composed a significant part of their texts in Castilian just as later Portuguese writers would write a significant amount of their work in French. Castilianization was important in the lead-up to the Iberian union: at this time, some Spanish writers wrote in Portuguese and works from Portugal were translated into Castilian.[193] Camões was part of a shifting literary tradition involving political change and translation. Not until 1655 did *The Lusiads* appear in an English translation, that of Richard Fanshawe, which is still reprinted and which I discuss in the next section.[194] The second ambition—the conquering of North Africa—led to disaster for Portugal. In 1578, the young King Sebastião invaded Morocco and, at Alcacer-Kebir, was defeated and slain, along with important members of the nobility. Two years later Philip II of Spain took up the crown of Portugal, and the Spanish ruled the Portuguese for 60 years.[195]

The story of the English connection to Portugal and Spain, then, began centuries before Columbus. As early as 1443, Prince Henry the Navigator (Dom Enrique) had became a member of the Order of the Garter.[196] The more immediate context of the 1480s and 1490s is also important for this connection. There seems to have been in those decades close trade among Iceland, Bristol and Portugal. England and Portugal were on friendly terms. From documents it is hard to say how much contact before 1480 the Bristol ships had with Madeira, the Açores [Azores] and Cape Verdes, the Atlantic islands, which the Portuguese came across and settled in the fifteenth century.[197] A Bristolian, William Worcester, who has given us the only account of the Isle of Brasil expedition in 1480, left two jottings about these Atlantic islands that show an interest in charting new lands and the surrounding seas.[198] In the Bibliothèque Nationale in Paris, there is a map made in about 1490 probably in Portugal of the Genoese type. It includes the Island of the Seven Cities and the Isle of Brasil that the Bristol expedition set out to find in 1480. The legend of the Island of the Seven Cities is that the Portuguese settled it and that, as Spanish sailors said, the sand contained silver.[199] By 1480, if not earlier, the English appear to have known about the voyages and maps of the Portuguese.[200] It seems that Columbus approached João II [John II] of Portugal in 1484–85 about his plans for a western voyage and then Spain in 1485–88. His brother Bartholomew, who was a chartmaker in Lisbon from about 1477 onward, presented the same scheme to Henry VII in London during 1488–89 and then sought Charles VIII of France's support in about 1491. Later, especially in 1501–02, there were Anglo-Portuguese voyages.[201] The relation between Portugal and England in exploration also involved connections with Iceland, Italy, Spain, France and other countries. Although there were rivalries, the push toward expansion was pan-European.

From this general background, well known to Portuguese readers, let me look more specifically at connections between England and Portugal that are less apparent and more specific. These links relate to explorations of the New World. The French and the English had to learn from Portugal and Spain while claiming that the Iberian nations had no right to lands such as Newfoundland and New France. Hakluyt used narratives from Portuguese and Spanish authors to provide information to the English government and nation in order to initiate permanent English settlement in North America, which was defined beyond the Portuguese and Spanish imperial domains. In 1498 Henry VII of England debated this treaty with Pedro de Ayala, the Spanish representative.[202] On July 25, 1498 De Ayala wrote from London to Ferdinand and Isabella to report John Cabot's discoveries in 1497 and the progress of his expedition of 1498:

> Los de Bristol ha siete años que cada año an armado dos, tres, quatro caravelas para ir a buscar la isla del Brasil, i la Siete Ciudades con la fantasia deste Ginoves.

In 1862 this passage was translated into English as

> For the last seven years the people of Bristol have equipped two, three, four caravels to go in search of the island of Brazil and the Seven Cities according to the fancy of this Genoese.[203]

David Quinn suggests a translation that provides a plausible alternative: "The Bristol men for seven years have fitted out yearly two, three, or four small ships to go in search, as this Genoese fancies, of the Isle of Brasil or the Seven Cities."[204] The crux is the Spanish word, "fantasia," which in addition to meaning fantasy was a nautical term that signified reckoning or estimating distances. This interpretative difference, which probably cannot be resolved, is between the view that John Cabot, a Genoese who was Venetian by adoption, inspired the Bristol voyages or that he was merely commenting on their objectives but did not participate in them. Without getting into Cabot's activities in Venice between 1476 and 1485 or in Valencia between 1490 and 1493 or debating whether there were two Giovanni Caboti/Juan Caboto/John Cabots or confirming the claim by the Bristol merchants, like John Day, that the English discovered America in about 1480–81, I want to look briefly at the relation of English colonization to Portuguese expansion from the fifteenth-century voyages from Bristol to the narratives of Hakluyt and Purchas in the late sixteenth and early seventeenth centuries.[205] Like Columbus, Cabot had been in Lisbon and Seville seeking support for his scheme for exploration.[206] It is also possible that the discovery of the isle of Brasil by the merchants of Bristol in the early 1580s became known to Portugal and Spain through trading contacts.[207] Although in "Discourse on Western Planting" (1584, pub. 1877) Hakluyt does not use the earlier claim by Bristol to give England a claim to North America, he does employ Cabot's voyage of 1497 for that purpose. England has to build an empire by differentiating itself from Portugal and Spain. Hakluyt's prose epic, *Principall Navigations* (1589), is part of a propaganda campaign to establish an English empire: it is promotional literature.

During the sixteenth century, English ideas about colonization, while owing something to classical and medieval concepts and to the involvement of England in Ireland, depended most on continental sources.[208] English promotional literature about America most often involved translations of continental authors, especially from Spain. The example of Spain was central in determining English attitudes to the New World and its inhabitants. In addition to Hakluyt, who translated or commissioned translations from the Spanish, other principal translators were Richard Eden, John Frampton and Thomas Nicholas. Although the English adapted Spanish writings that glorified the Spanish conquest for their own purposes—providing propaganda to encourage potential investors and settlers—they often adopted Spanish representations of the New World and the Native.[209] The Spanish authors most translated into English, such as Peter Martyr, Oviedo and López de Gómera, emphasized the glory of Spain in the face of Native American betrayal and barbarism even if they sometimes advocated conversion and condemned Spaniards for mistreating the Natives.[210] Only one edition of Las Casas's *Brief Relation of the Destruction of the Indies* appeared in English as *The Spanish Colonie* in 1583. This translation was filtered through the French translation from which the preface is taken. The preface encouraged support for the Dutch revolt against Spain.[211] Until after 1590, English promotional literature did not take up the anti-Spanish and pro-Native stance of the Black Legend, so often associated with Las Casas. In the introduction to *Virginia Richly Valued* (1609) Hakluyt assumes the Spanish view that the Natives are liars and dissemblers and suggests that if the inhabitants of America could not be converted, then English soldiers trained in the Netherlands against Spain should prepare the Natives for the hands of English preachers.[212] In *Principall Navigations* Hakluyt does not pay much attention to the champion of the Indians—Las Casas.[213] Whereas the first edition contains no mention of Las Casas, the second alludes to him directly just twice. Only in a work that remained unpublished until the nineteenth century—the "Particular Discourse"—did Hakluyt show a clearly anti-Spanish and pro-Native stance.[214] Whether this is an accident of publishing history or whether this contrary position of Hakluyt as a proponent of the Black Legend is his private rather than his public view or whether there was a shift or tension in Hakluyt's thought is something that probably cannot be settled, but it was for others who sought to promote English colonization in the New World to emphasize the Black Legend. Walter Ralegh's *Discoverie of Guiana* (1596) tends toward the anti-Spanish and pro-Native position of the literature of the Black Legend, although here as in his unpublished tract arguing that the Spanish conquest was an illegal act that killed 20 million, Ralegh's argument also is one of outconquesting the Spaniards and finding even more gold.[215] It is quite possible that Ralegh distributed his tract to the queen privately, and Hakluyt might have done the same, as if there was a gap between the public promotion and secret matters of state in the case of the New World.

The English never found a sustained Black Legend to apply to the Portuguese. For the most part, they tried to learn as much as possible from Portuguese accounts of the New World. On one occasion Hakluyt included Portugal with Spain in qualifying the heroism of their exploration and settlement of the New World. The prefatory matter of the various editions of *Principall Navigations* and Hakluyt's dedication to his translation of an anonymous Portuguese account of Hernando de Soto are instructive examples of the English use of the Portuguese model while England, however haltingly, was attempting to establish an empire.

In the Epistle Dedicatorie to the first edition of *Principall Navigations* (1589), which addresses Francis Walsingham, principal secretary to Elizabeth I, Hakluyt speaks of his early reading of "discoveries and voyages" in ancient and modern European languages, including Portuguese.[216] The paradox of

Hakluyt's enterprise is that he is attempting to create a distinct patriotic and "nationalistic" framework for an English empire while relying on narratives from other modern empires, like Spain, and rival nations with imperial ambitions, like France, to define that patriotism and nationalism. In the preface to the first edition, which is addressed to "the favourable Reader," Hakluyt sets out his method: "Whatsoever testimonie I have found in any authour of authoritie appertaining to my argument, either stranger or naturall, I have recorded the same word for word, with his particular name and page of booke where it is extant."[217] Besides advocating literal translation, Hakluyt is also asserting the accuracy of his scholarship and the transnational nature of his enterprise. The Portuguese Hakluyt translates have had actual experience with voyages and discoveries and so are more reliable than unnamed and inexperienced cosmographers like André Thevet. Although Hakluyt says that he has collected English narratives about English exploration, he admits that in some places he had to rely on

> some strangers as witnesses of the things done, yet are they none but such as either faythfully remember, or sufficiently confirme the travels of our owne people: of whom (to speake trueth) I have received more light in some respects, then all our owne Historians could affoord me in this case, Bale, Foxe, and Eden only excepted.[218]

This qualification of these English narratives, in which Hakluyt finds foreign sources for English voyages more helpful than native sources, with only a few exceptions, demonstrates the ambivalence of his enterprise. His is a kind of cosmopolitan "nationalism" that shows the tensions between international humanism and affairs of the English state.

The Portuguese, in this same preface, are linked with Spain with whom, at this time, they are politically joined. Hakluyt mentions the recent Portugal expedition after the defeat of the Spanish armada the year before his preface appeared.[219] He also mentions the English trade with Brazil.[220] Some of the maps in the edition are "collected and reformed according to the newest, secretest, and latest discoveries, both Spanish, Portugall, and English."[221] The only explicit mention of Portugal in the Epistle Dedicatory to the first volume of the second edition (1598), which Hakluyt dedicates to Charles Howard, lord admiral of England, is of the English attack on Faraon on the coast of Portugal.[222] In the preface to the second edition (1598), once more addressed to the reader, Hakluyt compares some great exploits of the English with those of other nations. For instance, he asks "Be it granted that the renowned Portugale Vasques de Gama traversed the maine Ocean Southward of Africke: Did not Richard Chanceler and his mates performe the like Northward of Europe?"[223] The heroic deeds of other nations are to be admitted, but only to amplify with their greatness the great glory of English deeds. Hakluyt wants to promote English colonization of the temperate zone of North America just north of Florida and uses the example of the Portuguese and Spanish:

> But nowe it is high time for us to weigh our ancre, to hoise up our sailes, to get cleare of these boistrous, frosty, and misty seas, and with all speede to direct our course for the milde, lightsome, temperate, and warme Atlantick Ocean, over which the Spaniards and Portugales have made so many pleasant prosperous and golden voyages.[224]

But Hakluyt soon betrays more ambivalence over the role of the Portuguese, who are now politically connected to the Spanish. He admits that they have endured hardships and tempests in their many voyages, "yet this dare I boldly affirme; first that a great number of them have satisfied their fame-thirsty and gold-thirsty mindes with that reputation and wealth, which made all perils and misadventures seeme tolerable unto them" and second their first attempts were no more dangerous than the English voyages to the Northeast.[225] Here is a hint of the motives that underpin the cruelty of the Black Legend but nothing more. While the Portuguese and Spanish had to sail farther than the English, they did not have to encounter cold, dark and ice. Moreover, whereas the Spanish had the Canary Islands and the Portuguese the Açores, Madeira and other islands to provide protection and supplies, the English had no such lands on their voyages Northeast. Whereas the Portuguese and Spanish had continual "allurements" that arose from their trade with Africa, such as sugar, slaves and gold, the English had nothing to look forward to in their northern journeys.[226] The motives are hardly as pure as Hakluyt's promotional work would have them. In fact, he comes to promote gold as well as God and the many commodities of the temperate region of North America that the Portuguese and Spanish possess through their colonies and trade. Hakluyt wants England to emulate Portugal and Spain in order to free itself from trade with them.

The trade practices and secrets of Portugal and Spain are to serve the imperial ambitions of England. One of Hakluyt's concerns in his Epistle Dedicatorie to the second volume of the second edition (1599) is that of trade with nations that differ ideologically from England, a problem that still arises. In the late sixteenth century Hakluyt wanted to justify trading "with Turkes and misbeleevers."[227] In making this justification he cites as a precedent the example of Spain and Portugal:

> And who doth not acknowledge, that either hath travailed the remote parts of the world, or read the Histories of this later age, that the Spaniards and

Portugales in Barbarie, in the Indies, and elsewhere, have ordinarie confedera-
cie and traffike with the Moores, and many kindes of Gentiles and Pagans, and
that which is more, doe pay them pensions, and use them in their service and
warres?[228]

As much as Hakluyt would like England to displace Portugal and Spain in
empire, he must use their practices against them. He also outlines the first
English trade with the Canary Islands, the Cape Verde Islands and other
Spanish and Portuguese possessions. Toward this end, Hakluyt sometimes
dramatizes his information as new and secret, such as "a late and true report
of the weake estate of the Portugales in Angola, as also the whole course of
the Portugale Caracks from Lisbon to the barre of Goa in India."[229] Just as
Hakluyt translates Portuguese narratives for the purposes of promoting an
English power, so too does he use English narratives, like that of Thomas
Stevens who in 1579 was a passenger on the Portuguese fleet from Lisbon to
India, to corroborate information about Angola and Goa. England should
have ambitions in the East. To amplify the theme of secrecy and espionage,
Hakluyt adds "I have likewise added a late intercepted letter of a Portugall
revealing the secret and most gainfull trade of Pegu," and names a Venetian
and an Englishman who will confirm this account of the trade.[230]

The subject of the third volume of the *Principall Navigations* (1600) is
America, or the "New World," a term Hakluyt says he prefers, though he
persists in his use of America.[231] He dedicates this volume to Robert Cecil,
secretary to Elizabeth I. While Hakluyt shows that he continues to draw on
the translations from other European languages, he makes explicit here the
English rivalry with Spain and the enjoyment Hakluyt derives from using
Spanish reports to reveal Spain's secrets to England, especially if the Spanish
do not seek a Christian peace with the English.[232] The memory of the
Spanish armada and the persisting tensions between the two nations are a
recurrent theme in Hakluyt's prefatory matter. Nine years later, he used
a translation of an anonymous Portuguese account of Hernando de Soto's
expedition in order to promote Virginia.

Hakluyt makes use of a Portuguese narrative while the colony in Virginia
is experiencing a crisis. At about the same time that the Virginia Company
had sent out a fleet in 1609, Hakluyt was dedicating his *Virginia Richly
Valued*, a translation of the Portuguese report of de Soto's exploration of the
lands to the south of Virginia from 1538 to 1543. A Portuguese "gentleman
of Elvas" who was a member of the company, one of the eight volunteers
from Elvas and perhaps Alvaro Fernandez composed the original account of
the expedition, *Relaçam verdadeira dos trabalhos*, perhaps from memory after
the author returned home. In 1557 it was published at Evora, Portugal.
Hakluyt himself was a member of the Virginia Company of London that had

founded Jamestown in 1607 and had issued stock for publication in 1609. He hoped that after more than 50 years this work from the Portuguese would help to enlist settlers for Virginia. During the winter of 1609–10, when Jamestown suffered through famine, Hakluyt issued another edition of *Virginia Richly Valued*, this time with a title more distanced from the colony itself, *The Worthy and Famous History of the Travels, Discovery, and Conquest of Terra Florida* (1611).[233]

Hakluyt is no different from Columbus in taking up the theme of gold and God.[234] In "The Epistle Dedicatorie," Hakluyt addresses his work "To The Right Honovrable, The Right Wordshipfull Counsellors, and others the cheerefull aduenturors for the aduancement of that Christian and noble plantation in Virginia" and then he proceeds to speak most about the rich metals and commodities of Florida and, by implication, of Virginia. The implied wealth of Virginia soon becomes apparent: the Native inhabitants point north to even richer metals. Rather than simply relying on the Portuguese account of de Soto's expedition to lure settlers with an early version of gold rush fever, Hakluyt also mentions similar stories of copper and gold that Thomas Harriot related at a meeting of the Virginia Company at the earl of Exeter's house. Hakluyt gathers his hyperbole when describing the abundance of pearls, the quality of the cotton and the multitude of oxen. To shore up his evidence, Hakluyt also calls on the Italian relation of Cabeça de Vaca and the relations of Vasques de Coronado and Antonio de Espejo that Hakluyt publishes in Volume 3. Mulberry trees for silk, dyes, grain, grapes, salt and other commodities are to be found in the vicinity of Virginia. In the account of de Soto's expedition Hakluyt finds two notices of the South Sea, which will allow a passage to Japan and China. Hakluyt also notes near the conclusion a description of the qualities of the soil, diversity and goodness of the fruit, animals and birds and other important information for potential settlers and not just his fellow sharers (shareholders) in the Virginia Company whom he is addressing.

After outlining the benefits of these commodities, Hakluyt then spends a brief time on the second category he sets out at the beginning of the Epistle—the inhabitants. The first attribute of the Natives that Hakluyt mentions is their speech. The Natives are eloquent orators as John Ortiz, who lived 12 years among them, says and as the anonymous Portuguese author corroborates. All this Hakluyt tells us, but not without qualification because, not surprisingly, Native speech means treachery. He has sought this Portuguese account to find gold and God, and the mediators between them—the Natives:

> But for all their faire and cunning speeches, they are not ouermuch to be
> trusted: for they be the greatest traitors of the world, as their manifold most

craftie contriued and bloody treasons, here set down at large, doe euidently proue. They be also as unconstant as the wethercock, and most readie to take all occasions of aduantages to doe mischiefe. They are great liars and dissemblers; for which faults often times they had their deserued paiments. And many times they gaue good testimonie of their great valour and resolution. To handle them gently, while gentle courses may be found to serue, it will be without comparison the best: but if gentle polishing will not serue, then we shall not want hammerours and rough masons enow, I meane our old soldiours trained vp in the Netherlands, to square and prepare them to our Preachers hands.

Here is Hakluyt's account of the Natives, which preaches gentleness more than Oviedo and other champions of the Spanish conquest, but behind it is a threat of violence similar to the propaganda from Spain. The narrative from the Portuguese is used to show how unreliable and treacherous the Natives are, so that they need to be conquered by the sword in order to be converted if they cannot be persuaded gently. Hakluyt has come full circle, a few words about Christianity at the beginning and a paragraph or so at the end of his Epistle Dedicatory.

The concluding paragraph includes a wish and a prayer. The wish is that the members of the Virginia Company will revere and cherish "the painfull Preachers," respect the soldier, embolden the coward, reward the diligent, relieve the weak and sick, suppress the mutinous, preserve "the reputation of the Christians among the Saluages," exalt "our most holy faith" and utterly extinguish "all Paganisme and Idolatrie little by little." Hakluyt then asks God to bless the Company's work of "the inlargement of the dominions of his sacred Maiestie" and the general good of those who undertake this colonization. The apparent chaplain of the enterprise, Hakluyt signs himself as "one publikely and anciently deuoted to Gods seruice, and all yours in this so good action." God must uphold gold. Columbus knew that. Hakluyt embodies that message in this dedication to the anonymous report of de Soto's expedition. It was a difficult task as the sheen and lure of gold, as Ben Jonson's Volpone experienced at his altar, tends to obscure God. The so-called intransigence or lack of cooperation of some of the Natives in the Portuguese account was an inconvenient fact and may have led to Hakluyt's stance as crusader or Christian soldier toward the end of the dedication. Other hardships must have presented problems for Hakluyt. De Soto died on the expedition: he was buried in the Mississippi river to hide from the Natives the fact that Christians were not, as de Soto had claimed, immortal. Only 311 of the 600 people on that expedition arrived in Veracruz, Mexico in the autumn of 1543, which would not be reassuring for a colony like Virginia, which was facing adversity, mutiny and death in its early years.[235]

This Portuguese account was translated for English purposes, to claim land in North America for their empire in order to assert their claims at least from Cabot onward and to oppose the division of the New World into Spanish and Portuguese spheres. Hakluyt uses the accounts written in Spanish and Portuguese to inspire the English to act against those great powers, especially Spain. Hakluyt refers to Portugal in passing in many places in his work. What I have concentrated on here is a turning point, the actual beginnings of a "permanent" English/British empire in the New World. At this key moment, to promote Virginia and an empire overseas, Hakluyt chose an anonymous Portuguese account of a Spanish expedition, which included an important Portuguese contingent. Hakluyt's dedication is dated April 15, 1609. During the summer and autumn of 1609, people awaited news in England of the Virginia Company's fleet. In November the English heard of a storm in which the Sea Venture apparently disappeared with the colony's leaders, Thomas Gates, George Somers and Christopher Newport. As yet no one knew of their survival on Bermuda. This is a story that shows up in a refracted way in Shakespeare's *The Tempest* (1611). Before Shakespeare used a source to give his play a still much-disputed New World dimension, George Chapman, Ben Jonson and John Marston had satirized the illusion of Virginia's riches in *Eastward Ho* (1605). Between those two plays, Hakluyt chose a Portuguese account to contribute to the debate on the imperial theme. To assert English national interests and ambitions in the New World, he called on an old ally and on his linguistic gifts and his under-standing of a more cosmopolitan and pan-European project that crossed the various cultural and geographic boundaries Hakluyt and others were seeking to redefine in the wake of the Latin Middle Ages: the encounter with the New World and the Reformation. Besides gold and God, Hakluyt celebrated the glory of expansion. Part of his enterprise was to encourage the English to enlist in this colonial enterprise. He could have quoted these lines near the end of *The Lusiad*: "Podeis-vos embarcar, que tendes vento / E mar tranquilo, per a Pátria amada" (or in Fanshawe's translation): "Ye may embarque [for Wind and Weather fit, / And the Sea courts you] for your *Countrey* dear."[236]

V

The Restoration of Portuguese independence took place in 1640. João IV (John IV) needed European allies to protect Portugal against Spain, but, it took the Holy See, where Spanish influence was strong, until 1668, to recognize that independence. Relations with the Dutch were also complex. The Netherlands had gained from the breakdown of official trade with Portugal by going directly to Africa, India and Asia, so that losing the advantages of the Portuguese overseas territories as part of the Restoration was a matter of concern for the Dutch. In 1641, Maurice of Nassau, who was set up in Brazil, was to take Angola. The Dutch secured good terms in negotiations with the Portuguese: the alliance between England and Portugal was revived in 1642 and built on the agreement with the Netherlands. The civil strife in England meant that the Portuguese had to find accommodations with the Spanish and Dutch. From 1650 to 1654, the Portuguese negotiated with the English commonwealth, which raised to treaty rights the privileges that English merchants had enjoyed and a limitation on custom duties on English goods. At the Restoration in England in 1660, the Portuguese were given permission to raise troops in England and, on June 23, 1661, the two nations signed an alliance and marriage treaty. Charles II was to marry Catherine of Braganza, the sister of the new king of Portugal: her dowry included Bombay, Tangier, 2,000,000 cruzados, and a limited type of free trade in Brazil and India. England provided Portugal with military aid. In February 1668, Sir Robert Southwell and Sir Richard Fanshawe, the translator of the *Luciads*, negotiated terms that Lisbon and Madrid accepted. Spain was weakened. Although Portugal had lost command of the trade in the East, it retained some control of Africa and Brazil, from where the Brazilians had expelled the Dutch. In 1666 Afonso VI married Maria-Francisca of Savoy, so that the English alliance was not the only one with Portugal. The French had had influence since Portugal gained its initial independence itself.[237]

Fanshawe's translation of 1655 of Luís de Camões's epic poem, which was published in 1572, came, then, at a time when England and Portugal were experiencing a rapprochement and about the time of Cromwell's Western Design, his attempt to take colonies from the Spanish in the West Indies. This Portuguese epic was an example to the English in their expansion and Portugal served as a counterbalance to Spanish power in Europe and the New World. The context of Camões's original poem can be partly discerned from the urging of King Sebastian, then 18-years old and dead six years later, to follow his ancestors in their achievement and, to stem decay, to revive those aristocratic values in church and state in the service of imperial expansion.[238] Sebastian, as we have seen, was among the 8,000 Portuguese dead at the hands of the Moors at Alcazar-Kebir in 1578, and Camões, who had warned of the decline of Portugal, died in 1580 just before Philip II marched into Lisbon and began 60 years of Spanish rule.[239] The very attempt at expansion that Camões exhorted Sebastian to follow was, despite his great navy and army, the cause of his demise. Portuguese crusading had, for a time, come to an end, and the Portuguese empire would never be the same. Why Fanshawe personally chose to translate Camões's *Os Lusíadas* is a puzzle, while he was a fluent translator of Latin, Spanish and Italian, he was probably not familiar with Portuguese in the early 1650s. Having translated Virgil, Horace,

Guarini, Fletcher and Mendoza, why did he turn to Camões rather than
Aristo, Boiardo or Tasso when he set out to translate an entire epic especially
when Fanshawe himself called the Portuguese language *"uncourted"*?
Fanshawe may well have mediated the translation of the Portuguese through
Spanish translations and later when he was ambassador to Portugal and then
to Spain, he used Spanish alone to communicate in the Iberian Peninsula.[240]
It is also possible that Fanshawe, as I have suggested previously, had political
reasons for seeking to translate the great Portuguese epic of empire. Besides
the rapprochement between England and Portugal, Fanshawe also had to
take into account the English Civil War through which he was living. As part
of the prefatory matter of his translation, Fanshawe translates, from
Petronius's *Satyricon*, Eumolpus's rules for writing epic poetry, recounting the
Roman Civil War in the style of Lucan's *Pharsalia*.[241] Through Portugal an
equation between Rome and England might well be wrought, a kind of
translation of empire and, perhaps, a hope for the restoration of order.
Whether Fanshawe is equating Caesar and Prince Charles is an open question in the ambiguous world of allegory. Whatever the intention, the poem
itself may well have helped Charles II, after the Restoration, to appoint
Fanshawe as ambassador to Portugal and then to Spain. From this context,
I wish to move to the text itself, discussing briefly a few aspects of this
intricate poem.

A prefatory poem combines the translation of poetry with that of empire.
Here classical and Renaissance Italian poetry are recalled and the fame of
Portuguese exploration is placed in the context of antiquity. Poetry allows for
memory and renown:

> SPAINE *gaue me* noble *Birth*: Coimbra, *Arts*:
> LISBON, *a* high-plac't loue, *and* Courtly *parts*:
> AFFRICK, a *Refuge when the* Court *did frowne*:
> WARRE, *at an* Eye's *expence, a faire renowne*
> TRAVAYLE, *experience, with*) *noe* short *sight*
> Of India, *and the* World; *both which I write*
> INDIA *a* life, *which I gaue* there for *Lost*
> On Mecons waues (*a wreck and Exile*) *tost*
> To boot, this POEM, *held up in* one hand
> *Whilst with the* other *I swam safe to land*:
> TASSO, a sonet; *and* (*what's greater yit*)
> *The honour to giue* Hints *to such a* witt
> PHILIP a Cordiall, (*the ill* Fortune *see!*)
> *To* cure *my Wants when those had new* kill'd *mee*
> My country (*Nothing—yes*) *Immortall Prayse*
> (*so did I, Her*) Beasts cannot browze on Bayes.[242]

The praise the poet gave his country is an example to the translator and the English nation that is now introduced to this epic in its own tongue. Fama, as Virgil recorded at the beginning of Book IV of the *Aeneid*, is important in the building of nation and empire. Literary representation is a key part of the imperial archive because it is, at its best, so memorable: the aesthetic allows the idea of empire to persist beyond its earthly power.

Literary merit and translation are an aspect of the transmission of this epic, both in how it is framed in the prefatory matter and also in the copy at Princeton, which may be a copy that Fanshawe had presented—"For my noble Nephew Mr Francis Compton"—because it is probably in his own hand and, in the same writing, contains changes to the printed text. "To the Right Honorable William Earl of Strafford, & c." represents Camões as a "*Poet* to rival your beloved TASSO...He FEARED NO MAN BUT CAMOENS: Notwithstanding which, he bestow'd a *Sonet* in his praise"; this text also emphasizes the rivalry between Tasso [*Jersusalem*] and Guarini [*Il Pastor Fido*].[243] The world of Renaissance poetry frames Camões's achievement and lends authority to his content, the quest of epic and romance. The imperial theme itself travels from Greek to Latin to Italian to Portuguese to English (through translation). A literary agon is also part of the imperial enterprise: "might my Potingall have retorted upon Him with reference to his own *Epick* way; IF HE HAD NOT SEEN MY LUSIAD, HE HAD NOT EXCELL'D IT." Tasso is to Camões as Horace is to Lollio: Horace "held himself accountable to *his* potent friend LOLLIO."[244] Fanshawe changes what appears in print in the second line here—"Whilst thou (Great LOLLIO) in ROME dost plead, / I, in PRÆNESTE have all Homer Read"—to "I, in PRÆNESTE, Homer twice have read."[245] The textual care becomes part of the record of this poet-diplomat: Fanshawe revises this Homeric antecedent. He says that he hopes to bring to his lordship "this TREASURE-TROVE." Fanshawe appeals to Lord Strafford, "however *dis-figured* in the *trans-lating*, yet still reteining the old *materials*, both *Politicall* and *Moral*, on a *truer* and more *Modern Frame* of *Story* and *Geography* then *that* of HOMER."[246] This translation of empire is also from ancients to moderns just as the Spaniards understood that the torrid zone, as Aristotle considered it, did not bear out their experience sailing to the New World.

Narrative and geography are transformed by European exploration even if some of the conventions remain the same and the invention of tradition is an aspect of coming to terms with new lands:

> *Now conquering* Rome *did all the world controle,*
> *From* East *to* West *from* one *to* th'other *pole:*
> *Yet was not satisfied. The plough'd up* Sea

With brazen keels, was made her common way.
If any nook *were hid, if any* Land
(*Which yellow* Gold *afforded) lay beyand,*
It was a foe, and covetous *anger seiz'd*
Whatever *wealth.*[247]

Rome is the imperial example—with gold and wealth as its pursuit—by land and sea. Here was the lord of the world, although being "covetous" was in control as well. The context, then, is rapture in Petronius's satire.[248] The "satirical" genre may present alternative, ambivalent or even oppositional interpretations of the scope and aims of empire. In his satire, *Gulliver's Travels*, Swift has the king of Brobdingnag speak of the English in unflattering terms: "I cannot but conclude the bulk of your Natives, to be the most pernicious Race of little odious Vermin that Nature ever suffered to crawl upon the Surface of the Earth."[249] From a satirical vantage, Roman, Portuguese and English imperial practices would fall short of ethical action. Applying the same standards over time to empires, it would be difficult not to criticize, or not to fault, the Spanish or Portuguese for seizing lands in anger because they coveted gold and other riches even though, in the case of Spain, this became part of the Black Legend. It is a question of consistency. There is sometimes an ironic patriotic or political gap between what one allows to rivals and what one says or does oneself. In "Discourse of Western Planting," for example, Hakluyt was especially hard on the Spanish while advocating an exploitation of the resources of North America.[250] Fanshawe seems to observe a connection between satire and epic, for in "The Translator's POSTSCRIPT" he sees Petronius as a model for Camões.[251]

Fanshawe, himself no stranger to politics, provides an aesthetic context for Camões's epic—one of his aims is

> to shew the *Rule* and *Model*, which (*indubitably*) guided our CAMOENS in raising his GREAT BUILDING, and which (except *himself*) that I know of, no POET ever *followed* that *wrought in great*, whether *ancient*, or *modern*. For (to name no more) the *Greek* HOMER, the *Latin* VIRGIL, *our* SPENCER, and even the *Italian* TASSO (who had a *true*, a *great*, and *no obsolete story*, to work upon) are in effect wholly *fabulous*: and LUCAN (though *worthily* admired) is as much censured by *some* on the other side, for sticking too close to *truth*.[252]

The choice of topics and relation between the fabulous and the true concerns Fanshawe in setting out this poet lineage, which includes romance, epic and satire. The translation of poetics from Greek to Roman to Italian, Portuguese and English successors is a matter of Camões's literary reputation and not simply one of a record and inspiration of empire. The achievement of

Camões's epic, and its introduction into English through translation, has aesthetic dimensions that, while overlapping with politics, are not entirely political. Rather than evoke a battle between ancients and moderns, a concern of neoclassical England, Fanshawe sets out a poetic lineage from classical to modern Europe. According to Fanshawe, Lucan is a historian and not a poet.[253]

An icon of Portuguese expansion is displayed in this translation. It includes an engraving of "Prince Henry of Portugall," dressed for battle, his library and instruments of navigation, mathematics and warfare (below the two shelves of books) to his right (our left). And to his left (our right) there is a crown and coat of arms with the motto: "Honi Soit Qui Mal Y Pense." Behind him is the battle before Ceuta, the name of which appears above the fortified city to the left of his left leg (our right).[254] This prince is a man of learning whose support of exploration, this image implies, helped to achieve the key victory of the Portuguese in North Africa. Richard Hakluyt had advocated an English school of navigation, which, whatever he said, would be indirectly inspired by Henry the Navigator. The next and facing image is of "Vasca de Gama," another important figure in Portuguese expansion, in ornate dress. His left hand grasps his sword and his right a staff.[255] Here is the navigator who, by finding a way around Africa by sea, opened up the East to the Portuguese just as Columbus allowed the Spanish to expand into the western Atlantic. In this English translation, Portuguese priority and glory appear in image and text up front and center.

The literary nature of this translation is something that the construction of the book emphasized. Facing the beginning of the poem is the reference, "TORQVATO TASSO. in his 6 Part. fol. 47," and then the verse in Italian followed by the English translation:

> VASCO, te [corrected to le] cui ardite Antenne
>   Incontro al *Sol*, che ne riporta il *giorno*,
>   Spiegar le vele, e fer colà ritorno,
>   Dove egli par che di cadere accenne:
> Non piu di Te per aspro mar sostenne
>   *Quel*, che fece a CICLOPE oltraggio, & scorno:
> Ne *chi* turbo *l'Arpie* nel suo soggiorno,
>   Ne diè piu bel *Subjetto* aColte *penne*.
> Et hor *quella* del coltro, e buon LUIGI
>   Tant'oltre stende il glorioso volo
>   Che j tuoi spalmati *Legni* andar men lunge.
> Ond'a *quelli*, a cui S'alza il nostro *polo*,
>   Et a chi ferina incontra j suoi vestigi,
>   Per *lui* del corso *tuo* la fama aggiunge.

> VASCO, *whose bold and happy ships against*
>> *The Rising* Sun (*who fraights them home with day*)
>> *Display'd their wings, and back against advanc't*
>> *To* where *in Seas all Night he steeps his Ray:*
> *Not more then* Thou *on rugged Billows felt,*
>> He *that bor'd out the Eye of* POLYPHEME;
>> *Nor* He *that spoyl'd the* HARPYES *where they dwelt,*
>> *Afforded Learned* Pens *a fairer* Theam.
> *And* this *of Learn'd and honest* CAMOENS
>> *So far beyond now takes it's glorious flight,*
>> *That thy breath'd* Sailes *went a less Journey, Whence*
>> *To* Those *on whom the* Northern Pole *shines bright,*
> *And* Those *who set* their *feet to* ours, *The boast*
> *Of thy Long* Voyage *Travails at his Cost.*[256]

In his own hand in this presentation copy Fanshawe corrects the Italian in the first line. Tasso's homage to da Gama, the explorer, and Camões, the poet, combines the poetry of empire with the empire of poetry. Fanshawe pays tribute to the Portuguese explorer and poet with his own implicit praise of Tasso. This great epic poet from Renaissance Italy, whose literary language is quoted, is used as a bolster to the Portuguese epic poet and language. Ever careful, Fanshawe, translator of Portuguese and negotiator with Portugal, corrects the various languages in his presentation copy.

The epic itself begins with an echo of the opening of the great Virgilian epic. This is also a story of a quest that affirms the glory of a nation that became a great empire:

> *Armes, and the Men* above the vulgar File,
> Who from the *Western Lusitanian* shore
> Past ev'n beyond the *Trapobanian*-Isle,
> Through *Seas* which never *Ship* had sayld before;
> Who (brave in *action*, patient in long *Toyle*,
> Beyond what strength of *humane* nature bore.)
> 'Mongst *Nations*, under *other Stars*, acquir'd
> A *modern Scepter* which to *Heaven* aspir'd.[257]

This heavenly aspiration of a Portuguese voyage is, despite the echo of the invocation of Virgil's Roman epic, well beyond the pale of anything achieved by sea by Rome or anything that Aeneas could conceive. The translation of epic and empire is about a simultaneous continuity and break with that tradition.

In Stanza 2 Fanshawe marks a correction in this copy, but the translation, even with the change, represents a mixture of Virgilian Fama as a memorial to heroic deeds and the Ciceronian motif of history as memory that

Camões effects:

> Likewise those *Kings* of *glorious memory*,
> Who sow'd and propagated where they past
> *The Faith* with the *new Empire* (making dry
> The *Breasts* of ASIA, and laying waste
> Black AFFRICK'S vitious Glebe[) as a correction]; And *Those*
> who by
> Their deeds at *home* left not their names defac't,
> My *Song* shall spread where ever there are *Men*,
>   If *Wit* and *Art* will so much guide my *Pen*.[258]

Art will make these famous acts in which Portugal subdues Asia and Africa. The metaphors are telling: Portugal dries Africa's breasts and lays waste to Africa, which is designated as "Black." Gender and color difference mark this triumph of a "*new Empire*." The act of writing becomes a celebration of nation and empire, a kind of translation that is emphasized by the very translation that Fanshawe has produced.

There has been an agon between ancients and moderns, which some poets during the Renaissance and beyond expressed, over their achievements in empire and poetry. Camões faces this theme squarely:

> Cease *man* of Troy, and cease thou *Sage of* GREECE,
> To boast the *Navigations* great *ye* made;
> Let the high Fame of ALEXANDER cease,
> And TRAIAN'S Banners in the EAST display'd:
> For to a *Man* recorded in this *Peece*
> NEPTUNE his *Trident* yielded, MARS his *Blade*.
>   Cease All, whose Actions ancient Bards exprest:
>   A brighter Valour rises in the West.[259]

The westering of empire means that Camões and his Portugal have surpassed Homer in epic story, for his nation has broken new ground and has out-produced Aeneas, Homer, Trajan and others in extending empire east and west. The fame of Alexander the Great cannot measure up to that of da Gama: Greece begot but has yielded to Portugal. Even the gods from classical mythology, Neptune and Mars, who provided a poetic language and framework for moderns, like Camões, must yield to the Portuguese bard and the valor of which he sings. Poetry and empire from antiquity are summoned as frames only to be succeeded.

By stanza 8 the Portuguese empire is one on which the sun does not seem to set. This is an imperial expanse of power and potential and already has subject peoples:

> You (pow'rful *King*), whose *Empire* vast the *Sun*
> Visits the *first* as soon as he is born,

And eyes it when his Race is *half-way* run,
And leaves it *loath* when his tyr'd Steeds *adjourn*.
You, who we look should clap a yoak upon
The bruitish ISHMAELITE, become your scorn;
On th'*Eastern* TURK, and GENTIL who still lies
Sucking the *stream* which water'd PARADISE.[260]

This empire elicits images born of the scriptures and not simply those from classical sources. The chosen people have been exiled from Eden and the Gentiles are those who now inhabit paradise. That the eastern Turks are mentioned seems to mean that one of the desires expressed is that the power of the Portuguese king be returned in a crusade against Islam. Gentiles, Turks and Ishmaelites ought to be brought under the Portuguese yoke. Here, although Camões does not mention it in this stanza, is an image of Portugal, born of the Reconquest of lands that Muslims had held on the Iberian Peninsula and sometimes helped by other European crusaders in that war, reconquering the holy lands from others, particularly the Muslims, who reign over them. The sun never sets on the translation of empire: providence and fame are concerns of the first stanza of Camões's epic.

Fanshawe continues to correct the lines of the printed translation. For instance, in Stanza 90, which describes the Omnipotent, the firmament and the elements, the translator makes his changes:

In all these PLANETS motions different
Thou maist perceive, some *speedy*, and some *flow*:
Now climbing nearer to the FIRMAMENT,
Now stooping closer to the *Earth* below,
As seemed best to the OMNIPOTENT,
Who made the *Fire* and *Ayre*, the Wind and Snow:
Those (clos'd within the *Heavens*) each other enter,
And *both* the *Waves*, and *Earth*: the common *Center*.[261]

Both these last lines are crossed out in ink and the following two lines appear in the author's hand (hardly legible in places): "W*th* Fire & Ayre, [*thou seest more neerer*[?]] ye pole/*And Earth & Water center of* y^e [*the*] *whole*." Fire and air sublimate the quest.

Cosmology is a concern throughout the epic and, as in the tenth canto, coincides with culture and politics. Some of these cultural and political comments reflect more on a Portuguese or European view of itself rather than any perceptive or novel ethnographical view:

See CHRISTIAN EUROPE, higher by the head
In *Arms* and *civill Arts* then all the rest!
See untill'd AFFRICK, covetous, ill-bred,

> Wanting ev'n things whereof shee is possest,
> With her great CAPE (by *you* discovered)
> Which NATURE towards the *South-Pole* addresst!
>   See all this *Neck* with People infinite
>   Almost, who neither *doe* nor *know* what's right![262]

Da Gama is the discoverer here while Europe is above all the rest, including uncultivated Africa, whose people do not, in this representation, have a moral sense. In this epic, unlike in the work of More, Léry and Montaigne, there is no sense in key places of the ethnological differences between Europe and other cultures, no ironic or satirical distance or typology that would call a European country or Europe itself up short. The beginning of the next stanza Fanshawe renders as "See the great *Empire* of MONOMOTAPE, / With naked savage People black and grim."[263] According to this stanza, in Africa, Gonsalvo was martyred for the martyr Christ. Nevertheless, the poem does embody, particularly at its end, advice to the king of Portugal, the monarch who was by heaven reserved "to scoure our Rust."[264] Like the English in regard to Columbus, the Portuguese sometimes lamented lost chances at "discovery" and glory: Fernão de Magalhães (Magellan), "(angry with his *King*) / Atchieves a great and memorable Thing."[265] What is more galling here is that this discoverer of the western route to Asia was a Portuguese, once loyal, who accomplished this feat in the service of Spain. A couple of stanzas later, he reappears, "MAGELLAN; / Who in reality of *Fact* shall be / A PORTINGALL, but not in *loyaltie*."[266] Between these representations of Magalhães is a brief praise to gold that is similar to the sun that is similar to the longer paean that Ben Jonson's Volpone gives in his opening speech. In this world divided between Spain and Portugal the poet refers to "Your Friend CASTEEL" and in the last half of the line personifies Castile as a female ("as her guerdon of worth").[267] Here, relations between Portugal and Castile are ambivalent: they are friends and rivals. The king of Portugal is advised to choose qualified men.[268] Like Richard Hakluyt the younger, who tried to get his monarch, court and compatriots to want imperial greatness, this epic poet (and in translation he is also an example for the English in their imperial expansion, later helped, too, by the marriage between the Portuguese and English royal houses) is trying to rouse king and country to maintain the course of empire, something they had developed far more than England had. Still, the address is to move the king: " '*Great sir*, let never the astonisht GALL, / The ENGLISH, GERMAN, and ITALIAN, / Have cause to say, the fainting PORTUGALL / Could not *advance* the GREAT WORK he *began*.' "[269] Whereas Hakluyt uses French disdain to light a fire under the English to get started in earnest on the course of empire, Camões employs the English, Germans and Italians to move the Portuguese to further their imperial ends. Camões represents himself as obscure and unknown to the king: " 'But *I*, who speak in rude and humble *Ryme*, / Not known nor dreamt of by my LIEGE at all.' "[270] Nonetheless, the poem ends with a representation of King Sebastian as an ideal conqueror, who, if he listens to this advice, as the verse implies, will be more feared in North Africa than the Gorgon was by Atlas and will be the ruler in whom Alexander the Great will "respire, / Without envying the MEONIAN LYRE."[271] Curiously, the king is portrayed as someone who will not feel rivalry with the poet in an analogy and allusion that yokes Alexander and Homer. Conqueror and poet— perhaps a little like philosopher and general, Phormion and Hannibal—have potential conflicts, but, in the last stanza of the poem, they are, at least ostensibly, allies in the course of empire. How much the neglected and impoverished poet, soldier and adventurer, Camões, resented his situation is difficult, if not impossible, to say, so that this possible textual undertow is something that can be suggested as an alternative but cannot be proved.

Fanshawe became the vehicle through which England was introduced to a coherent story of the Portuguese empire and to Portuguese literature, although Hakluyt and others had included English translations of Portuguese texts in their works and collections. In 1659, Francisco de Melo, Portuguese ambassador in London, praised Fanshawe's translation; the orator in Lisbon in 1661 welcomed Fanshawe as the envoy sent to finalize the arrangements for the marriage of Catherine of Braganza and Charles II and as the one who taught the Portuguese Prince of Poets to sing in English; when in 1666, as ambassador to Spain, Fanshawe visited Portugal, Francisco Manuel de Melo, a Portuguese poet, wrote to him in Spanish and praised his "remarkable book," saying that more than in the first age Portugal, Camoens and Gama are more fortunate for being "reimmortalized" through Fanshawe's "sublime muse."[272] This poem may well have helped Fanshawe live out his last years as an ambassador to Portugal and then Spain, where he died in June 1666.

The dowry of Catherine of Braganza included Bombay. Fanshawe's translation allowed the English to read this Portuguese epic of da Gama. In 1776, when the first British empire was amid a civil war that would involve the loss of 13 of the North American colonies, William Julius Mickle published a new translation of Camões's epic, and in the nineteenth century seven more translations, including one by Sir Richard Burton (1880), were made of the poem.[273] As England reached the height of its empire and Victoria was deemed, from 1876, empress of India, a translation of empire, and of India, came from the Portuguese and its epic poet more directly than it had ever done before, despite the fondness for classical allusion to Homer and Alexander, from Greece. After Portugal, Spain, France, the Netherlands, England (Britain) and others pursued the imperial mantle of the ancients, of pagan empires made Christian, of learning and experience modifying the models of antiquity. The translation of empire was an epic struggle beyond that cliché.

VI

The English and French could make life difficult for the Iberian trade with Brazil. For instance, from 1589 to 1591, English privateers captured 69 ships and the French corsairs and Barbary rovers also disrupted shipping. A Spanish spy reported that as a result of English privateering sugar was less expensive in London than in Bahia or Lisbon.[274] From about 1600 onward, the Dutch, who were in the process of a long break with Spain while Portugal had drawn closer in an Iberian union, created great problems worldwide for the Portuguese empire.

The Netherlands rebelled against Spain in 1568 and the rebellion persisted on and off for 80 years. In the final years of the sixteenth century the Dutch attacked Iberian colonies, when Spain and Portugal were united under Philip in an arrangement that prohibited Spaniards from settling or trading in the Portuguese empire and the Portuguese from doing the same in the Spanish empire. This long colonial war was for the sugar trade in Brazil, the slave trade in West Africa and the spice trade in Asia. The Portuguese won the war in Brazil, drew in West Africa and lost in Asia.[275] The Dutch East India Company, founded in 1602, controlled cloves, nutmegs and mace in the Moluccas, cinnamon in Ceylon (Sri Lanka) and pepper in Malabar. The Dutch had a monopoly in European trade with Japan after the ruling Tokugawa family had expelled the Portuguese in 1639, and, by 1663, the Dutch had secured from the Portuguese trade in Asian waters between Arabia and Japan. The success of the Dutch in the East alarmed the English and Danes, who sought peace with Portugal in the 1630s. In 1648, a Luso-Brazilian expedition from Rio de Janeiro saved Portuguese fortunes against the Dutch in Angola. In Brazil itself, the Dutch attacked Bahia in 1624–25, invaded Pernambuco in 1630, and in 1645 they controlled most of the sugar producing areas of the northeast. In 1654, after nearly ten years of war, Recife and the last Dutch holdings capitulated in a war in which both sides used Native American auxiliaries as the French had in the wars that Léry refers to in the sixteenth century, the Tupís allied with the Portuguese and the Tapuyá with the Dutch. In the Pernambuco campaign of 1644–54, the Dutch and Portuguese accused each other of inciting their Native American allies to commit cruelties and atrocities. Mulattos, Blacks and various peoples of mixed backgrounds made up many of the Luso-Brazilian forces at this time; the original leader of the revolt against the Dutch was João Fernandes Viera, son of a Mulata prostitute and a Madeira Fidalgo; Camarão, a Native American, and Henrique Dias, a Black, were among their best regimental commanders.

The loss of "Netherland Brazil" was, according to C. R. Boxer, particularly hard for the Dutch because they had been defeated largely by an army of color, and the Portuguese possession of the sugar trade in Brazil was qualified by improved methods of cultivating sugar and grinding cane that Luso-Brazilian Jews probably helped to introduce in the English and French West Indies while the Dutch occupied Pernambuco.[276] The soldiers of the East and West India companies were mercenaries that included Dutch, Germans, French, Scandinavians and (before 1652) English soldiers, all of whom seemed much better fed and trained than the Portuguese soldiers they faced, some of whom were prisoners and children, in contrast to the well-trained Spanish army. Portugal was exhausting itself in maintaining its empire. After the marriage of Charles II with Catherine of Braganza in 1661, which saw Bombay and Tangier being given to England as part of her dowry, the Portuguese sought English help to secure peace with Spain and the United Provinces in 1668–69.[277] The Dutch did have successes against the Portuguese in Asia: for instance in the Indian Ocean, Malacca fell in 1641, Ceylon in 1644 and 1656, Quilon in 1658, Negapatam in 1660, and in Arabia, with the help of the British and Dutch, the Arabs expelled the Portuguese from the Persian Gulf and Arabia. In 1657 the Dutch attacked Portugal and blockaded Lisbon for three months; a peace treaty was finally signed in 1661. This peace gave Portugal some benefits because from 1661 to 1665 the Spanish launched great offensives, which, with the help of mercenaries and German and French military advisers, the Portuguese repelled. In 1662 and 1667 two *coup d états* occurred in Portugal and, after much maneuvering between the French and the English, a peace treaty was signed between Portugal and Spain. The Spanish kept Ceuta alone.[278] Despite the Dutch challenges to the Portuguese empire, they themselves admitted that local populations preferred the Portuguese language, religion and cultural practices.[279]

Portugal, although exhausted by the end of the 1660s, could have lost more in these wars with the Netherlands and Spain. The final chapter involves discussions of the Netherlands and the United States, the one who fed on the Portuguese empire and challenged Spanish power in Europe and across the globe and the other who took up in the wake of all these empires and including those that France and Britain had established, but with a new twist, a little like Venice but on a much vaster scale—an imperial republic—perhaps a little reminiscent of republican Rome and its growth into an empire. That is to jump ahead because in the seventeenth century, as Portuguese power had subsided, France and England sought to emulate the success of the Spanish empire, which was now the strongest of the western European empires, as well as to contend with and displace it. France and England would, despite the great challenge the Netherlands presented to

Spain, become the great beneficiaries of this challenge, particularly in the eighteenth century. In that century, when Britain (now a union that brought together the various kingdoms including Scotland and England) was able to become the great European colonial power, it lost its greatest colonies in America, whose independence France and Spain helped to achieve. This rivalry among Spain, France and England was long-standing and was particularly intense at the turn of the seventeenth century. Spain was the leading colonial power and France and England learned from it and found ways to challenge that lead.

Chapter 3 ～

Spain, England and France

S pain was on the minds of its rivals long after the turn of the seventeenth century. Texts in England and France particularly paid close attention to the case of Spain in the New World. In the early decades of that century, as permanent settlements in northern America seemed to be taking hold, the English continued to consider the Spaniards and Natives side-by-side and in ambivalent ways depending on self-interest and context. Sometimes this concern with Spain occurred in places in which school and official history and national myths have not ventured. For instance, William Bradford's account of Plymouth Plantation tells about key events in the history of the English (British) overseas empire and, after its printing in the 1870s, helped to emphasize the seminal role of the Pilgrims in the birth of an American identity and nation: that there are some representations of Spain in his narrative changes some of the focus to the priority of Spain away from the birth of the English or first British empire or the story of religious freedom and the key event and reference in beginnings of the United States and its liberty. Jamestown itself, as important as it was, could, particularly after the debates over slavery and in the aftermath of the American Civil War, be occluded in the construction of national identity in the United States. Northern liberty, industrialism and the melting pot might well find in Bradford and the Pilgrims matter more conducive to their story and history. Whether Roger Williams, and other related dissident figures—some well known and others not—like Anne Hutchinson and John Throckmorton, moving from Salem and Boston to Rhode Island and beyond, should have provided models for plurality and free speech much earlier is a question for another day.

Another approach taken in this chapter—and I leave off from giving away too much—is something one might expect but does not find discussed enough, that is the ways French officials represented Spain and Spanish interests in the shifting political and trading patterns and maps of the Caribbean. In the various typologies this study is discussing in its comparison of empire, it is good to remember the importance of the Caribbean or West Indies, not just in their relation to Europe, but also to the East Indies and Asia and to the mainland of the Americas. The French officials give us glimpses into the changing realm of the Caribbean. Governor Bradford and these French governors and other state officials are not necessarily promoters of empire in the sense of historians, collectors and courtiers who were promoting the idea of empire, but people in government on the ground and in the place and culture, trying to make things work for the colony they helped to lead and maintain. They represent every day concerns about ideas and doctrine. How Spain crops up in unexpected places and in unexpected ways in predictable places is part of a larger pattern. It is not surprising that the powers that entered the Caribbean relatively late—England and France—could not entirely ignore the precedence of Spain in the region even if their own myths or ideology could try to suppress, ignore, undermine or correct the Spanish connection or origins in the European contact and settlement of these places.

The various texts beyond but including Bradford and the French officials themselves offer unpredictable aspects and complicating factors. Although Spain had not wanted other European nations except for Portugal settling in the New World, it could not stop the French, English, Dutch and others from developing economic interests and colonies there. Spain, though the great power of Europe and the New World in the sixteenth century, was sometimes exposed by the very attention other nations paid it, not to mention the piracy and conflict over trade that was a part of both seascape and landscape at this time. In what follows I will discuss some key instances, principally from the early seventeenth century onward, of this preoccupation with the actual and possible power and vulnerability of Spain as a colonial power.

I

In a translation in 1612 of Peter Martyr's *De nouo orbe*, for example, Michael Lok [Locke] made additions to Richard Eden's translation decades before and included a preface "To the Reader," in which he spoke about how Martyr's book "containeth the first discouery of the west Indies, togetherwith the subiection, and conquest therof."[1] Lok's title page gestures to the acts and adventures of the Spaniards and includes Psalm 95 as its epigraph: "*In the handes of the Lorde are all the corners of the earth*." God seems, he implies, to want the English to share these corners of the earth that the Spanish occupy. The address to the reader emphasizes what the book is supposed to accomplish:

> We are chiefly to consider, the industry, and trauailes of the Spanyarde, their exceeding charge in furnishing so many shippes, for this intended expedition,

their continuall supplyes to further their attemptes, and their actiue and vndaunted spirites, in executing matters of that qualitie, and difficultie, and lastly, their constant resolution of Plantation. All whiche, may bee exemplary vnto vs, to performe the like in our Virginea, which beeing once throughly planted, and inhabited with our people, may returne as greate benefitte to our Nation in another kinde, as the Indies do vnto the Spanyard.[2]

Lok called attention to the example Spain set for England, a success of a different "kinde" but an exemplary success nonetheless. The Spaniards, who showed "industry" and "active and vndaunted spirites," won admiration, sometimes grudging, among some English authors. The riches of Spain haunted the English, but their texts also included critiques of the Spanish in the colonization of the New World:

for although it [Virginia] yeeld not golde, yet, is it a fruitfull pleasant coun-trey, replenished with all good thinges, necessary for the life of man, if they be industrious, who inhabite it. But wee leaue this to them, who haue authoritie, and good purses, to further a matter of suche important consequence, and returne to our purpose. Besides the first discouery of this countrie of the West Indies, this historie likewise declareth the conquest, and subiection of the people, the manner howe, and what myriades of millions of poore naked Indians were slaughtered, and subdued through the conquering sworde, and the number of the Spanyardes, that attempted, and performed the same.[3]

The sympathy with the Natives as casualties of the Spanish conquest is something echoed in English texts during the sixteenth and seventeenth centuries. This ambivalent attitude in these works toward the Spaniards long persisted: the relation to the Natives was also ambivalent. The Puritans to the north in New England also embodied this two-way movement in attitudes toward the Spanish and the Natives.

William Bradford, English Pilgrim and governor of Plymouth Plantation, also mentioned the example of Spain, so that the voyage of the Mayflower and the settlement it built near Cape Cod were not in a vacuum. During a truce with Spain—for 11 or 12 years, in Bradford's estimation—the Pilgrims had lived in Leyden, which was part of the Netherlands, a publishing center for illustrated narratives of voyages to the New World, Bradford would have picked up positive and negative attitudes toward the Spanish and the Natives.[4] A typology of Spanish and Native cruelty, as something the English had to face, soon became evident in Bradford. Owing to the various diffi-culties the Pilgrims experienced in the Netherlands,

The place they had thoughts on was some of those vast and unpeopled coun-tries of America, which are fruitful and fit for habitation, being devoid of all civil inhabitants, where there are only savage and brutish men which range up and down, little otherwise than the wild beasts of the same.[5]

Here the notions of civility and occupation of the land echoed Portuguese claims about indigenous peoples in Africa and the papal donations of the "unknown" world to Portugal and Spain: the Natives did not occupy or possess the land, so they were bestial and could be displaced by a European civil society. Along with Aristotle's theory of natural slavery, this attitude toward the Indians led to their displacement and slavery. In *Of Plymouth Plantation 1620–1647* (pub. 1856), Bradford illustrated that the anti-Indian positions of some of the Spanish accounts had an influence on his views of what awaited the Pilgrims once they left Leyden. The Pilgrims feared hardship, disease and death in the New World:

> And also those which should escape or overcome these difficulties should yet be in continual danger of the savage people, who are cruel, barbarous and most treacherous, being most furious in their rage and merciless where they overcome; not being content only to kill and take away life, but delight to torment men in the most bloody manner that may be; flaying some alive with the shells of fishes, cutting off the members and joints of others by piecemeal and broiling on the coals, eat the collops of their flesh in their sight whilst they live, with other cruelties horrible to be related.[6]

These Pilgrim exiles had to choose between this graphic Native cruelty if they sailed for America and Spanish cruelty if they remained in the Netherlands as war loomed on the horizon. Although less sensational and descriptive about Spanish violence than Native abuses, Bradford makes explicit the typology: "The Spaniard might prove as cruel as the savages of America, and the famine and pestilence as sore here as there, and their liberty less to look out for remedy."[7]

Bradford presented the divergent arguments amongst the Pilgrims for staying in the Netherlands or for settling in Guiana or Virginia. Guiana is, as in Ralegh's description, rich, fruitful and not under firm Spanish control: "As also that the Spaniards (having much more than they could possess) had not yet planted there nor anywhere very near the same."[8] This was the kind of argument that the English monarchs, Henry VII and Elizabeth I, as well as François Ier of France had made in response to Spanish and Portuguese claims, through the papal donations and treaties, to the "unpossessed" world. In Bradford's report the English did fear that if they encroached on Spanish power in the Americas, they would suffer retribution:

> Again, if they should there live and do well, the jealous Spaniard would never suffer them long, but would displant or overthrow them as he did the French in Florida, who were seated further from his richest countries; and the sooner because they should have none to protect them, and their own strength would be too small to resist so potent an enemy and so near a neighbour.[9]

The memory of the Spanish crushing the French colony in Florida served as a negative example to the Pilgrims in deciding whether or where to establish a colony in the New World. This kind of triangulation was not uncommon when the English or French followed Spain in colonization.

Some of the Pilgrims used the terrors and dangers to argue for staying in the Netherlands or delaying the departure for the New World and seemed to prefer to equate the cruelty of the Spaniards and Natives as opposed to the equation of Spanish cruelty to Natives and to the Dutch found in the translations of Las Casas and the pictures of De Bry. Perhaps the Spanish authors, like Gómara, who emphasized that the Indians were natural slaves or cruel savages, influenced these English exiles. Rather than pretend that the hardships were imaginary, Bradford faced them squarely. When rations were short, Bradford reported that the stoicism of the English settlers reminded him of the earlier fortitude of the Spaniards:

> Yet they bore these wants with great patience and alacrity of spirit; and that for so long a time as for the most part of two years. Which makes me remember what Peter Martyr writes (in magnifying the Spaniards) in his 5th Decade, page 208. "They" (saith he) "led a miserable life for five days together, with the parched grain of maize only, and that not to saturity"; and then concludes, "that such pains, such labours, and such hunger, he thought none living which is not a Spaniard could have endured."[10]

At first glance, then, the Spanish were heroic because Martyr portrayed them as such, but they had to endure only for five days whereas Bradford's compatriots endured two years even if their condition might not have been precisely the same. Bradford then mentioned that the Spaniards sometimes had to put up with such scarcity for two or three months and, citing Martyr once again, said how some Spaniards "were fain to eat dogs, toads and dead men, and so died almost all."[11] God, Bradford reported, kept "His people" from such extremities: the Spanish do not seem to be as anointed as the English Pilgrims.[12] Nevertheless, Bradford quotes Martyr who said that through their miseries these first Spanish settlers opened the way to the ease and feasts of their compatriots who followed them and, by implication and analogy, the Pilgrims would do the same, if not more, for others who came from England to New England to settle. Still, the Pilgrims had, like Moses and the Israelites, been exiled from their own land—an allusion Bradford used—so that England was not necessarily a united land of pure motive and gave birth to a new land, a shelter from persecution.[13]

In addition to the internal divisions amongst the English, Bradford's account also reflected the strains between England and Spain as well as the friendship with the Netherlands. He told of Thomas Cromwell, "who had taken sundry prizes from the Spanish in the West Indies" but whose sailors scattered sin and money in Plymouth and Massachusetts Bay.[14] Edward Winslow, without the consent of the government of Plymouth, took on employments with the government and, later, along with Admiral Penn and General Venable, became a joint head of the force that captured Jamaica in 1655, a part of Oliver Cromwell's Western Design.[15] An interesting triangulation, which began with the Dutch and English attempting to establish Plymouth and New Amsterdam during the 1620s, was the ghost of Spain in those settlements. The Dutch, who themselves had settled New Amsterdam, also feared the Spanish desire to be lords of the world. On March 9, 1627, Isaack de Rasieres wrote to Bradford from Manhattan in Fort Amsterdam about the friendship between the English and Dutch:

> it hath pleased His Majesty upon mature deliberation to make a new covenant, and to take up arms with the States General of our dear native country against our common enemy the Spaniards, who seek nothing else but to usurp and overcome other Christian kings' and princes' lands, that so he might obtain and possess his pretended monarchy over all Christendom, and so to rule and command after his own pleasure over the consciences of so many hundred thousand souls, which God forbid.[16]

In reply to the letter on March 19, 1627, Bradford confirmed this view of friendship between the Netherlands and England and expressed his thanks for the "freedom and good content" the Pilgrims had found in the Low Countries.[17] Like Rasieres, in this context of ancient friendship between the two countries, Bradford sketched an aspect of what would later be called the Black Legend of Spain: the union of these allies allow them "to resist the pride of that common enemy the Spaniard, from whose cruelty the Lord keep us both, and our native countries."[18] The Pilgrims and the Dutch at New Amsterdam shared a common cause against the Spanish: they came after Spain and feared that Spain would come after them.

II

In the early seventeenth century, there was also an anxiety in France and England of losing people to Holland and Spain because of their flourishing economies, so that national borders were not as fixed and patriotism not as deep as the ruling elites would have desired. Thousands of French artisans and merchants had crossed into Spain after the expulsion of the Moriscos in 1610.[19] The Flemish and Swiss were French and then French-speaking as such a distinction became possible. The Pilgrims lived in Holland and those who feared assimilation left for America, but those who did not stayed. National feeling and anti-Spanish sentiment, which is only part of the example of Spain, while present and important, was not a fixed entity, but, rather, was qualified by religion, region, language and commerce.

Anti-Spanish sentiment was not universal as the French Catholic missionaries to America remembered the example of their Spanish counterparts before them.[20] During the 1630s, the Jesuit missionaries worked amongst the Hurons, and there the Iroquois killed both Jean de Brébeuf and Gabriel Lalemont in the late 1640s.[21] The Jesuits, like the Recollets, often looked to the success of Spanish Jesuits for inspiration.[22] Like Protestant sects, Catholic religious orders complicated loyalties to language and nation in a period where regions and national boundaries were in flux.[23] French Catholic religious writing in and about the New World was also indebted to Spanish influences even as, in some instances, the writers resisted Spain or felt ambivalent about its colonization, particularly in its treatment of the Amerindians. Between 1632 and 1672, the Jesuits partly published their annual relations. Paul Le Jeune was the Jesuit superior at Québec during the 1630s, but although the French Jesuits were well aware of the example of the Spanish Jesuits, they did not, in their relations, dwell directly on Spain and the Spanish empire.[24] From Huronia (Ouendake), Le Jeune could write in 1637 about the success of turning the Paraquais from cruel cannibals to gentle lambs of God and of the good results of Portuguese conversions of the American Indians.[25] The accounts of America in French in the sixteenth century had been overwhelmingly Protestant, whereas in the seventeenth century they were Catholic.

Influences on Catholicism in France derived from Italy, from the Council of Trent, which attempted to restore Christianity to its essence. The spiritual works of Spaniards, which emphasized internal renewal, especially the spiritual exercises of Ignatius Loyola that set out a model of how to be a missionary, increasingly affected the French.[26] As some objected to the means of converting the Natives and cruelty toward them, an ambivalent attitude toward Spain occurred in France in matters of religion. Possibly, part of the suspicion of the Spanish amongst the French was derived from Jacques de Miggrode's translation of Las Casas in 1578, which Lescarbot, who questioned the godliness and zeal of the Spaniards, made popular (Lescarbot even inflated the number of Native dead that Las Casas had given). Nonetheless, the *légend noire* was not the only view in France, so that the Thevet of *Singularitez* thought that God had rewarded the Spanish with America for taking Granada.[27] The work of Louis Hennepin and the translation of Las Casas in 1698, also illustrate the ambivalence in the use and example of Spain in religious accounts in French.

Rather than discuss all these works, I would like to concentrate on a crucial period of the relations amongst the Europeans in the New World and between the French and Natives in New France: the 1630s and 1640s.

An example is Gabriel Sagard's *Histoire dv Canada et voyages qve les freres mineurs Recollets y ont faicts pour la conuersion des Infidelles* (1636). Sagard, a Recollet who traveled among the Huron or Ouendat, focused on conversion from 1615 to the fall of Québec to the English in 1629.[28] Sagard said that America was named after Vespucci but reminded his reader that the honor was due to Columbus, who discovered the New World five years before.[29] This rehashing of the origins of America and the first European contact with it occurred, almost as an obsession, in French and English writing from the sixteenth century onward. Sagard used Las Casas as a source for Hispaniola and recalled the conquest of Mexico by Cortés.[30] A more telling aspect is the account of a Spanish Recollet baptizing 400 Natives, an example for this French Recollet historian and missionary and one that served his theme of conversion and cut across the secular concerns of rival empires.[31] Sagard followed up with a description of the Recollet conversion of the kingdom of Voxu, a province in eastern Japan.[32] The Spanish Recollets in America and the Far East became a model for the French amongst the Hurons.[33] Sagard's history, which talked about conversion and profit, had a promotional element to it: he mixed commerce with religion.

From the 1630s onward, Spain still haunted the rivalries amongst the European nations in the Americas. England and France fought with each other and the Netherlands grew in power, so that these two powers became anxious over the success of the Dutch while having to contend with the continued strength of Spain in the New World. What is surprising is the staying power of the example of Spain in the imperial purview of France and England. Long after Sagard wrote, the ghost of Spain was still wandering the streets of Paris and London, not to mention those of Québec and Boston.

III

The legal and political questions started early in the history of European expansion to the western Atlantic and depended on the discovery and possession of territory. England followed Spain most closely in exploring the New World. Henry VII seems to have ignored the papal bulls and treaties between the Iberian powers during the 1490s dividing the world-to-be-discovered.[34] After the accomplishment of John Cabot, the English began to lag behind the French, who were in Brazil, as traders and pirates and who challenged the Portuguese there until they were driven out in 1603. François Ier, unlike Henry VIII, made a concerted effort to explore and claim new territories in the Americas and, like Henry VII, ignored the authority of the pope to donate these lands to Spain and Portugal. He built up a policy of discovery, conquest and settlement that challenged the bulls, which was, as in Henry VII's case, a version of *terra nullius*. The French use of the principle of "no settlement, no possession" goaded the Portuguese and the Spanish, and was a position Elizabeth I took up.

Precariousness marked the French and English efforts at colonization in the New World during the sixteenth century as opposed to the established Spanish settlements. Spain and England were united in the 1550s during the brief reign of Philip and Mary. What seems to have crystallized Elizabeth's action in colonization was Spanish actions against Protestants in Florida and the Netherlands, although she played both sides against France and Spain as she tried to gain a foothold in the Caribbean.

Anti-Spanish sentiment appears to have intensified at the height of Spanish power during the late sixteenth century and sometimes camouflaged the positive responses that the French and English received in this period. Before the translations of Las Casas, which are traditionally set out as the beginnings of the Black Legend of Spain, the Huguenot attacks on Spain during the 1560s began the Black Legend in earnest. Despite the propaganda against Spain from the Netherlands, France and England during the 1570s and 1580s, Spanish power was still supreme in Europe.

Spain may have been declining from the defeat of the armada to 1621, but was still a superpower. From 1621 to 1640, Spain began to collapse under the pressure from France and the Netherlands. During this period of decline, France and England established permanent colonies in North America. Just when Spain seemed invincible, joined with Portugal from 1580 to 1640, the Dutch, the French and the English "triumphed." They became rivals to one another. France and England became chief contenders in North America, and the claims and counterclaims over Hudson Bay were just one aspect of that rivalry. In 1722, in the epistle dedicatory, to the duke of Orléans, the regent of the kingdom, in *Histoire de L'Amerique Septentrionale*, which covered the period 1534–1701, Claude Charles Le Roy Bacqueville de la Potherie concentrated on the triumphant French voyage to Hudson Bay in 1697.[35] His work on the northern reaches of America supplemented Belleforest's. The myth that the Natives loved the French and, as a result of that love, worked side-by-side with them against the Spanish and other Europeans was something that began with the French narratives about Brazil and Florida in the sixteenth century, but in Bacqueville's "Epistle" the French, like the Spanish before them, experienced conflict with the indigenous population, and Bacqueville represented the heroism of the French in their overcoming of hostile Natives and nature. The heroic model died hard.[36]

Nonetheless, despite the decline and collapse of Spain, the specter of its power never left the rhetorical world of these texts, and this was especially true in times of war and crisis. Spain remained a power in America and Asia long after its diminishment in Europe, so that as late as 1737, those trustees establishing the colony of Georgia could speak with concern about the threat of Spanish might.[37] In the eighteenth century Spain continued to haunt the British as it did the French. In an address to the king of Great Britain, the trustees of Georgia, formerly the southern part of South Carolina, in the words of the secretary, Benjamin Martyn, pleaded for protection from Spain for their colony:

> being very much exposed to the Power of the *Spaniards*, and become an object of their Envy, by having valuable Ports upon the homeward Passage from the *Spanish West-Indies*, and the *Spaniards* having increased their Forces in the Neighbourhood thereof; The Trustees, in consequence of the great Trust reposed in them by your Majesty, find themselves obliged humbly to lay before your Majesty, their Inability sufficiently to Protect your Majesty's Subjects settled in *Georgia*, under the Encouragement of your Majesty's Charter, against this late Increase of Forces, and therefore become humble Suppliants to your Majesty, on the Behalf of your Subjects settled in the Province of *Georgia*, that your Majesty would be pleased to take their Preservation into your Royal Consideration, that, by a necessary Supply of Forces, the Province may be Protected against the great Dangers that seem immediately to Threaten it.[38]

This passage expressed some of the same anxieties the Huguenots had in Florida during the 1560s and suggested that the Spanish force, which defeated the English "Western Design" during the 1650s, had not withered away.

A few of the findings in this chapter should help to qualify received opinion. Although the Black Legend was important in the representation of Spain in France and England, it was only part of the story. French Catholics, like Marc Lescarbot, were capable of resenting Spain's power, success and presumption. It was not until the revocation of the Edict of Nantes in 1685 and the Glorious Revolution of 1688 that France and England went their separate Catholic and Protestant ways, and it was not until the Bourbons occupied both the French and the Spanish thrones before Spain and France could, at least while Louis XIV lived, put their differences aside. In Louisiana, however, the Spanish did not want the French there even if their king, Philip V, was the grandson of Louis XIV. National self-interest often cut across the lines of religion.

This textual surprise or evidentiary imperative was one of the pleasures of exploration as I had to shed ignorance and preconceptions like an Old World. Just as in their ethnographical writing Bartolomé de Las Casas, André Thevet, Jean de Léry, Michel de Montaigne and others used other cultures to criticize European culture, following classical works like Tacitus's *Germania*, which used the manly German barbarians to reproach the effeminate Romans, so too does the otherness of the past provide a critique of stereotyping or oversimplifications of the past. The "Germania syndrome," to borrow Peter Burke's phrase, could be used as a skeptical tool to create a more complex understanding of the English and French uses of the example of Spain.[39] In discussing the polemical conflicts surrounding the Spanish colonization of the New World, particularly from about 1566 to 1626, the "history of prejudice" is another description of one of the principal concerns of this precedence of Spain, when countries like France and England followed Spain in the colonization of the Americas, that is, the negative aspect of the example of Spain. Nonetheless, the intricacy of the textual representations, both internally and in relation to other texts (what I have called the "context"), also implied positive views of Spain, which, together with the negative elements, created ambivalence or contradiction, something that prevented a straightforward and unqualified generalization about the relations among the Spanish, English and French in their image and colonization of the New World.

It was quite apparent that by the end of the sixteenth and the beginning of the seventeenth century the Spanish, English and French, not to mention the Dutch and the Portuguese, all contended in trade and war in the New World. By the eighteenth century the rivalries continued and the English still seemed to rejoice in having Spain as an enemy, so that the War of Jenkins's Ear (1739–48) was like old times. For instance, the opening paragraph of the Anonymous *The British Sailor's Discovery: Or the Spaniards Pretensions Confuted* (1739) began by distinguishing amongst titles, conquest and actual possession. Besides the title in the margin, "*Spain's* Pretensions vain and boundless," the anonymous author challenged Spain's right to America and its questioning of British rights there; Spain "by an arbitrary, and unwarrantable Authority, pretends too set Limits and Boundaries in the greatest of *Oceans*, whereby to exclude all others from sailing past the same."[40] The author then presented an "Introduction towards a Review of the Discovery by *Columbus*," the source of this pretense, wherein he compared the "Iniquity" of Spanish discoveries and the "Equity" of English ones and concluded "that the much boasted *Right* of *Spain*, here taken notice of, is founded upon *Possession* obtained by unjust *Conquests*, which were attended with most execrable *Murders, Cruelties, Devastations,* and other Acts of *Inhumanity,* unbecoming one fellow Creature to act towards another; much less for those who professed Christianity."[41] The rivalry and the obsession with origins and the Black Legend endure well beyond the period examined in this chapter.

How much of the ground of British and French identities in mid- and late eighteenth-century North America was set by the example of Spain, especially the relation of the French and British to the American Indian as against the influence of earlier experiences of Spain in this kind of cultural encounter and definition? The answer is multifold but one of its aspects is this—the example of Spain was much greater than they may have known or we may think.

Ambivalence and contradiction complicated these English and French texts that represented Spain. Spain was an example to follow and avoid. In time the French and the English slowly abandoned the example of Spain as Spanish power declined in Europe, although its strength in the Americas was something to be reckoned with well beyond that decline. This moving away from Spain as an exemplum also occurred in France and England when there appeared to be no obvious evidence of precious metals in North America. The political cultures of France and England were also changing in a way that made the Spanish model of conquest and settlement less attractive. By the time of the Enlightenment, among Whigs and *philosophers*, Spain and its empire were becoming images or tropes of feudalism and reaction. The staying power of the example of Spain, as well as its complexity, make simple generalizations difficult, so what I am describing here is based on wide reading and evidence but should be taken as tendencies and trends in these texts and in this discursive history and not, in some sort of personification, as the motives of entire nations, such as France and England.

What I have argued here and elsewhere is that legal, political, economic and religious elements in English and French uses of the example of Spain are blended in a complex representation and that ambivalence and contradiction arose in imitations that denied they were imitations, that moved away from the model of Spanish colonization even as that exemplum was inescapable owing to its precedence in law, history and narrative. In the example of Spain, conquest was central but should not be isolated or overemphasized because other aspects contributed to that model. Some of these aspects that complicated a simple shift from conquest to settlement or the Black Legend were the shifting alliances amongst Spain, France and other European powers, which tempered and altered the rules of the pursuit of God and gold.

I have also tried to call attention to the ambivalence that English and French texts displayed toward the legal, political, economic and religious precedence or exemplarity of Spain. For instance, Richard Eden saw the marriage of Philip and Mary as a means of expressing the imperial union of Spain and England, which involved English expansion, but it is possible that his ambivalence even in his triumphal vision of the 1550s led to his dismissal.

Here, I wish to elaborate on a representative example: the pursuit of riches in the Amazon basin and in South America. In the last two decades of the sixteenth century and the first two decades of the seventeenth century this quest played out differently in England and France, but both powers had to contend with the legacy and power of Spain in the region. Myths, God and gold haunted the English and French as they had the Spanish.

Ralegh's challenge to the Spanish, his conquest of the conquerors, his more golden El Dorado, did not fare well with James I, who made peace with Spain in 1604. The conqueror turned liberator, following the lead of Humphrey Gilbert, was conquered, and the dream of gold, which had also possessed Cartier, Roberval and Frobisher, faded but did not go away as, in 1609, Robert Johnson could still hold out hope for precious metals in his tracts on Virginia. After the defeat of the French (whose leader was the Huguenot Vice Admiral La Ravardière) by the Portuguese at Maragnan in Brazil in 1612—partly because the queen mother, Marie de Médici, did not choose to reinforce the French colony as she preferred her son's Spanish marriage to it (as Portugal was joined with Spain at this time)—the French were less intense in their interest in the Amazon as a shortcut to El Dorado in Peru but still sought that end during the rest of the seventeenth century.[42] This search for precious metals in Spain's South American territory persisted for a long time. Three expeditions during the ministry of Cardinal Mazarin (1642–61) left for Guiana, which was considered the entry to El Dorado, but the more successful French efforts in the colonies stemmed from their commercial relations with the Dutch in the Antilles.[43] More and more, the imitation of the example of Spain also involved a shift away from it.

Paternalism, displacement, exploitation and conversion of the Natives were also part of the example of Spain, a pattern the English and French followed in modified forms, so that they could not turn away from this Hispanic model. France and England devised representations of liberating the Natives from Spanish oppression. While the English and French either represented scenes, as Ralegh had, of liberation of the Natives from Spanish tyranny, or a better way of coexisting with the aboriginal population, as Lescarbot did, both English America and New France found themselves at war with the Natives: the French with the Iroquois and the English in Virginia and, later, in the so-called King Philip's War during the 1670s.[44] The fictions of turning away from the Spanish model of conquest, paradoxically, came up against the actuality of Natives who did not want to succumb to a "conquest" called by many other names but a conquest nonetheless.

These fictions of history and political identity were related closely to legal fictions, which were resilient and persistent long after their original articulation. Laws and legal strategies from the late fifteenth century, sometimes backed by earthly or spiritual power and at other times rhetorical claims, endured in some form or as tropes and examples in arguments into the seventeenth and eighteenth centuries. The instances of *terra nullius* and the papal donations of the 1490s are cases in point. *Terra nullius*, as John Winthrop had noted in New England, meant that the Natives did not occupy the land and could be displaced.[45] As David Ramsey observed after the War of Independence in his history of the revolution, the English colonists in America, while criticizing the papal donation of the New World to Spain and Portugal, used similar terms to distinguish between the rights of heathens and Christians, so that his view corroborates the idea, in my study, that even in contradiction there is imitation.[46] These legal and political fictions served ambivalence and contradiction in the French and English use of the example of Spain. Even during the revolutionary break from Britain, British Americans used Spain as a model to claim legal and political right to the lands from which these colonists had dispossessed the Natives. How different were these rites of possession from those employed by Europeans early in the expansion of Europe to the New World?

As the cases of Ramsey and some jurists testify, certain instances of the paradoxes of ambivalence and contradiction within the French and English (later British) positions became apparent to the Europeans themselves. Despite "ceremonies of possession," to use Patricia Seed's phrase, the French and English still occupied and wanted to occupy the lands of the Natives, something that, with good reason, met with resistance, even as they differed from more horrific forms of Spanish possession—like the one Las Casas focused on, the *Requerimento*, or Requirement, which traced the history of creation, gave the grounds for Spanish possession and threatened the Natives in a language they could not understand with enslavement and loss of their lands if they resisted.[47] The differences, legal and religious, the French and English set out in contrast to the Spanish, sometimes having to do with the authority of the pope in temporal matters, at other times the differences within Catholicism or national traditions in religion and at still other times between Protestantism and Catholicism, could then be used, had they the power, by the Natives to undermine any claim that France and England might have to the New World. This logic, as I have suggested, had not been lost on some European jurists and intellectuals since Vitoria. It increased the refractory nature of the French and English uses of the example of Spain, which often included a representation of the Spanish and Amerindians. The apparent contradictions and ambivalences also qualified the Bourbon occupation of the thrones of France and Spain over which Europe went to war at the opening of the eighteenth century: after the death of Louis XIV, Spain did not necessarily side with France even if both were ruled by the same family.

Like law, the justifications of the possession of territory, religion or patriotism were not always predictable factors in the English and French representations of Spain. A telling example was the clash between the French Protestants and Spanish Catholics in Florida during the 1560s. In his account of the Spanish massacre of the Huguenots in Florida, Le Challeux, who was not an eyewitness but had escaped with Laudonnière from Fort Caroline, was sometimes more interested in seeing a providential punishment for the

French who had left their families to gain a living or riches in a far-off land, in being anticolonial and in seeing the personal betrayal and suffering in the atrocities the Spanish committed. It was Dominique de Gourges, who led the unauthorized reprisal against the Spanish forts in Florida in 1567.[48] Elizabeth I and John Hawkins seem to have waited to see whether legal trade with the Spanish in the Caribbean was more profitable than joint piracy with the Huguenots against Spain. Colbert ordered the translation of Thomas Gage to use against Spain, which had kept secrets about its American colonies, even though this author had turned from Catholicism to Protestantism.

In writings about the New World in French and English, a tension existed between an attempt to transcend partisan national and religious interests and to use what I have called the typology between the New World and the Old for polemical advantage and propaganda. Personal and national self-interest, as well as the ability of some historians—like La Popelinière, who was forthright about the tragic consequences and stupidity of French Catholics and Protestants destroying each other and about the envy France had for the Spanish and Portuguese discoveries—to transcend, at least in part, the partisan political and religious interests of their faction or government, meant that a simple split between Catholics and Protestants, even during the Wars of Religion, in France or a completely chauvinistic division between European nations is too one-eyed a view.[49] They often saw the horror of Spanish atrocities in the New World in the terror in a France divided by civil war. Léry witnessed cannibalism in France as well as in Brazil just as Montaigne, who never traveled to the New World, saw cruelty in Spanish America and his own country. On the other hand, in this typology, as the French translations of Las Casas published in Amsterdam in 1620 and 1630 revealed, the Revolt of the Netherlands helped to set up a typological relation between earlier Spanish atrocities in the New World with later ones in the Netherlands. This is an example of the double movement this chapter has examined where Spain was both a positive and negative example to those who represented it in English and French publications. Politics and religion were mixed in ways that were sometimes unforeseen, and matters of national loyalty and interest, as they might have been defined in the nineteenth and twentieth centuries, were not always clearly defined.

In French colonization, internal religious conflict may be illustrated by Champlain. He sailed with Spain, whom his uncle served, worked with de Monts, a Protestant, in Acadia and then founded a colony in Québec that was centered on orders like the Jesuits and Recollets, which often looked to Rome and Spain for models, even as they also expressed Gallicanism. In fact, Champlain complained about the friction between Huguenots and Catholics being one of the causes of the slow growth of New France.[50] More generally, self-contradiction in French views of the role of religion in France and its colonies complicated its ambivalent and contradictory relations with Spain and its American empire. Even during the Wars of Religion, Catholic and Protestant moderates viewed Spain's power in Europe and America with caution and ambivalence. Members of the Catholic League were staunch allies to Spain.

Most of these aspects of colonization—legal, religious and economic— which constitute parts of the example of Spain, had refractory political implications. Europeans born in America began to complicate the relations among Spain, England and France, so that, eventually, in the late eighteenth and early nineteenth centuries, these European American views complicated examples of the polity and civil society that moved from colony to independent nation. This shift in identity for the Americans, as Ramsey saw, employed some of the dynamics of the English use of the example of Spain as a means of achieving independence. This tension between the crown or church and its "American" landowners and prominent citizens can be seen as early as the second decade of Spanish settlement in the West Indies. As Las Casas reports in Book III of his *History of the Indies*, in December 1511, Father Antón Montesino, a Dominican or Black Friar, preached two Advent sermons in which he condemned the Spanish colonists for enslaving the Native population much to the ire of the colonists, who protested to the king. The Spanish crown shifted positions over the rights of the colonists and the "Indians." The line between politics and religion was blurred in the church and at court as these were the same Dominicans who had directed the medieval papal inquisition and, afterward, the royal inquisition in Spain. These Dominicans also acted as missionaries in Portuguese and French as well as Spanish colonies, so the transnational nature of religious orders complicated national interest in the expansion of Europe. Later, in the English and French colonies, a native-born elite, was also developing its own views of colonization, so that their concerns with Spain or with their rivals was more local and American and not necessarily a part of a European theater of politics, economics and religion. Another distinction now made among the French, as it was among the Spanish, was that between Americans and Europeans. Pierre Boucher was such as example.[51] Bacqueville, or the printer, had advertised Bacqueville's birth in Guadaloupe and now he used it as a means of expressing praise for the duke through the topos of inexpressibility. It was not, he said, for an American like him ("un Ameriquain comme moi") to undertake such a high endeavor ("à prendre un effort si haut") to expand on the heroic virtues ("les vertues Heroïques") that shine in his royal highness, so that he would leave them to the delicate pens of the French to treat material so elevated ("je laisse donc aux plumes délicates des François à traiter une matière si relevée").[52] The French and the British would not be able to avoid the split between the American and French part of the empires. That shift was gradual and effected great changes; New France fell in the Seven Years' War (1756–63) before independence might have come; most of the British North American colonies won independence in 1783; the Spanish colonies separated during the 1830s, so that this movement also was slow and uneven.

Some of the key earlier colonists, regardless of their religion, when France and England were trying to establish permanent settlements in precarious circumstances, looked to Spain as a positive and negative example of a European nation that had firmly established colonies in the New World. As we have seen, beyond the obvious uses of Las Casas, a Spanish Dominican, amongst the French and English for the purposes of propaganda, other important colonists and writers—like Marc Lescarbot and John Smith— were wary of embracing the example of Spain on the whole. Another French Dominican tradition that built on Spanish Dominicans, like Las Casas, was the idealization of the Natives (in this case the Caribs, whom Columbus had described in such negative terms) and a critique of the French for beginning the wars or conflicts with the Amerindians in the Caribbean.[53] As France and England were establishing permanent colonies in North America, Marc Lescarbot, a Catholic and a lawyer who was conscious of the precedent of the Spanish discovery and sometimes used the language of "conquest," condemned the Spanish treatment of the Natives and was not taken with the model of colonist as conqueror and used them as negative examples for French colonization. Lescarbot differentiated the French from the Spanish: "The most beautiful mine that I know of is wheat and wine, with feed for beasts. He who has these, he has silver. We do not live by mines."[54] John Smith, although fashioning himself on the heroic model of Cortés and commending Columbus and Queen Isabella for having the vision to back him, could proclaim: "And though I can promise no Mines of gold, yet the warlike *Hollanders* let vs imitate, but not hate, whose wealth and strength are good testimonies of their treasure gotten by fishing."[55] As early as 1603 the Flemish humanist, Justus Lipsius could declare of Spain, "Conquered by you, the New World has conquered you in turn, and has weakened your ancient vigour."[56] The shift away from the Spanish model of conquest and settlement was perhaps more uneven than other historians have indicated because the anxieties over, and mythical recreations of, the discovery of America, Spanish wealth by precious metals and the Black Legend persisted for a long time.[57] The use of the example of Spain declined in the seventeenth century but not as rapidly and as evenly as one might expect given the decline of Spain in Europe: one reason, as we have observed, is that Spain was still strong in America and Asia.

IV

The French also showed anxiety over the power of Spain in the New World and the desire to displace them, to undo what Columbus had done. In addressing the king, Samuel de Champlain notes that he explored with Sieur de Monts, the king's "Lieutenant in New France," but when he addresses the "Queen Regent Mother of the King," Champlain ignores the fact that de Monts was a Protestant and declares: "what made me navigate & skirt [costoyer] a part of the lands of America & principally of New France, where I have always a desire to make flourish there the Lily [le Lys, emblem of France of the ancien régime] with the unique Catholic, Apostolic & Roman Religion."[58] There is an implied rivalry with Spain, which was not as riven by civil wars fed by religious difference: French writers about the New World in the early decades of the seventeenth century, like Champlain and Marc Lescarbot, wanted France to be the champion of the church, which they often saw as its rightful place among nations and saw Spain as a threat to that preeminence. Champlain also speaks about his desire to help in the augmentation of "glory," a French preoccupation in the colonization of the New World especially in the sixteenth and seventeenth centuries.[59] Part of the front matter of the edition of 1613 is a poem by "Ange Paris" about the voyages of Champlain. The poem includes as one of its themes the audacity and arrogance of strangers or foreigners ranging the seas that should be France's. Stanza 4, which celebrates French military prowess in different continents, ends with the line: "*These peoples are witnesses of their warlike acts*". Aristocratic warrior culture, with its love of honor and glory, is never far away, so that the Spanish conquests in the New World must have been a goad to those in France that held to the ideals of prowess in battle and the subjugation of those less able in war. Stanza 5 becomes more explicit about the figure of France deserving more than a equally personified Spain:

> Thus I your mother in arms so fecund
> I make tremble beneath me the three parts of this world,
> The fourth only my arms have not tasted.
> This new world that Spain parched,
> Jealous of my praise, alone glorifies itself,
> My name more than its must be planted there.[60]

The verses admit that Spain alone has the glory in America but seeks to change that because France should have its due as it does in all the other parts of the world, something of a fiction at this time. The final stanza begins with an address to the king in the sweep of a trope of the translation of empire, "Your arms, o my King, o my great Alexander," the "Your," being in the familiar form, creating a bond with a kind of informal formality, an address to a great king who might be as familiar as a friend or loved one: the

official and the personal come together. This poem ends with Champlain's
"planting" that helps the king in his grandeur to soar to the heavens in an
apparent apotheosis in the final line. The last three stanzas—14, 15 and
16—are a rousing address to the dead Henry IV and his son, the king
regnant, to have France expand and to allow glorious Champlain to plant. In
an ode by Motin, "TO MONSIEVR DE CHAMPLAIN on his book & his
nautical charts [cartes marines]," there is more on his "glorious voyages" and
is addressed to Champlain, who overcomes dangers with his "courage blind
to dangers" and represents a new idea of immortality of the explorer as an
"author" and as someone who creates "renowned charts," a maker of maps as
a kind of art.[61] The description of the fourth voyage is one of hardship and
scurvy in cold and snow—35 of 79 died and more than 20 came close to
death—and in which all drinks except "the wine of Spain" freezes.[62] Without
being too facetious, even Spanish wine has adapted well to a new world,
which the French hope to master. Champlain describes a conspiracy in which
Iean du Val, a locksmith, sought to have Champlain put to death ["fait
mourir"] and to hand the fort over to "Basques or Spaniards" who were at
Tadoussac.[63] After Champlain found out and du Val made his admission,
"We decided that it would be enough to be put to death the said du Val as
the mover of the undertaking, & also to serve as an example to those who
remained, to behave wisely in the future in doing their duty and in order that
the Spaniards and Basques who were many in the country did not
triumph."[64] As a result of the sentence that Champlain passed, "the said Iean
du Val was hanged & strangled at Québec, & has head put on the end of a
pike to be planted [planté] in the most prominent [eminent]" place in the
fort.[65] This almost novelistic description of the ravages of scurvy and the
attempted revolt is the kind of pain, death and violence that challenges
French glory just as, in a different way, the story of the Pizarros qualified
Spanish notions of glorious conquest.

   In the Caribbean, the French in the seventeenth century also had
Spain on their minds, although in the official government correspondence
between Guadeloupe, Martinique and adjacent islands with France from
the 1660s paid more attention to England, particularly as regards commerce.
For instance, Monsieur de la Baar wrote on December 26,1669 from
Guadeloupe: "a Spaniard who seemed by chance in these Islands," something
that appears remarkable enough to note; his letter also suggests that there was
conflict among the various leading French officials as well as with the
Spanish.[66] From Martinique on February 24, 1670 he lamented, "I wrote to
the Company to send two or three men who knew how to make Rope-soled
shoes like the ones they make in Spain" but to no avail.[67] The frustration
here came from the lack of heeding advice from the Islands to France about
the imitation of a Spanish success.

Still, like the Dutch and English, the French came after Spain in time and pursuit, and they underestimated their power in the Americas. In the 1560s, as we have seen, the French had tried, after setbacks in Canada and Brazil, to found a colony, something that Spain ended swiftly with force and that created controversy and ill-feeling between the French and Spanish. However, the French Protestants could never convince the king to act against Spain, so this would indicate some division or weakness within France. A memorandum in 1669 revisited the possibility of Florida as a French colony, saying that it was appropriate "to make beautiful and large colonies."[68] It is as if the French had forgotten their earlier interest and the reasons for it. In the memorandum, article 2 claimed that Florida "is near the Strait of the Bahamas by which [ships] pass necessarily and the fleet of Spain and several vessels that carry riches to Spain" and, in a passage reminiscent but not explicitly aware or alluding to Duplessis-Mornay, an earlier Huguenot leader, noted: "if we were some day to have War with the Spaniards or if we were to make it all the time as the English do we would occupy a passage that could diminish, or perhaps restrain [rayner] one day their commerce and their finances." Article 5 maintained, "The wine there is becoming as good as several places in Spain," so that, by implication, such a place could provide competition to the Spanish. The memorandum proposes in article 8 that the French settle in a place that is not distant from St. Augustine where the Spanish are "feeble" and where their fortress is not well guarded because they "hold more lands throughout America than they can guard" and that they fear that some other nation will "seize the coast of the Gulf of Mexico, one of the most beautiful countries of America & much inaccommodate the Spanish fleet and vessels returning to Spain from passing as we have said except by the Strait of Bahama that joins Florida." Another germane document is "Memorandum de Francois [T]ourillon of Marseille who made several voyages in Spanish Mexico, with the Spanish and in their service, having lived there several years both in the islands and on the main land [terre ferme] always in the company of the Spanish."[69] Here was someone who would turn his experience with the Spanish in America to French advantage. This memorandum had as its premise: "If His Majesty had some thoughts of making conquests of this coast there, it would not be difficult for him to augment the number of islands that He possesses there and which are better and more considerable than those that she had there now."[70] The document suggests in detail how the French could defeat the Spanish: for instance, the rendezvous would be at La Tortue because it is closest to the Spanish island; the French coureurs de bois ("boucanier") who are used to fatigue and hide in the woods when they are hunting the Spanish wild oxen (chasse des boeufs), should prove "very useful" in this expedition.[71] What this French equivalent of Cromwell's "Western Design" on the Indies in 1655 was leading up to was a sense that if the French took the two key Spanish islands in the Antilles, including Cuba, then they could hold in "subjection all the main land of New Spain and the rest of Mexico."[72] The author used an argument similar to that which Ralegh had employed in his work on Guiana in 1596, except here the case is extended to all the people, including descendants of the conquerors, and not just the Natives: they will welcome a change because "the inhabitants are much maltreated by the viceroys" and other officials "sent from Spain to govern them that they have little affection for the government."[73] From his experience in the service of Spain, the author has noticed that the Spanish ships en route to Spain from Mexico have to stop in Havana for water and, if the French possess that place, it "would interrupt the commerce from Mexico to Spain," which includes the treasure on which the Spanish monarchy subsists, comprising also of silver from Peru, which, "since the conquest of the West Indies," Spain has fought for "than against the men subject to its empire."[74] This kind of talk had been going on for at least a hundred years, whether it was Humphrey Gilbert, Duplessis-Mornay or Hakluyt the younger, and Spain had not given up the ghost in the New World yet.

The conflict between the French and the Spanish over the divided island of St. Domingue continued. From there, on February 28, 1678, Monsieur de Louançay recorded his campaign of three weeks "in the Spanish lands" and told of how the French killed seven or eight men and "wounded a large number" and that the Spaniards retreated.[75] This friction with Spain had its costs and he reminded his unnamed addressee ("Monsieur") of the many and "considerable" expenses that have indebted him "extremely," so that "I take the liberty of addressing you a memorandum and to beg you in the desire that you speak to Mgr. Colbert in order to obtain more easily from him the appointments that give me the means to continue the Service with the same zeal."[76] De Louançay ended this memorandum by pointing out that all the other governors of the islands have such appointments and that the charges were falling on him alone, as the monarch spent nothing on his colony, so he hoped that "Monsieur" will show him his "favour" and support him "and I shall have this obligation to you of which I shall all my life acknowledge[.] I kiss very humbly your hands and am with respect Your very humble and very obedient servant."[77] For this governor, Spain became a financial and diplomatic problem with his own court. From La Tortue, De Louançay wrote on January 9, 1679, about the conflict, saying there are bruits there that "peace must be made with Spain as it was with Holland and that the war continues in Germany."[78] The problem of rules governing the treatment of prisoners between the Spanish and the French in the West Indies is something De Louançay, governor of "la Tortue" and "Coste St. Dominigue," also addressed here.[79] On July 10, 1680, his Spanish counterpart, also had to consider his role as a representative of the crown and the wars in Europe when considering peace and conflict and the question of prisoners.[80] De Louançay's response, on July 27, 1680, concerning the articles of peace was diplomatic but complained: "as until now I have seen little disposition to peace on the part of the subjects of the King of Spain who live on this island, I have reason to believe that they will do the same as they have in other preceding peace [agreements]."[81] The killing of cattle by Spanish inhabitants in places they were accustomed to do so and communication with the king and with Count d'Estrées, the French Vice Admiral, were other concerns for De Louançay.[82] In a memorandum in 1682, De Louançay, reporting that Count de Blenac sent him a copy of a letter that ordered him to prevent French subjects from "navigating to the coasts of the lands and islands of America inhabited by the Spaniards without the consent of Monsieur de Maintenon," said that the colony remained feeble and "exposed to the insults of the Spaniards."[83] On October 18, 1685, Le Sieur de Cussy wrote from St. Domingue, appealing to many of the same topics as his predecessors: the treatment of slaves by the French and Spanish, the conflict between the two nations in the Antilles, the lot of prisoners and the need for money in the colony.[84] The Spanish governor of Cuba wrote to one of his French counterparts in the Caribbean on July 3, 1688, discussing the movement of "Negroes" and "Spanish Negresses" in an apparent attempt to regulate the movement of slaves.[85] The everyday life of government officials in the Spanish and French West Indies included, especially in times of armed conflict, communication with one another.

Spain required cooperation as well as contention. The references to Spain and the Spanish in the New World in these letters and memoranda were not part of a systematic representation but were more scattered or quotidian in response to the pressures of the moment. The officials of the incipient or recent French colonies were feeling their way, so that divisions within the administration as well as differences of opinion with the court and government in France were as much or often more a concern than the presence of Spain.

V

It is possible that the French and English proponents of expansion, explorers, colonizers and settlers, found it hard to get over their admiration and envy of Spain, as if they desired what the Spanish had found and profited from while attempting to displace the great power, and that these nations remembered, long after its decline, the sting of the power of Spain as a kind of trauma. To call attention to the mixed reaction to the example of Spain expressed in these French and English documents is not to ascribe simple

and naive emotions and reactions to their writers. Psychoanalytical interpretations of history, such as those by Peter Gay, may be appropriate for an
analysis of such emotions, but I have chosen to focus on another direction,
one that is more in terms of a historical or contextual poetics, which concentrates on representation and rhetoric—modes of analysis that the period
under consideration shares with our own. The texts yield an emotional aspect
in a complex of rhetorical tropes, schemes and strategies in which the writer
seeks to persuade the reader. Relations that the text sets out between the
writers and the audience possess other elements that are beyond the scope of
this book. It would, however, be oversubtle, especially in the works of propaganda, not to observe the appeal to emotion, and some of those feelings,
however embarrassing they might be to scholarly detachment, are raw and
direct. These emotions, like the allegorical characters of medieval morality
plays whose names represent each of the Seven Deadly Sins, are hard to
ignore. One of the reasons I have chosen a close examination of texts is that
I thought it best that the reader of my book experience this dimension of
textual messiness. It is easy for historical truth to present itself at such a
distance that another kind of truth gets lost. Even as the truth seems to
recede in the quest for it, it is important not to begin at too great a distance
from the documents under examination. Critical distance is necessary for
history to have a shape but too much leaves history without a texture. This
textuality is an integral part of this book.

The texts under discussion here form a kind of textuality, an intricate
collocation of texts. Part of my argument is to point beyond itself because
the interpretation of texts—historical, literary, philosophical, legal or of
whatever discipline is, in Edmund Spenser's words, endless work. A direction
I would like to suggest as an end to these concluding remarks and to this
chapter is conquest—one of the ways France and England, no matter how
much they might have denied it, displayed, or had traditions that involved,
the very characteristics they criticized or trivialized in Spain—well into the
eighteenth century and beyond. Conquest among some of the key French
and English writers about and in the New World was something to be
emulated and, often in a later period, to be avoided. While not writing
psychohistory, I might suggest, nonetheless, that it is a kind of return of the
repressed. *Conquistadores*, like Cortés, never seem to go away entirely in
French and English texts concerning the New World.

The French had their own history of conquest that they failed to bring up
when criticizing Spain for being conquerors. In France, as well as Spain, there
was a tradition of conquest despite what the French would later deny,
although they do not seem to have used it extensively in Brazil, the Caribbean
or New France. In 1744, Pierre Charlevoix, a Jesuit and thus another part
of the representation of the New World (although Le Jeune, a Jesuit, had

recommended military action), claimed that the French, unlike the Spanish, had no conquerors like Cortés and Pizzaro on the stage of the New World, a statement that was true if measured by his term *éclat* but was not accurate if the would-be conquerors, pirates and lords of the French (and often Norman) in the Caribbean were taken into consideration.[86] The term, "*éclat*," can mean a burst of noise, the glitter of a gem, or brilliance, all appropriate for the conquerors regardless of whether Charlevoix intended all these meanings. In the "Advertisement" Charlevoix said that some people thought that he should have included the Spanish conquerors, such as Cortés and Pizarro, in his description of San Domingo, so that "the History of Saint Domingue would have been that of nearly all the Spanish Empire in the new World."[87] It is sometimes forgotten that the Norman nobles, who were still settling the Caribbean islands during the seventeenth century and hoped to be lords and to supplement their income through plunder, had a long tradition of piracy and conquest, from before the Norman conquest of England to that of Sicily and the Canary Islands (which they then yielded to Spain).[88] A literature of piracy or buccaneering in the Caribbean developed in the 1680s.[89] The "Epistle," signed by De Frontignieres, declared that he had something new to teach about the example of Spain: "For example you will learn there [in his *Histoire*] many curious particulars, unknown until now, regarding the King of Spain. You will see there in what manner he governs the Indies, the Dignities, whether Temporal or Ecclesiastical in which he is endowed, the revenues to which he has a title; so that these Kingdoms of New Spain are worth more to him than all those of Old."[90] De Frontignieres then talked about the triumph of the French under "LOUIS LE GRAND," so that imitating the example of Spain and French triumphalism coexisted ambivalently.[91] Having touched on glory, the "Preface" added that it was nearly "impossible to know well the grandeur of their adventurers' ('aventuriers') enterprises."[92] It declared "he [the author] makes seen the treatment they [the adventurers] give the Spanish when they take them and that which they receive from the same Spaniards when they are taken."[93] Old habits died hard.

In the late seventeenth century John Dryden could reduce the story of Cortés to a historical romance, and not of the kind Bernal Díaz wrought with El Cid and romance ringing in his ears, as if the Spanish were now a curiosity and something tame enough to remove to a fantasia. In their own way the English devastated the Native population through a conquest of property. England had developed its own varieties of conquest, some of which bore some textual relation to Spain's; these texts explored legal, political, social and religious implications of possession of Native lands.

The religious and economic aspects of conquest were as significant in French and English America as they were in Spanish America. A few examples will specify this claim. Conquest and the mining and forced labor it entailed, as opposed to agriculture, fishing and other means of working with natural resources, was not the only dimension of the example of Spain: religion, as we have observed in Las Casas's critique of Spanish colonization, was another important aspect of the model of Spain. Proselytizing the Natives was supposed to be the primary reason Alexander VI had donated the New World to Spain and Portugal. Religious orders crossed national borders and were centered in Rome. The French and English Jesuits in New France and in Maryland respectively, followed the example of Loyola and the Spanish Jesuits in the New World in the framework of spiritual exercises and gained inspiration from reports of large numbers of converts. But, rather surprisingly, they largely ignored their Spanish confreres in the details of their reports.

Within a decade France and Spain were at war, the death of Louis XIV perhaps making the conflict within the ruling Bourbons easier. A few instances will suggest the ways in which the relations among Spain, France and England in the Americas continued to change. In 1714, an English translation of a French volume, which included translations of Spanish accounts of America published the year before in Paris, appeared in London. The publication of *The Travels of Several Learned Missioners of the Society of Jesus, Into Divers Parts of the Archipelago, India, China, and America* showed that neither political nor religious differences could stem the demand for, and flow of, information about the New World and other exotic countries. Although the anonymous preface concentrated most on India and China, it did call attention to the extract of a Spanish relation by Baraza, printed in Lima in 1704 and in Madrid in 1711, about how he "first convey'd the Light of the Gospel, bringing together and civilizing an infinite Number of Barbarians, who liv'd dispers'd, like Wild Beasts in the Woods and Mountains; building several large Towns, and Baptising above Forty Thousand Idolaters."[94] The civilization of Europe was more the theme here than the division between powers. A letter concerning Hudson's Bay and another about Acadia, both disputed territories in the wars between France and England, "may be the more acceptable at this Time, as having been yielded up by the last Treaty of Peace by the King of *France* to the Crown of *England*."[95] In the extract from Cyprian Baraza, S. J., he talked about barbarians and described Amazons, suggesting that not as much had changed from Columbus to 1704 as his successors would like to think.[96] The letter about Hudson's Bay, by Gabriel Marest, S. J. to F. de Lamberville, S. J., was a balanced account of the exploration of Hudson's Bay and the differences between the French and English. It also contained two murders among the French (the smith did it and confessed).[97] The next letter, which described Acadia, was by a French gentleman to an unnamed Jesuit. It represented the

Natives and the ingenuity of the French inhabitants.[98] The volume ended with a letter from a mission in the Mediterranean, which the editor hoped the reader would find acceptable. In 1718 Joseph François Lafitau, a Jesuit, presented his *Mémoire* to "Le Duc D'Orleans, Regent du Royaume de France," in which he proclaimed that he found the ginseng of Tartarie in Canada, but, more important for our purposes, he connected the Jesuit experience in New France with that in Brazil and Peru.[99] While shifting tensions remained among Spain, France and England, the writings of the religious show that the French and English now had each other in mind as much as they did the Spanish.

In the seventeenth century, France often shifted its policy on religion in the New World, sometimes resembling Spain's religious politics and sometimes not. Religious directives also had racial and economic dimensions. In order to encourage the growth of the white population in the islands, like Martinique, during the 1660s, Colbert advocated the tolerance of Jews and Huguenots, a divergence from the Catholic-only policy that Spain had followed and that France had considered when Richelieu assumed power in the 1620s. The "Code Noir" (1685)—which was instituted under Colbert's son, Seignelay—repealed this tolerance and the liberal conditions for African slaves, Huguenots and Jews.[100] Article I gave the Jews, "the declared enemies of the name of Christian" three months to leave the islands.[101] The Huguenots and galley slaves were forcibly transported to the French colonies in the Caribbean during the 1680s.[102] Slavery, which occurred in the French and English colonies that relied on tobacco, sugar and cotton, is one of the most shameful examples of a way that the French and English, as much as the Spanish, were lords and conquerors, ruining lives and working others to death all for gain. Once again, to paraphrase Lipsius, the conquerors were conquered. Once more, the "liberalization" or movement to a progressive and enlightened empire was not a matter of an even development.

Even when England used a rhetoric of triumphalism in the face of the fear of a new universal monarchy that joined Spain and France under the Bourbons, there was an uncertainty and some unexpected anxieties and differences that the English, and their rivals, experienced. The translations of Spanish works, and the fascination with the Spanish origins of European settlement in the New World and with their conquests, even while that attraction was denied, continued into the eighteenth century but did not always seem to have the same urgency. Las Casas, however, was still used for political ends, as with the English translation of 1656 in Cromwell's Western Design. It is also possible that Comte de Pagan's *Relation* (1655), a translation of Spanish texts on the Amazon, was, as Philip Boucher has suggested, part of French plans for an assault on the Spanish colonies in South America, a kind of French counterpart to the Western Design.[103]

In the "Epistle Dedicatory" of the English translation of 1661, the translator, William Hamilton, explained to Charles II that the work was first addressed to "Cardinal *Mazarine*, in order to have set his Majesty of *France* on conquest of the great Kingdome of the *Amazone* to himself."[104] Hamilton exhorted the king to seek out this land unpossessed by the Portuguese and Spanish, "For it is possest by the barbarous Natives only."[105] A similar narrative of liberation arose here: "And the Natives not only in their forlorn condition, but by singular junctures of providence, call for the Christian religion from us, while others cease from that duty."[106] As Spain, Portugal and France had not pursued this design, England should, and Hamilton quoted Pagan, whose noble background he provided to prove how easy this "design" would be, and reminded the king of his own family's service to the royal family; Hamilton even sought reparations for his lost estates from "the troubles of the times."[107] This was a balder proposal than Ralegh's advice to Elizabeth I concerning Guiana. Even as the French and English moved on to commerce from conquest, with a far bit of backsliding or sidestepping, and their colonies grew in strength, they could not ignore the example of Spain. John Dennis could write a political poem dedicated to Queen Anne on the triumph of Britannia as the preeminent empire, but the "British" still feared the growth of French power and in 1730s still respected Spanish military might in America.

The rivalry between France and England in the northern half of the New World refracted and sometimes overshadowed their relations with Spain and its American colonies. Still, the importance of Spanish America for France and England persisted. The connections between European empires in the New World became increasingly complex from the early sixteenth to the late seventeenth and early eighteenth centuries. When the French and Spanish crowns became related, although not joined, under the Bourbon dynasty, even in Louisiana, the French and the Spanish could not always cooperate in the face of English encroachment. In 1762 France ceded Louisiana to Spain as recompense for the Spanish alliance against Britain during the Seven Years' War (1756–63) because Spain had lost Havana to the British and had had to cede Florida to get it back. The English and French, as can be seen in the genealogy of "collections" from Thevet through Hakluyt, Lescarbot and Purchas to Thevenot, Harris and Stevens, influenced each other, including in their representation of Spain, although they were great rivals in North America. They also kept their eye on the Dutch, whose commercial success was eclipsing the wealth of Spain. During the seventeenth century, both the English and the French imitated the trading companies in Holland, another illustration of a movement away from the example of Spain. Working the land with European farmers was another shift in this direction: for instance, Jean Talon, an intendant in New France (1665–72), promoted agriculture by encouraging subsidies for small tenant farmers, although the fur trade had the allure of an adventure not entirely divorced from the Spanish image of conquest as it involved expeditions and broke the routine of farming or civic life. This tension between a community of farmers and the wandering of *coureurs de bois* was a major conflict in New France throughout the seventeenth century, exemplified in the differences between Champlain and Étienne Brulé, Bishop Laval and Governor Frontenac.

To look backward now can make it difficult to consider the uncertainty in the rivalries amongst Spain, England and France in the period in question. One French point of view from our time illustrates that a historian can sometimes see something that was not so clear to those who lived between the late fifteenth century to the last decades of the eighteenth century. In looking back on the struggle of the Europeans in the Americas, Étienne Taillemite, Inspecteur général honoraire de Archives de France, says that an insatiable curiosity and the thirst for knowledge were the staying motivations of the Europeans in the New World. He also noted the shared hardships: "French, English, Spanish had united their efforts to reach at the end of two centuries, in the hardest material and sanitary conditions, a knowledge, as perfect as the techniques of the time admitted, of the continent and its inhabitants"[108] Of the period from 1492 to 1795, Taillemite thinks that perhaps the greatest consequence is "the triumph of England."[109] Taillemite explains English ascendancy in the following terms: "The strength of naval power assured it a liberty to manœuvre almost universal of which neither France nor Spain" could maintain, so that "Great Britain acquired, from the middle of the XVIIIth century, positions of supremacy and domination that only the two world wars" called into question.[110]

VI

The first main encounter in the New World was between Native and Spaniard, which grew more complicated as the variety of American Indians became apparent and rivalries developed between Spain and its European neighbors. Spain was surprisingly persistent in the New World texts of France, England and other rivals. An ambivalence arose about the model of Spain, which provoked envy and emulation, so that Spaniards were represented as heroic and cruel. The French and English, like the Spanish, represented the Natives as noble and cruel. A typology between Spanish cruelty in the New World and in the Netherlands was qualified by Spanish success at permanent colonization and descriptions of Native cruelty. The rivals of Spain revisited it as a negative and positive example again and again long after its decline in Europe. Despite that loss of power in Europe, Spain was a force to be reckoned with in the Americas long after the War of the Spanish Succession.

The endurance of Spain, even as the Netherlands, France and England became the chief rivals of the later seventeenth century, is one of the surprises in a comparative historiography of European expansion. Even if Hakluyt's hope that England would rival Spain had come to pass, other rivals grew stronger, and in 1713, it was far from certain that the English would come to dominate North America as Hakluyt had dreamed.

That dream was realized for a brief moment and, with the American Revolution, the First British Empire came to a close. Britain was still strong in North America but not dominant, and its former 13 colonies along the Atlantic seaboard became its greatest rival in what was to become the wealthiest continent. Mutability, then, is a great theme in comparing empires. It was not Spain alone that had to contend with surprises, miscalculations and fatal weaknesses. Britain later turned to other places in the world, despite the expansion of Canada, to expand on a grand scale. Along the way, however, it contended with and imitated other empires, for instance, its great commercial rival of the seventeenth century: Holland.

Chapter 4 〜

From Portugal to the United States

lthough Spain was a prime force in the colonization of the
New World, Portugal deserves close attention in the historiography
of European expansion. That is one reason, in providing a wider
context for the European contact with peoples in the western Atlantic,
I began the body of this book with Portugal and gave Portugal's earlier experience in exploration and trade in the Atlantic and Africa. Even though Spain
was a preoccupation for Europeans thinking about the New World, and
some of its rivals came after Spain, the role of the Portuguese in the seaborne
expansion of European trade and colonies helped to set the stage and is
significant, as it is when considering the Netherlands, mainly because these
are relatively small countries with small populations, that can be elided or
forgotten all these years later. Nonetheless, in the translation of empire and
comparison of empires, these key states and their colonies should be considered and represented. The title of this concluding chapter yokes the first
seaborne European culture in all its smallness and distance with the greatest
of European colonies, a great nation and economic empire today, here and
now, in the western Atlantic—the United States.

In this final journey from Portugal to the United States, we will make
brief stops in the imperial endeavors of the Netherlands and Britain, leaving
Spain aside, except in the culmination of the book—that is a brief discussion
of the Spanish-American War. This final blow to Spain in the Americas, after
having lost most of its possessions to independence in the early nineteenth
century, came just over 400 years after Columbus's landfall amid the very
islands Spain yielded in this war with the United States. Before we move on
to that conflict, what follows will be another look at the Portuguese in Brazil
and how the Dutch tried, sometimes successfully and sometimes not, to
displace them there and in the East. In unwinding some of these threads it is
interesting that past events, which involve the translation of empire and the
comparison of empires, are offered up for interpretation and become part of the

story of a present moment, now past for us. That Spain could be important to the United States in 1898 seems surprising until we look further, just as it is not readily apparent, though more so, why the Dutch focused on the Portuguese.

I

European expansion did not begin with the Iberian powers. The Italian contribution is always worth remembering. In the late 1200s the Italians had factories that ranged from the Black Sea through the Levant to Egypt connecting Asia to Europe: the friars John of Plano Carpini, in 1246, and William Rubruquis, in 1253, and the Polo brothers, Marco and Maffeo, had written of such a cultural contact.[1] The texts of Marco Polo, like those of Columbus afterwards, have a complex textual history involving several languages and a filtered or mediated aspect to the transmission. Polo, like Columbus and Shakespeare, does not really have an undisputed, authentic painted portrait to provide to posterity an image of a "cultural hero."[2] That has not prevented imaginary renderings after the death of these figures to become part of the mythology and interpretation of them and their place in the history of culture. Polo's Venice had been in conflict with Genoa long before Columbus was born. During this war, Polo was taken prisoner and shared a cell in Genoa with a Pisan, Rusticiano or Rustichello, the scribe and apparent romance writer who wrote down Polo's travels. This tale was mediated and its original language has been disputed, whether it was French, a dialect of Italian or Latin, although French seems to be the favored alternative. Besides the Old French text, there are Ramusio's Italian version and an Irish text: the textual intricacies are a warning about the precariousness of key documents in culture, whether they are meant to be historical, literary or mythological.[3] The Italian precedence in trade, exploration and writing often underlay the accomplishment of the Portuguese and Spanish. Italian banking, credit and commercial skills also underwrote the Iberian expansion into the western Atlantic.

Europe in the late Middle Ages was short of gold, which was available through African trade routes. The Iberian merchants in the thirteenth century wanted to expand into North Africa and to challenge the Italian and Muslim merchants there. Although Aragon and Castile tried to divide regions of Africa between them—Tripoli and Tunis to Aragon and Algeria and Morocco to Castile—they used different methods of expansion. The crown of Aragon, on behalf of its Catalan subjects, sought to establish factories in the ports of North Africa, in competition with Italian merchants and Muslim pirates, whereas the crown of Castile preferred military action and dominion over lands in the tradition of the *Reconquista*, a tact that cost the Castilians in terms of life and finances. Even though Aragon and Castile signed a treaty of demarcation—something Portugal and Spain would do later in the 1490s, they did not control North Africa or the Atlantic islands off Africa and southern Europe. In the late 1200s the Catalans also appeared on the Atlantic coast of Morocco and the Genoese navigators seem to have reached islands inhabited by Neolithic inhabitants, the Canaries, where in the mid-fourteenth century, the Genoese, Mallorcans and Andalusians traded and slaved, and, by which time, European mariners had come across Madeira, which was uninhabited. Through a dynastic marriage Peter III (1276–85) of Aragon acquired claims to Naples and Sicily, which the French contested with help from the pope, and during the 1340s, Peter IV (1136–87) conquered Ibiza, Minorca and Mallorca from the Moors. Catalan merchants benefited from and supported this expansion. Strife, warfare, famine and plague in fourteenth-century Europe slowed expansion into the Atlantic, and although Castile, Aragon and Portugal took advantage of dynastic marriages that brought them closer to a united Hispania in one respect, these kingdoms fought each other in a changing balance of alliances involving France and England, who were also engaged one against the other in a conflict that endured for a hundred years.[4]

A legal framework was developed as the Iberian powers expanded. Until the fifteenth century, relations with Islam had been a significant political and juridical consideration. In Iberia or Hispania the Moors were thought to inhabit *terra irredenta*, lands that needed to be restored to legitimate Christian rulers, whereas pagan lands in Africa were *terra nullius*, uninhabited lands in the sense that these people lived without civility or a polis. Earlier writings, like those of Hortensius (Cardinal Henry of Susa, d. 1271), were used to justify Portuguese claims in Africa: Christ embodied temporal and spiritual lordship over the world, and this dominion was passed on to his representatives, the pontiffs or bishops of Rome, who could also delegate lordship over non-Christian lands. This doctrine imbued a papal bull in 1452, which donated to the crown of Portugal sovereignty over subjects in the lands they had discovered, and another in 1454 over peoples in lands that the Portuguese might discover in Africa as they proceeded south. The crown was obliged to convert these peoples, who could be conquered if they resisted trade with, the dominion of and evangelization by Christians. In these bulls the pope gave Portugal a monopoly in the expansion south of Morocco on the Atlantic coast of Africa.[5] The Portuguese and Spanish, in pursuit of their delegated monopolies, enslaved Africans, who were considered pagans and savages, and sold them in Portugal, Spain and the Atlantic islands. In the fifteenth century the Black Slaves were sometimes considered to be ill-formed and inferior; therefore, whereas this racial attitude was not yet a developed, systematic racism, as occurred in the nineteenth century onward, it was there and insidious nonetheless.[6] The Treaty of Alcáçovas in 1479 attempted to divide these lands between Portugal and Spain. On the eve of the Columbian landfall, this was an important strand in the legal and ethnological aspect of Iberian culture and its expansion, so that Pope Alexander VI's bulls in 1493 and the treaty between Portugal and Spain at Tordesillas in 1494, which moved the line of demarcation of the papal donations to Spain 270 leagues further west, follow on earlier bulls on religious, cultural and political aspects of Italian or Iberian expansion.[7] In about 1511 a printed version of the "Inter Cætera," the famous bull of May 4, 1493, which exalted the Iberian powers for spreading Christianity and which had proposed a dividing line between their spheres, 100 leagues west of the Azores and Cape Verde, appeared in northern Spain.[8]

II

Texts in different languages charted the Portuguese expansion into Africa and the Atlantic. For the most part, this section will focus on a few key instances of those works concerned principally with the Atlantic. Books about navigation were important for the dissemination of the knowledge that permitted expansion by sea. For instance, Abraham Zacuto, a Spanish Jew, who was royal astronomer from 1495 to 1521 at the courts of King João II and King Manuel, wrote his *Almanach*, an influential work that circulated in manuscript from about 1473 and that was printed in Hebrew at Leira in 1496 and was translated into Spanish and Latin by one of his students, José Vizinho, also a Jew who later became astronomer to the Portuguese court.[9] The Portuguese expansion also required narratives of voyages and histories. The multicultural and multilingual nature of the spreading out of Portugal, and of other European powers, is something that is readily noticed when examining the early texts. In 1508 there appeared, for instance, a Dutch edition of an influential work by Amerigo Vespucci, an Italian, who sailed for Portugal and encountered Natives in Brazil, including Guanabara Bay and the site of what is now Rio de Janeiro, full of woodcuts and Vespucci's narrative that told of the good health and long lives of the Natives as well as their incest, polygamy and anthropophagy.[10] Later the Netherlands would take a direct political and economic interest in the Portuguese colonies in Asia, Africa and America. In Venice in 1534, Benedetto Bordone gave an account of the charting and settlement of the islands to the south and west of Portugal and Spain, including Madeira (from ca. 1425), the Azores (from ca. 1427) and the Cape Verdes (from 1455–56).[11] A German soldier in the service of Portugal, Hans Staden, was among the Tupinamba, who had captured him in 1554 and kept him prisoner for nine months, just before Jean de Léry, who, owing to the circumstances of his travels and the French Wars of Religion, was unable to publish his work until years later. Both

Staden and Léry, whose books contained illustrative woodcuts, described the customs and manners of the Tupinamba and did not shy away from the question of cannibalism.[12] In the sixteenth century Brazil was sometimes kept as a secret in Portugal or was neglected in favor of trade with the East; in 1576 Pedro de Magalhães Gandavo praised Brazil, which other countries were trying to colonize.[13] The early religious history of Brazil concerned the Franciscan and Benedictine friars, but it was not until the arrival of the Jesuits in 1549 that a systematic attempt at evangelization of the Natives occurred. In 1663, Simão de Vasconcellos published an account of the Society of Jesus in Brazil, from their appearance in 1549 to 1570, including the founding of the Colégio de São Paulo, an important moment in the Jesuit contribution to education in the colony.[14] Another work represents the key role of António Vieira, a Jesuit father, in a key point of Iberian and colonial history—the separation of Portugal from Spain in 1640 (they had been joined in 1580) and the expulsion of the Dutch from Brazil in 1654.[15] The Dutch West India Company had captured the northeast of Brazil in 1630 and, in order to exploit the sugar production of Pernambuco and the region as a whole, they granted religious freedom and offered good conditions for work and trade to the Portuguese on whom the Dutch relied in the specialized world of sugar plantations. Willem Piso, physician to the governor of Dutch Brazil from 1638 to 1644, edited a key book from this brief Dutch sojourn in this area of Portuguese influence.[16] The Portuguese traded with Brazil and Africa, where they found gold, ivory and slaves. During the 1630s, the Dutch, who employed many Germans in the Dutch West India Company, attacked the Portuguese in Brazil and their slaving stations on the Atlantic coast of Africa. One such German employee was Michael Hemmersam, who was in Brazil from 1639 to 1644, and who described the slave trade and the peoples of West Africa.[17]

Prince Henry the Navigator may have become interested in African trade when he was at the capture of Ceuta in 1415. That trade involved the caravans of slaves, gold, ivory and ebony from beyond the Sahara to the ports of Barbary, where Christian galleys brought European goods to the Moorish merchants who controlled the trade. As early as the Catalan Atlas of 1375, there is some idea of the markets and trade routes of the Niger basin, so that before the Portuguese voyages along the coast of Africa, an acquaintance with the Niger and the Gulf of Guinea is evident, implying, as G. R. Crone has suggested, that these expeditions from Portugal were not "thrusts into the unknown" but an attempt to take control of this lucrative trade from others of different cultures.[18]

Alvise Cadamosto's narrative—which has a complex textual history and seems to have been begun in 1463 and was completed by 1468, first appeared in the collection, *Paesi*, in 1507, was translated into Latin in Milan and into German in Nuremburg both in 1508, and into French in Paris in 1515—claimed that he sighted the Cape Verde Islands in 1456, which led to their colonization, although many authorities credit Antonio da Noli with the discovery in 1458 or 1459. Cadamosto appears to have left Portugal for his native Venice in 1463 or 1464.[19] The popularity of Cadamosto, who described the Atlantic islands and West Africa, derived from Giovanni Ramusio's *Navigazioni* in Venice in 1550. In English, neither Richard Hakluyt the younger nor Samuel Purchas included Cadamosto's voyages in his collections: Hakluyt had asked John Pory to translate Leo Africanus, and this translation and amplification was supposed to appear in Hakluyt's compilation, *Principall Navigations*, but a translation of Cadamosto into English, an abridged version of the text in Ramusio, did not appear until 1745 in the first volume of Thomas Astley's *New General Collection of Voyages*.[20] This text, like others concerning travel, exploration and geography, had distinct histories of translation and transmission in each country in western Europe.

Cadamosto's work is of particular interest because it is earlier than the "travel" texts that are better-known today—those of Columbus and Vespucci—but he described before they did a sense of wonder and strangeness over a world new to Europeans and because he represents Black Africa, a region that was so crucial in the slave trade for Islamic North Africa, for Europe and for the Americas. His *Voyages* begins with a chapter that appears in *Paesi* but not in the two earlier manuscripts, so that some ideological or interpretive editing or amplification might well have occurred here. This version called attention to these two aspects of wonder and Black Africa : "I, ALOUISE DA CA DA MOSTO, was the first of the noble city of Venesia moved to sail the ocean sea beyond the strait of Zibeltera [Gibraltar] towards the south in the land of the Blacks of lower Ethiopia. On this my journey I saw many things new and worthy of some notice. In order that those that shall come after me may be able to understand what my thoughts were in the midst of varied things in strange new places,—for truly both our customs and lands, in comparison with those seen by me, might be called another world—I decided that it would be laudable to make some record of them."[21] This new start to the text honors "Don Hurich," brother to Don Dourth [Duarte], king of Portugal, for being the first, since Adam, except for Hanno, to whom Pliny referred in his *Natural History* (book 6, chapter 36), "to initiate the navigation of this portion of the ocean sea towards the south of the land of the Blacks in lower Ethiopia."[22] This heroic brother to the king fought in the service of Christ against the Moors. Chapter 2, which seems to have been the original introduction, began a little more personally, although Cadamosto ends up in the second paragraph with "the Lord Infante Don Heurich" in Reposera near Sagres and in Algarve, of which Prince Henry was Governor: "In the year of Our Lord 1454, I, Alvise da Ca' da Mosto, then about aged twenty-two years, found myself in our city of Venice. Having sailed to various parts of our Mediterranean Sea, I then determined to return to Flanders, where I had been once before, in the hope of profit."[23] Although he then mentions qualification and honorable distinction as his other motives, it is important to remember the role of profit in this or any of these voyages: the motives and motifs of getting on in the world and making something of oneself are as central as formulations of faith and service to one's native or adopted God, country or city state.

In Cadamosto's account there is the kind of ethnographical description later found in narratives about the New World. He noted that the Portuguese settled Madeira, "which had never been inhabited," but saved many observations of cultural difference and conflict for his writing about the Canary Islands: "the inhabitants of the four Christian islands are wont to go by night with some of their galleys to assail these islands, and to seize these heathen Canarians, both men and women, whom they send to Spain to be sold as slaves."[24] The slaving of the Old World affected the conquering and settlement of the New. Cadamosto continued with a description of what happened when these slaving raids went awry: "And it happens that at times some from these galleys are taken prisoners: the Canarians do not put them to death, but make them kill and skin goats, and prepare the meat, which they hold to be a most vile and despicable occupation, and they make them serve thus until they are ransomed by some means or other."[25] The Canarians showed leniency toward those who would enslave them. The Guanche, as they came to be known, would also sometimes commit suicide in honor of a newly chosen lord, were "the most dexterous and nimble race in the world" and would paint their skin, red, green and yellow, esteeming these colors "as we do fine clothes."[26] Cadamosto also described cultures in Africa, mentioning peoples at Holden or Timbuktu: "They are Muhammadans, and very hostile to Christians."[27]

The presence of the Portuguese in the African trade is something Cadamosto noted: "You should know that the said Lord Infante of Portugal has leased this island of Argin to Christians [for ten years], so that no one can enter the bay to trade with the Arabs save those who hold the licence."[28] The Portuguese exchange alchezeli (perhaps a rough cloth), corn, cotton, woolen cloths, silver, carpets and cloaks for "slaves whom the Arabs bring from the land of the Blacks, and gold *tiber*" or dust.[29] For Berber horses, an item of trade that Arabs brought to Blacks, "Ten or fifteen slaves are given for one of these horses, according to their quality."[30] For slaves and gold, the Arabs also traded silver and Moorish silk from Granada and Tunis. The slaves were bound for Sicily, Tunis and Portugal. The Portuguese had expanded rapidly the African slave trade since 1448 when Gomes Eannes de Azurara had described it, for Cadamosto reported: "every year the Portuguese carry away from Argin a thousand slaves."[31] The organization of the slave trade, terrible in and of itself, replaced practices that were also insidious:

> Note that before this traffic was organized, the Portuguese caravels, sometimes
> four, sometimes more, were wont to come armed to the Golfo d'Argin, and
> descending on the land by night, would assail the fisher villages, and so ravage
> the land. Thus they took of these Arabs both men and women, and carried
> them to Portugal for sale: behaving in a like manner along all the rest of
> the coast, which stretches from Cauo Bianco to the Rio di Senega and even
> beyond.[32]

This river divided Arab from Black Africa, and here the Portuguese were
involved in raids not unlike those the Spanish practiced in the Canaries. The
Iberian experience in Africa and the Atlantic islands provided precedents
for the ways Spain and Portugal overcame and settled the New World.
Apparently, the Lord Infante of Portugal hoped that the Azanaghi, or
Sanhaja, would give up Islam for Christianity.[33] These poor people "are
the biggest thieves in the world" and "wear their hair in locks down to their
shoulders, almost in the German fashion."[34] Seemingly, the peoples on
the coast thought the Portuguese caravels, which could travel fast on their
slaving raids, must be phantoms. Cadamosto provided a context on trade, religion, war and other aspects of culture. Two groups of Black Africans exchanged
salt for gold: the king of Senega had slaves. Religion continued to be a concern
for Cadamosto: "The faith of these first Blacks is Muhammadanism: they
are not however, as are the white Moors, very resolute in this faith, especially
the common people. The chiefs adhere to the tenets of the Muhammadans
because they have around them priests of the Azanaghi or Arabs."[35] The
Black chiefs were continually at war.

Cadamosto described his trading of horses and goods for 100 slaves, something he initiated through his own "negro interpreter" with Lord Budomel,
who gave him "a handsome young negress, twelve years of age, saying that he
gave her to me for the service of my chamber"; praised a Black swimmer who
swam three miles in rough seas to deliver a letter for Cadamosto for his
"marvellous action" and "concluded that these coast negroes are indeed the
finest swimmers in the world"; observed that despite poverty, the lords, who
deserve to be called that owing to ceremonies and the following of the people,
"receive beyond comparison more obedience than our lords"; Budomel had
nine wives, each with "five or six young negro girls in attendance," and "it is
lawful" and does not give offence that the lord sleeps with them as with the
wives; more generally, Cadamosto called this group of Black Africans, men
and women, "lascivious"; Budomel allowed more freedom to Christians (he
also permitted an Azanaghi priest to approach him in his own apartment)
than to his own Black subjects.[36] As in later narratives of the New World, the
hope for conversion is part of the Iberian and European stance. Cadamosto

debated religion with Budomel: "Finally I told him that his faith was false, and that those who had instructed him in such things were ignorant of the truth."[37] This lord could laugh during the debate and, despite their differences, Cadamosto could say, "In this he showed good powers of reasoning and deep understanding of men."[38] Cadamosto still showed hope that Budomel or his nephew would convert to Christianity. Nonetheless, he could also assert that the Blacks were "great magicians" who could charm snakes and used as corroboration the word of a certain unnamed Genoese.[39]

The meeting of cultures was intricate and left many ironies, intended or not. Cadamosto turned the lens back on himself, although he did not always necessarily comment explicitly on the ironies that might come from his own cultural blindness in regard to the Black Africans he met: "These negroes, men and women, crowded to see me as though I were a marvel. It seemed to be a new experience for them to see Christians, whom they had not previously seen. They marvelled no less at my clothing than at my white skin." This marveling is a two-way representation and exchange: despite the comment on clothing and any thought that Prester John might be brown or black, Cadamosto identified Christians with whiteness. Differences in color also apparently concerned the Black Africans as the Portuguese and other Europeans, for Cadamosto said: "some touched my hands and limbs, and rubbed me with their spittle to discover whether my whiteness was dye or flesh. Finding that it was flesh they were astounded."[40]

Trade was also at the heart of the exchange between Africans and Europeans. The shortage of gold in Europe during the later Middle Ages helped to drive Europeans to find new sources and at this market sought "further strange sights" but also "to find out whether any came thither with gold for sale," although "there was little to be found."[41] Columbus would later be in search of gold in the New World. The Arabs and Azanaghi brought horses from Barbary and exchanged them for slaves: "A horse with its trappings is sold for from nine to fourteen negro slaves, according to the condition and breeding of the horse."[42] A chief will send for his horse charmers after he has bought a horse, so that this animal took on a spiritual or supernatural role as well as being a product in trade: this animal was worth many human slaves. It is quite possible that the charms worn on horses contained texts from the Koran (Quran). Sometimes the admiration or marveling was a matter of point of view. In such moments it is almost possible, all these centuries later, to feel the divide of cultural difference, in which the author and the people he is representing are at right angles or are caught in unintended ironies: "I then told them that a mortar would slay more than a hundred men at one shot, at which they were astonished, saying that it was an invention of the devil's."[43] What might well have been for the author a means of impressing these Black Africans with Christian power, impressed them as something diabolical. Cadamosto also demonstrated to these people how to extract honey from wax to show them how to makes candles, as they had no such thing among them: "On seeing this, they showed much wonderment, exclaiming that we Christians had knowledge of everything."[44] Knowledge became a commodity and a means to have power over someone, perhaps even a tool for conversion, showing that God had blessed Christians with know-how and technology. This kind of description of the wonder of Natives at the knowledge and technological power of Christians was, then, something that preceded similar stories or reports in many narratives of the New World from Columbus onward.

Another proleptic aspect of these texts of early European expansion into Africa for those accounts of a similar spread into the western Atlantic is the representation of the "bad" tribes or peoples. The Barbazini (Barbacenes) and Sereri (Serer) partly play this role: "They will not recognize any lord among them, lest he should carry off their wives and children and sell them into slavery, as is done by the kings and lords of all the other lands of the negroes. They are exceedingly idolatrous, have no laws, and are the cruellest of men."[45] They seem to be without class, religion, law, restraint and civility. Even though the king of Senega has tried to subdue these peoples, he has suffered at their hands, presumably their poison arrows had been too much to overcome. A certain unruliness and danger, a group escaping but needing control, created a tension that would welcome later European intervention.

Another group that occurred in Cadamosto's text that also appeared in the accounts of Columbus and his successors were interpreters, who acted as linguistic go-betweens and cultural mediators.[46] On reaching the Rio de Senega, Cadamosto reported: "we cast anchor, and debated whether we should send ashore one of our interpreters on board brought from Portugal, who had been sold by the lords of Senega to the first Portuguese to discover this land of the Blacks."[47] After first contact, an intricate relation developed between the Europeans, which included Portuguese and Italians, and the Africans, of which there were many groups. The crown of Portugal must have realized that interpreters were necessary to their success in trading in Africa. Cadamosto gave some further background concerning these interpreters: "These slaves had been made Christians in Portugal, and knew Spanish well: we had had them from their owners on the understanding that for the hire and pay of each we would give one slave to be chosen from all our captives. Each interpreter, also, who secured four slaves for his master was to be given his freedom."[48] Language and religion were part of the Black African's training, and only enslaving others would free him. Spanish, rather than Portuguese, was the language taught to the slaves: Cadamosto gave no reason for this choice. The king of Senega, it seems, had unleashed a new force in Africa as an aspect of his trade in slaves. As part of this plan to land a slave on the coast during Cadamosto's voyage, the masters drew lots to see whose interpreter was to go ashore, and it fell to the Genoese, who sent off his slave, who "was instructed to ascertain the condition of the country, to whom it was subject, and whether gold and other objects of use to us were to be obtained there."[49] The interpreter-slave was left by himself and encountered a great number of people ashore who "had lain in wait" for the Portuguese: "They conversed for a short while; what he said to them we do not know, but they began furiously to strike at him with their short Moorish swords, and quickly put him to death, those in the boat being unable to succour him."[50] This victim of both European and African group dynamics—his master drew the lot without his having a say and the Africans slew him— baffled Cadamosto, who did not know what he said and the cause of his death. Interpreters were often subject to suspicion on both sides of the cultural divide. The Portuguese must have suspected that this landing would be dangerous, but this unnamed African interpreter, owing to the chance of a lot, was sacrificed, despite the time he took to become a Christian and to learn Spanish. His death led Cadamosto and those around him to the following conclusion: "When we were informed by our men of this, we were left stupified, realising that they must be very cruel men to do such a thing to a negro of their own race, and that they might reasonably be expected to treat us much worse."[51] The theme of cruelty recurred in this conflict between Blacks. The example of the poor, nameless, dead interpreter set the sails and the Portuguese proceeded south.

At the Gambra (Gambia), the Portuguese also wished to avoid a fight with the Blacks because "we had come thither to trade in the country peacefully and with their approval, which would be more fittingly accomplished by tact than by force."[52] In each of the canoes, there were about 25 to 30 Blacks, and each "remained for a while gazing upon a thing which neither they nor their fathers had ever seen before, that is ships and white men."[53] After more sailing but nearby, they engaged in a fight with Blacks who fired arrows at them; the Portuguese had heard much about poison arrows and were afraid of them. Despite the efforts of one of the interpreters with speech and signs, in a kind of parley, nothing peaceful could come of this meeting, at least from the Portuguese point of view, because this group of Africans replied that "they firmly believed that we Christians ate human flesh, and that we only bought negroes to eat them: that for their part they did not want our friendship on any terms, but sought to slaughter us all, and to make a gift of our possessions to their lord, who they said was three days distant."[54] Here was another reversal, this time of the European fear of cannibals, because the Africans feared that the Portuguese ate the slaves they bought in Africa. Embedded in Cadamosto's report about the Africans, even if through the "doubtful" medium of an interpreter, is their opposition and hostility to the Portuguese based on their part in the slave trade. Although the captains wanted to proceed a hundred miles upriver to find more peaceful peoples with whom to trade, the sailors opposed this move vigorously, but Cadamosto and the officers "agreed to give way in order to avoid dissention, for they were pig-headed and obstinate men," and so they set sail for Spain via Cape Verde.[55] In Gambra "the people of the coast were so rude and savage that we were unable to have speech with them on land, or to treat about anything."[56] The indigenous peoples could not be understood by speech or signs.

The next year, Cadamosto, and Usodimare, the same Genoese with whom he traveled on the first voyage, outfitted two caravels under the authority of the Lord Infante and sought to navigate the river of Gambra (the Senegal river). In another cultural encounter Cadamosto reiterated his tropes of wonder, clothing and color but added trifles to the exchange. The Black who could understand Cadamosto's interpreter, marveling at the caravel, "was overcome with astonishment at the sight of us white men, and marvelled no less at our clothing, so different to his—principally in that most of them went naked, or, if clothed, in a white cotton singlet. We made much of the negro, giving him many trifles of little value, with which he was exceedingly pleased, and asked many questions."[57] The use of trifles in trade and cultural exchange also became a staple of exploration and settlement in the New World. The trading of knowledge is another dimension of this meeting of cultures. Interpretation is part of the process, although Cadamosto also observed that the Blacks sometimes sold "some trifles of theirs."[58] Through an interpreter, Cadamosto traded with Lord Batimaussa, exchanging many articles for gold and slaves. Differences in values and valuation occurred in this relation between the Portuguese and the Blacks of Gambra: "Gold is much prized among them, in my opinion, more than by us, for they regard it as very precious: nevertheless they traded it cheaply, taking in exchange articles of little value in our eyes."[59] These Africans spoke many tongues and traded varieties of colorful cloth, apes, baboons, civet and wild dates and did not venture from their own country because they were "not safe from one district to the next from being taken by the Blacks and sold into slavery."[60] Besides gold and slavery, Cadamosto also described the hunting of wild elephants, the physique of the river horse or hippopotamus, other animals and resources. Near the Rio Grande (later called the River Jeba) Cadamosto came across another group but was unable to make progress in communicating with them. Unlike Columbus afterward, Cadamosto was often refreshingly frank when he came up against barriers in communication: "Then I, wishing to gain information of this people, caused my interpreters to speak with them, but none of them could understand what was said, nor could those on the other caravels: on realizing this, I was greatly disappointed, and at last they left without our having been able to understand them."[61] The difficulty of understanding is a central concern for Cadamosto, so much so that the Portuguese expedition left off when it came to a point where the peoples encountered spoke dialects that these Europeans could no longer comprehend.

In the last three chapters Cadamosto reported what a friend on Piero de Sinzia's expedition, sent out by the king after Prince Henry's death in 1460, told him: once again the Portuguese came into contact with peoples they could not understand. This report included descriptions of the idolatry and bodies of the Africans as well as their food, customs and lands. The end of Cadamosto's narrative emphasized the account of the taking of a Black African precisely because the Portuguese could not understand him: "This they did in obedience to His Majesty the King, who had enjoined them that, from the farthest land they reached, if it chanced that the people were unable to understand their interpreters, they were to contrive to bring away a negro, by force or persuasion, so that he might be interrogated through the many negro interpreters to be found in Portugal, or in the course of time might learn to speak, so that he might give an account of his country."[62] It is remarkable that at this early time there was a large group of Black interpreters in Portugal. This later expedition did carry an African back to the king, who had different Blacks speak with this kidnap victim. There is a twist to the usual sad endings of such kidnappings later in the New World: "Finally a negress, the slave of a Lisbon citizen, who had also come from a far off country, understood him, not through his own language but through another known to both. What this negro told the king through this woman I do not know, save that he said that among other things found in his native country were live unicorns."[63] This bilingualism and ability to tap into legend, mythology and even credulity appears to have saved the captive. The king, according to the narrative, showed mercy, as if he had had the right to kidnap and had then done a good deed: "The said lord, having kept him several months, shown him many things of his Kingdom, and given him some clothes, very charitably had him carried by a caravel back to his own country."[64] The go-between was left to his own devices, although what happened on his return is left unsaid or was unknown. The lack of knowledge and of communication is something that Cadamosto stresses in the final stages of his account, something suggestive for those who might envision dogma and an insistence on filling up the void of ignorance with certainty and dominion.

III

This was not, however, the beginning of the story of contact between Europe and Africa or Asia. Origins have a way of receding beyond the letter of history. Alexander the Great had gone as far as India, and the Roman Empire had connections by sea with India and by land with China (via overland caravan). In the translation of empire, Constantinople presented itself as the successor to Rome and Venice had acted as its middleman by the thirteenth century. Even with the fall of Constantinople in 1453, the eastern Mediterranean, although now under the influence of Islam, was still crucial in the trade between Asia and Europe. Portugal, as we have seen, began to challenge the place of Venice in this trade: following on earlier voyages along the western coast of Africa, Bartolomeu Dias in 1488 and Vasco da Gama in 1497, through their voyages round the Cape of Good Hope, affected the commerce among Africa, Asia and Europe. Early in the fifteenth century, China had sent fleets that ranged from India to Kenya, but the Ming Dynasty soon concentrated its energies on the Mongolian threat. The Portuguese upset the Muslim dominance of the trade among Indonesia, India and eastern Africa: they defeated an Egypt–Calicut alliance in 1509, took Goa in 1510, seized Malacca, the emporium of Asian trade, in 1511 and Hormuz in 1515. Whereas no power could defeat Portugal in the Indian Ocean, it was possible for the Chinese in the China Sea. However, they found it convenient, in about 1557, to permit a controlled Portuguese settlement near Canton at Macao, so that China, which had prohibited contact with Japan because of its piracy, could trade silks for Japanese silver. Similarly, in 1571, the Japanese allowed the Portuguese to settle at Nagasaki: perhaps because of the power of these two countries the Portuguese behaved as peaceful merchants rather than those who enforced trade with military power as they did in the Indian Ocean. The Portuguese brought with them the Jesuits, who were involved in the trade between Nagasaki and Macao; and the Spaniards, who in the wake of Columbus had crossed the Pacific from Mexico and established Manila during the 1570s, carried Dominican and Franciscan missionaries with them. By 1600 there were perhaps hundreds of thousands of Christian converts in Japan and, in reaction, Japan expelled the Portuguese in 1639. Lisbon was the great European center for Asian trade, but the distribution of these imports lay in the hands of the Netherlands, which, owing to its experience in the fisheries of the Baltic and North Sea, had the largest merchant fleet in Europe.[65] This relation between the Portuguese and Dutch was soon a cause for friction. King Sebastian's death during his invasion of Morocco in 1578 led to the union of Spain and Portugal under Philip II in 1580: the Spanish Netherlands fought for its independence at this time and sought the help of Elizabeth I of England. Although Francis Drake sailed round the world in 1580 and James Lancaster searched out Portuguese ships to plunder and reached the northern part of Sumatra in 1591, the English did not do as much as the Netherlanders to challenge Portuguese trade in Asia. Owing to a long association with

Portugal, the Dutch—including Catholics in the Netherlands who had served with the Portuguese in Asia—were able to use their maps and knowledge of sailing and this Asian trade to make inroads. In 1595 the Dutch set out to Asia and by 1602 this commerce was important enough to set up the Vereenigde Oostindische Companie or the United East India Company. The English themselves, perhaps sensing a threat to their Levant trade from the Dutch in the 1590s, formed the Company of Merchants of London Trading into the East Indies. A multiple rivalry among the Portuguese, Spanish, Dutch and English had, owing to the union of the Iberian crowns and the Dutch Revolt, arisen from political as well as economic pressures.

These rivalries, being intricate and refracted, cannot be addressed here, but can be seen in Andrew Marvell's depiction of the Dutch in the poem, "The Character of Holland" (anon. ed. 1665, 2nd ed. 1672); views of the Portuguese, Dutch and English are set out in the *Tratados historicos* (1676) of the Spanish Friar, Domingo Navarrete; and representations of the Dutch can be found in François Valentijn's *Oud en Nieuw Oost-Indien* (1724–26), that is, the old and new East Indies. Marvell's poem about Holland was probably written after February 20, 1653, when the English defeated the Dutch in a sea battle near Portland.[66] The poem begins its satire with a barb at Holland as a land literally and as a country: "Holland, that scarce deserves the name of land, / As but the off-scouring of the British sand; / And so much earth as was contributed / By English pilots when they heaved the lead" (lines 1–4). Holland is England's refuse, a land made flush by the English navy. The Dutch are like dung-beetles making a "dunghill soul" and build "their watery Babel" (lines 9–22).

In alluding to Hugo Grotius's *Mare Liberum* (1609), in this context of the presumption of the Dutch to claim freedom of the seas and to conquer the sea (and thus the image of their dykes as a Babel) through reclamation, the poem evokes the conflict between the Dutch and the Commonwealth, which required ships in their waters to salute the English flag (lines 23–26).[67] In satirizing the Dutch who live in a state in which "The earth and the water play at level-coil" (line 28), a Christmas game in which one participant displaces another from his seat, Marvell amplifies the various images that insult the Dutch in this halfway or between state, including the lines "For these Half-anders, half wet, and half dry / Nor bear strict service, nor pure liberty" (lines 53–54).[68] Nothing in this pun could make Hollanders whole. In the context of the English Commonwealth the following charge, which comes in the middle of the satiric imagery and indictments against the Dutch, is curious: "Therefore necessity, that made kings / Something like government among them brings" (lines 37–38). Is the Dutch republic really so ill-governed that it shares the distained reputation of kings among the Puritans and those who supported them?

In this swim of images, which includes lines like "The fish ofttimes the burger dispossessed, / And sat not as meat but as a guest" (lines 29–30), Marvell identifies the Dutch with the fish: "And oft the tritons and the sea nymphs saw / Whole shoals of Dutch served up for cabillau; / Or as they over the new level ranged / For pickled herring, pickled *Heeren* changed" (lines 31–34). Besides likening the Dutch to cod (though its French name), Marvell uses further puns to bring man and fish together in Holland. In such a fishy situation it is no wonder the Dutch were fish, fisherman or fishers of men: "How could the Dutch but be converted, when / The Apostles were so many fishermen?" (lines 57–58). The next lines play with the Heeren worshiping herring as gods—themselves and fish—and turn John the Baptist or Evangelist into "Poor-John" or dried salt fish (see lines 59–62).[69]

The image of diversity shifts from Babel to an ark of religion, which splits on the rocks and leads to pillage: "Hence Amsterdam, Turk-Christian-Pagan-Jew, / Staple of sects and mint of schism grew, / That bank of conscience, where not one so strange / Opinion but finds credit, and exchange" (lines 71–74). The very tolerance of the Netherlands is held up to ridicule, as if religious belief should not be treated as opinion because if it were it would be like a commercial exchange that deserved no credit. To which Marvell adds: "In vain for Catholics ourselves we bear; / The Universal Church is only there" (lines 75–76). Is all this religious and cultural latitude really just as bad as the much maligned Catholic Church? This is satire and can hardly be fair in its pursuit of truth.

The satirical verities proceed, so the deluge of insults continues. Marvell continues the litany of witty insults and his unmoved movement of satiric imagery. The speaker of the poem chides the Dutch for choosing a village, The Hague, for their court and concludes: "How fit a title clothes their governors / Themselves the *Hogs*, as all their subjects *Bores*!" punning on the title the Estates General used—Hoog-mogenden, or high and mighty, and Bores for Boers and boars—to identify Hogs with boars who are the tedious Dutch (lines 79–80).[70] The denial and depreciation of Civilis, a Batavian leader who in A.D. 69 (C.E.) battled against the Romans, is an attempt to play with or play down Dutch history and leads to more satirical images, such as the mermaids melting and reeking over the chafing dish that the Dutch brought to church "While the fat steam of female sacrifice / Fills the priest's nostrils and puts out his eyes," an imagery as violent, scatological and possibly misogynist as it is liturgical (lines 91–92, see 85–90).

The nub of the complaint against the Dutch is in the following verses in the middle of this poem of 152 lines:

> When their whole navy they together pressed—
> Not Christian captives to redeem from bands,

Or intercept the Western golden sands—
No, but all ancient rights and leagues must vail,
Rather than to the English strike their sail;
To whom their weather-beaten province owes
Itself—when as some greater vessel tows
A cockboat tossed with the same wind and fate—
We buoyed so often up their sinking state. (lines 104–12)

Rather than do something for Christianity or commerce, the Dutch have turned on the nation that helped them to independence: in May 1652, on two occasions, the Dutch breached custom on the seas by failing to salute the English in their own waters, something that began, or was used as a pretext for, the protracted struggle between England and the Netherlands.[71] Part of the grievance in these lines is the refusal of the Dutch to defer to the English as the greater ship of state, implying that the English resented the very success and independence of the Netherlands that they helped achieve. The Dutch had become a prosperous rival who had dominion over the seas, and was now a threat to the English. Marvell is fond of throwing Grotius back in the face of his native land: "Was this *Jus Belli & Pacis*?"—a reference to *Concerning the Law of War and Peace* (1625) by this important figure in the foundation of international law.[72]

Amidst jokes and images of butter and cheese—rather a battle of the dairy than a battle of the books—Marvell does allude to the Dutch defeat of the English in November 1652 while calling the Netherlands the "hydra of seven provinces," an allusion he returns to with his use of Hercules, whose second labor was to defeat this many-headed monster (lines 93–95, 119–38).[73] Marvell identified England with Rome against Civilis and with Hercules against the hydra, so that, by implication, it was the poet's country who was to succeed in this translation of empire. It is all or nothing with the Dutch in Marvell's poem: "Their tortoise wants its vainly stretchèd neck / Their navy all our conquest or our wreck" (lines 139–40). This is like an arms race for supremacy with no room for two strong powers. The identification of Rome and England becomes more explicit as the poem reaches its climax and end as Marvell continues from the choice between triumph or ruin: "Or, what is left, their Carthage overcome / Would render fain unto our better Rome, / Unless our Senate, lest their youth disuse / The war (but who would?) peace, if begged, refuse" (lines 141–44). The Dutch are Carthaginians, the English Romans, so although the Punic War was hard fought, the Romans triumphed (whence came Cato's famous phrase "Cathage must be destroyed"). A metonymy for the English Parliament, this translated Senate of this "Better Rome"—England—is key to future events and must remain united. The translation of empire in this poem, while it is about myths of foundation and amelioration, also depends on a pep talk, an attempt to raise the spirits of the nation in the face of this challenge, and an evocation of triumph: "For now of nothing may our state despair / Darling of heaven, and of men the care, / Provided that they be what they have been; / Watchful abroad, and honest still within" (lines 145–48). This, then, is triumphalism with a caveat, a cautious projection of victory with conditions. The final four lines of the poem have the Generals-at-Sea, Monck, Blake and Deane (who was to die in June 1653) steeling Neptune, who shakes his trident, "while Jove governs in the highest sphere, Vainly in Hell let Pluto domineer" (lines 151–52). In late February 1653 the English had defeated the Dutch at sea near Portland, and this poem leaves off in the middle of things, the future of England and empire unresolved but with measured and conditional potential and optimism in the air. If the "Darling of heaven," England, is honest at home and watchful abroad, great things in this providential history will be waiting. Implicitly, it might be that if all goes well as the speaker hopes, the Dutch, the butt of this satire, will not soar with Jove but will enjoy a renewed classical underworld, dwelling in vanity with Pluto.

Domingo Fernández de Navarrete, born in Spain in 1618 and died in 1686 in Santo Domingo, where he was archbishop of the Spanish Indies, provided views not just of the Dutch but of the Portuguese and English, not primarily in a European context but how Europeans functioned in Africa, America and Asia.[74] Navarette, like Las Casas before him in the West Indies, advocated the cause of the Natives the Spaniards encountered, this time in the Philippines, particularly in the face of Spanish greed and mistreatment.[75] The focus here, however, will be his view of other Europeans, as an illustration of the cross-section of various states in their imperial expansion.

The rivalry between the Portuguese and Spaniards, particularly in Asia, is something that arises in Navarrete's writing.[76] Navarrete described the island of Macasar (Macassar) that 80 years ago "was an inconsiderable country but since then has throve mightily by reason of the Fairs kept there for Ships met there from Manila, Goa, Macao, English and Dutch, so that abundance of rich Commodities were brought thither from all Parts of that Archipelago, and Trade enrich'd the Country, making its Sovereign powerful."[77] In describing his time in Macasar, Navarrete did something the English, French and others, often in the service of the Black Legend of Spain, did in quoting or using Las Casas to speak against his own compatriots: "Discoursing about the taking of Ceilon by the Dutch from the Portugueses, one of the Franciscans, and he, who spoke these words in my hearing, was himself a Portugal, said, 'It was bound to be lost; for if not, then Fire would have fallen down on it from Heaven and consum'd it, for such was the Wickedness and Iniquity of the Portugueses there.'"[78] Here the Franciscan spoke against his country and, therefore, is supposed to have given more credence to the critique of the Portuguese in Ceylon (Sri Lanka). When Navarrate was on his way with the Portuguese to Macao, probably in March 1658, an unnamed Englishman warned them that a Dutch ship would batter them with its cannon from a safe distance and added a further criticism of how Portugal was handling its expansion: "'You Portuguese Gentlemen have order'd your Empire very poorly, for you have only taken care to build a Nest in one place, and another in another place, which divides your Force, and so secures nothing.' The Portugueses own'd that the English Man was in the right, and that made them sometimes rail against their Government, and complain of their having cast off our King."[79] Navarrete, a Spaniard, made the point that the Portuguese sometimes yearned for the period between 1580 and 1640 in which Spain and Portugal were ruled under the Spanish crown, so between the Portuguese and the Englishman Portugal came in for some criticism.

Nonetheless, Navarrete was not so direct and plain in his representation of Portugal and the Portuguese or the difference between that country and Spain, for he began his chapter on his voyage from Macasar to Macao, which followed immediately this critique of Portugal, with something more positive: "It is most certain the Portuguese Nation are devout, godly, and religious, which I know by Experience, as I first discovered upon this voyage. I was treated by them with great Civility, Courtesy and Generosity; and what is more, I prevail'd with them, never to discourse with me, even at Macao, about the Differences then betwixt our two Kingdoms."[80] This balance, at a time of friction, is impressive and shows the intricacy of Navarrete's representation of others. Later, in about 1672, describing his stay in Lisbon and his journey to Rome, Navarrete once more was able to represent the contradictions in the relations between Portugal and Spain. Navarrete found the rivers in Lisbon and Goa to be fine, but while regarding the beauty of Lisbon, he observed the closed points of view of those who have not traveled and could not compare two places or more: "all that have not been abroad imagine there is nothing in the World so good as in their Country; a great Absurdity, which some are so far led away with, as even to conceit there is no good Wine in Spain."[81] Travel overseas led to relativity, a transformation of Europeans who made the journey, but on their return would still catch Iberians in the rivalries between Portugal and Spain. Navarrete was well treated in Portugal, and courtesy was shown to him by the president of the Inquisition. The attitude toward Spain in Portugal was something he paused to represent: "At that time there were some Rumours about a War with Spain; the Nobility were for it, saying, they should get their Bread that way. The People opposed it, and the Religious Orders more than the rest: Sermons were preach'd in several Monasteries against those restless Spirits."[82] In Macao during the revolt of Portugal against Spain in 1640, the Jesuits, according to Navarrete, worked against Spain, and they painted a picture of Philip IV of Spain on the gallows and their own king, João [John] IV, as the hangman and displayed it in a public place. Navarrate turned this insult around as he noted that in China it was the nobles who were hanged and the commoners beheaded—the opposite of the practice in Europe—but that the hangman is "the vilest thing that is throughout the world."[83] The Portuguese king is reconstructed as the butt of this visual affront. Navarrete was also present at several disputes between the Portuguese and Spaniards over who lost Brazil and Malacca. Navarrate agreed with "Emanuel de Fonseca, a worthy Portuguese," who told him at Canton that the Portuguese had lost Muscat (Muscate), the center of Portuguese power in the Persian Gulf after the fall of Ormus, because, contrary to the orders of the king of Spain, they had tolerated a synagogue there, to which Navarrete added: "Avarice made them permit those infamous People there."[84] This same worthy man informed Navarrete that at Diu, the Portuguese had allowed "a Moorish Mosque" and Father Torrente, a Jesuit in Canton, said that in some towns on the coast, "the Portuguese Commanders us'd horrid Injustice towards the Natives."[85]

In this bitterness between Spain and Portugal over the union of the two countries under one crown and over the loss of the Portuguese colonies in that period, Navarrete was constructing, while praising Portugal in some places, a Black Legend of Portugal, and partly, as the rivals of Spain had in constructing the Black Legend of that country, did so out of the mouths of subjects of that nation. Navarrete had an epic catalogue of Portuguese shortcomings: a Jesuit Father Ferrari heard from someone among the enemy who had been at Ormus or Ormuz when it was lost and had said that the Portuguese did not return for the fight after they were beaten "and left us Conquerors and possess'd of all."[86] Along with a Persian army, the English, with ships under the command of Captains Blyth and Weddell, captured Ormus in February, 1622. Another instance was set out by a Portuguese Jesuit, Antony Gouvea, who, speaking of the loss of India, said at Canton: "God had taken it from them for two Reasons; one was, the inhumane usage of the Natives, especially by the Portuguese Women, towards the Black Women, and the other for their Lust."[87] The power of Providence to punish sin is something that recurred in the writing of this time in the ebb and flow of colonial fortunes.

Navarrete pointed a moral about blindness and insight—the irony of judgment in and of history. In the middle of listing these Portuguese losses, which they brought on themselves through sin, disobedience to the Christian God and cruelty in relation to Natives, Navarrete turns these complaints on himself and his own country as well as on the Portuguese: "These and such-like things friar de Angelis might have inserted in his General History; what the Spaniards did in America we know and abhor. It is unreasonable to see the faults of others, and be blind to our own."[88] There might be, except for Navarrete's accusation that the Jesuits were behind the Portuguese revolt against Spain in Macao in 1640, another division, too, between the clergy and laity. This divide and the internecine struggle between different orders in the church were also expressed in the works of Antón Montesino, Bartolomé de Las Casas, Toribio de Motolinía and others.

This recognition and irony did not, however, prevent Navarrete from continuing the litany against the Portuguese in Asia even as he enrolled them to testify against themselves. Concerning the fall of Cochin in 1663, Navarrete reported that the Portuguese Jesuits blamed ill-fortune and the Natives for assisting the Dutch, but a layman said, " 'we Portuguese are the most barbarous People in the World, we have neither Sense, Reason, nor Government.' "[89] He also criticized the Jesuits. Moreover, Navarrete recorded the words of the ambassador's secretary to Father Gouvea to the effect that the ruin of Macao was the fault of Brother Manoel dos Reyes and Li Pe Ming; all these examples are set down "to prove that the Portuguese have no reason to complain, that our [Spanish] king was the cause of their losing India."[90] This interpretation is different from the one Abbé Raynal later gives in which he thinks that the Portuguese had a point in their case against Spain's contribution to the loss of colonies. For Navarrete, "their own Sins, and not those of others, have brought all these Misfortunes upon them."[91] He then proceeded to recount some of the sins: for example, the Portuguese are lewd in their use of Native women; one near the king of one of these territories said " 'the Dutch are satisfy'd with one Woman, but the People of Macao are not satisf'd with many'; he also told of Jesuits leading a large force of armed laymen against the Dominicans who saved their lives only by securing their Monastery."[92] Tensions between Spain and Portugal and their subjects overseas, lay and religious, were intricate, and some of these examples give a glimpse of some of the divisions between the two states under the person of the Spanish monarch. The Dutch fought the Spanish for independence at a time when Portugal was joined to Spain and Portugal bore the brunt of many Dutch attacks.

When the Netherlands concluded a 12-year truce with Spain in 1609, its independence was tacitly recognized, although the Spanish crown did not abandon its claims to the Northern Netherlands until 1648. From the turn of the seventeenth century, these United Provinces became a great sea power that challenged Iberian power from Europe through China to Peru. Whereas England concluded a peace with Spain in 1604, the Dutch left in ruins a Portuguese fleet off Malacca in 1606 and a Spanish fleet off Gibraltar in 1607. In the truce of 1609 the Dutch gained some rights to trade in the East Indies but much less so in the West Indies. Since 1602 the Dutch East India Company had made incursions into the Iberian monopoly in colonial trade. This example gave credence to those, like Willem Usselincx (1567–1647), who wanted to found a West India Company. He argued that natural resources, like dyewoods, pearls, indigo and sugar, were more valuable to the Spaniards in the New World than gold and silver, so that Usselincx wished to establish Dutch colonies in America based on agriculture and such natural production. For him, Brazil, which produced no gold and silver at that time but possessed abundant natural products, was a case in point.[93] Like François Ier of France and Elizabeth I of England, Usselincx maintained the view that no occupation meant no possession of a territory: he advocated that the Dutch settle Guiana and the region south of Rio de la Plata because the Spanish and Portuguese did not in fact occupy them. Guiana was the place that Walter Ralegh had recommended as a place for a colony to Elizabeth in 1596. Like Ralegh, who insisted that the Natives of Guiana supported England's ambitions and were about to throw off Spanish domination, Usselincx thought the Natives were restless under Spanish rule.[94] Usselincx advocated free rather than slave labor.

Between 1609 and 1621, the Dutch concentrated most of their efforts in Asia, although trading posts were expanded in Guiana and founded at Fort Orange on the Hudson River in 1614. Between 1623 and 1630 the Portuguese destroyed all the trading posts where the Dutch, Irish and English traded in the Amazon region. In coastal Brazil and in the Gulf and Guinea in West Africa the Dutch had their greatest success, so that by 1621 the Dutch, who maintained low prices for trade goods, had supplanted the Portuguese as the main traders in gold and ivory on the Gold Coast. At the end of the truce with Spain in 1621, the war between the Dutch and the Spanish was renewed and in June 1621 the West India Company was incorporated. This company, although modeled on the East India Company, subordinated its commercial activities to naval and military functions, which was opposite to its prototype venture in Asia. Both companies divided the world in two for Dutch power and influence.[95] The Portuguese found rivals in the land of the True Cross (as they first called Brazil), first in the French in the sixteenth century and then in the Dutch in the seventeenth. Nonetheless, connections existed between the Portuguese and Dutch there: the Portuguese officials helped to break the laws of the king of Spain, so that the Dutch had somewhere between a third and two-thirds of the carrying trade between Brazil and Europe. In May 1624 the Dutch captured Bahia, a key to Brazil, but they were defeated at Bahia, Puerto Rico and Elmina (São Jorge da Mina in Western Africa) in 1625 by an Iberian force.[96] The Dutch inflicted heavy losses on the Iberian fleets from the New World, and between 1630 and 1636 there was a struggle with the Dutch over Pernambuco, in the northeast of Brazil and the richest region in the world for the production of sugar and the most prosperous part of Portugal's colonial empire. The Spanish and Portuguese could not work together to send an Iberian armada to Brazil and blamed each other for this situation: the Spaniards, fearing that

Brazil was a launch for Dutch ambitions in Spanish America, complained that the Portuguese were relying too much on Spain and the Portuguese maintained that they were overtaxed and that their union with Spain had drawn them into a conflict with the Dutch. In this struggle the Spanish crown was willing to sacrifice some of the interests of its subjects in Flanders to those in Portugal. The Dutch were prevailing but the West India Company was bearing great financial burdens despite the booty from the 547 Iberian ships taken between 1623 and 1636.[97]

Between 1637 and 1641 Johan Maurits, the Dutch governor general in Brazil, proved successful in expanding Dutch holdings and influence in this region. The local Portuguese, subject to Roman–Dutch law, were guaranteed equal rights with the subjects of the United Provinces, and Maurits permitted Jews and Roman Catholics freedom of conscience and worship, allowing as well some French Capuchin friars to enter the colony. The Dutch had also been weary of or had opposed the slave trade with Africa: in 1596 the city fathers in Middleburg had freed a hundred slaves brought as cargo there and in 1608 Usselincx had opposed the use of Black slaves in Dutch America, but the demand for slaves after the Dutch capture of Paraíba and Pernambuco in 1634 to 1636 changed the Dutch position and, rather than opt for German labor, Maurits chose to go the route of African slaves in the sugar mills. Protestant and Catholic theologians in the Netherlands and elsewhere in western Europe gave their blessing to slavery, although there were exceptions like Alonso de Sandoval, who wrote different versions of *De Instauranda Aethiopium Salute* (1627, rev. 1647). The Portuguese did not wholeheartedly accept Dutch rule and were sometimes bitterly opposed to it: Antonio Vieira preached an anti-Dutch sermon on the eve of the Portuguese Revolution. In Brazil Maurits surrounded himself with 46 artists, scholars, scientists and craftsmen from the Netherlands, and their work, some of it published, was influential; he also established a legislative assembly. Despite wealth and sea power, the Dutch lost Brazil to Portugal, one of the poorest countries in western Europe. The weakness and unfocused efforts of the Dutch West India Company and the States-General from 1645 to 1650 meant mishandled policies toward Brazil owing, as Charles Boxer has observed, to the lack of will in Amsterdam to find the money for the proper blockades before war broke out with England. By 1657, France and England were strong enough to resist the tough policies of the States-General because they had their own designs on the Brazilian trade. The Portuguese, on the other hand, united under João IV (John IV). George Downing wrote home to his government in England in 1664 that it was the divided and shattered government of the Netherlands that contributed to its problems, and Cromwell's government in the late 1650s and that of Charles II in the 1660s were glad to see it that way. Charles, now married into the House of Braganza, which had helped him so much, brokered Luso-Dutch negotiations, but did not wish to give the Dutch equal access to the Luso-Brazilian trade: England wanted to displace the Netherlands in America and Asia.[98]

François Valentijn's work, which is more like a chronicle, noted the arrival of the Portuguese in Ceylon. Emanuel, king of Portugal, had as his representative, Payo de Sousa (Lelagius Sousa), who was to demand an annual tribute of 250,000 pounds of cinnamon in exchange for protection. The king or emperor regretted this treaty and slew some Portuguese and the violence persisted for some years.[99] The Portuguese pitted one group against another, so they could get into Candi and become masters.[100] Valentijn represented the cruelty of the Portuguese and included Native reports on this behavior: "After everything was at peace regarding the natives, the character of the Portuguese again came to the fore, who, beginning now to become lawless and wanton, did not hesitate to hurt the susceptibilities of the natives in various places and commit such crimes that they were forced to complain over this to the Queen, who, after hearing of Janiere's death, prophesied their fall and decline."[101] The Cingalese (Sinhalese) cruel revenge against Portuguese cruelty suggests the bitterness of the strife: "Many were taken captive by the Cingalese, to some of whom, out of revenge for the cruelties inflicted on their wives and daughters, they cut off the noses, ears and genitals and sent them back to let their companions know what they would expect from the Cingalese," an action that made the Portuguese abandon Ganoor for Walane.[102] When the Dutch came on the scene in Ceylon and elsewhere in Asia, the Natives were sometimes ripe for revolt, the kind of situation Walter Ralegh had hoped for in Guiana against the Spaniards. The French, like the Dutch, observed the Portuguese and other empires in their own amassing of knowledge in support of their own expansion and sense of the kind of France they wanted at home.

IV

The French, after losses in the Seven Years' War (1756–63), were keen observers of the history of European expansion overseas, including their own contacts with peoples in these locales, as well as colonization and the British Empire: they also had a hand in the War of Independence that gave the thirteen colonies their independence. France had been at various times a key rival for empire to Portugal, Spain, England and the Netherlands since each of those nations set out to expand trade and to establish colonies overseas. Here, I wish to focus briefly on two main aspects of the French representations of empire: the Portuguese past and the British and American present and future. As this section is meant to be suggestive rather than exhaustive about representations of Portugal, Britain and the United States (America), it will limit itself to a discussion of a few examples of aspects of eighteenth-century texts by Denis Diderot, Guillaume-Thomas Raynal, Jean-François Marmontel and Jean-Antoine-Nicolas de Caritat, marquis de Condorcet and a nineteenth-century work by Alexis de Toqueville.

In the *Encyclopédie* Diderot includes entries that have to do with places and peoples that some of the texts in this study have represented. Under "Calicut ou Calécut," the place the Portuguese found so strategic in India from the beginning, the entry emphasizes two main themes about this city and kingdom on the Malabar coast. When the king marries, he has the priests sleep with his wife, so that the only child to succeed him is his sister's, and the inhabitants follow suit by not having any difficulty in giving "their wives to their friends," so that a wife, who "can have up to seven husbands, if she becomes pregnant, ... can attribute the child to whom it looks most alike."[103] The entry continued that the inhabitants believe in a God who does not get mixed up in the government of the universe but leaves that to the care of the devil, to whom the inhabitants offer sacrifices. Nowhere is European contact with this kingdom mentioned centuries after this encounter. Diderot also has an entry for the Caribs or Cannibals, the group that Columbus represented early on, but centuries later, the ethnological detail is almost generic, mythical and stereotypical: "They are in general sad, dreamers and lazy," but they have a good constitution and so can live to 100 and their women are not jealous of one another, something that "Montaigne regarded as a miracle in his chapter on these people."[104] At this point, discussions of colonialism had become recursive and allusive, so that there were interpretations of interpretations: the Natives were presented in at least two removes. The fascination with eating human flesh persisted well beyond Columbus, Léry and Montaigne: The Caribs "eat their prisoners roasted, and send some pieces to their friends."[105] This text of the Enlightenment does not sound that different from Columbus writing in the 1490s. The entry under "Ceilan, Zeylan or Ceylon," began with an observation that "the Dutch ['Hollandais'] possess almost all the coasts, and the king of Candi is master of the interior of the country, which contains seven kingdoms."[106] Although the entry mentioned that the Candi were idolaters and later returned to "the cinnamon, ginger, ivory, precious stones" and so on that are in Ceylon, this description, like the two previous accounts, dwells once more on sexual difference from customary European codes: the woman chooses the man and the first wedding night "is for the husband, the second is for his brother, and if there is a third or fourth brother, up to the seventh, each has his night; in this manner a woman suffices for the entire family."[107] How much this is ethnological description or prurient and voyeuristic interest might be hard to say for the contemporary reader. The political contexts and comparison of empire give way to a fascination with the exotic,

the forbidden and the erotic. Only in passing, as a periphery to social
description and ideas, are the Dutch mentioned: the Spanish and Portuguese
have vanished into an interlinear obscurity or an extenuated and unspoken
subtext. Politics might well get in the way of the apparently direct access
Diderot gives to his readers.

Raynal, with a different goal in mind, played up the role of the Portuguese
and others in the settlement of the two Indies. He began his history with a
declaration of the epochal changes that the Spanish and Portuguese made in
the closing years of the fifteenth century: "There has not been an event so
interesting for the human species in general and for the peoples of Europe in
particular, than the discovery of the new world and the passage to the Indies
by the Cape of Good Hope."[108] These two voyages of separate Iberian
nations are linked as a single event. There was no priority of national accomplishment or of whether the East was more important than the West. Here
the whole world opened up to Europeans. Raynal described the contacts
Gama and Cabral had in Calicut and he praised Alfonso de Albuquerque,
who thought that Goa by the Malabar coast should provide a base for his
country in India, as "the most enlightened of the Portuguese who made a
passage to India."[109] Raynal also represented the military actions of the
Portuguese, of figures like Tristan D'Acugna, but he focused most on
Albuquerque in this context, who found himself in a struggle in and about
the Red Sea where means and ends did not always match in a "disquieting
and cruel politics."[110] After representing these problems and reservations,
Raynal concluded that after Albuquerque's "expedition, Portuguese power
found itself solidly enough established in the gulfs of Arabia and of Persia,
on the Malabar coast, so that it could consider spreading out in the east of
Asia."[111] Raynal addressed the topic of the violence of this expedition and
said that Albuquerque, who set the scene for the Portuguese taking part
in the commerce of Asia, provided a sense of justice to "diminish the hatred"
that must have naturally been attached "to the Portuguese name."[112] After
the taking of Malaca, Siam, Pegu and other places the local rulers asked for
an alliance with the Portuguese. Raynal also discussed the history of Portugal
and the influence of France and England in establishing chivalry at the
Portuguese court and described the "marvels" ("merveilles") of the Chinese
"empire" that had not just awaited the Venetian, Marco Polo, whose relation
"had passed for fabulous" but had been confirmed during the embassy of
Fernão Peres de Andrade there.[113] As in the Black Legend of Spain, which
was often upheld during the Enlightenment, in an account of the blacken-
ing of the reputation of the Portuguese, Raynal set up an interpretation that
the Portuguese came to be corrupted by their own success:

> So many advantages could form a mass of solid ("inébranlable") power; but the
> vices and ineptitude of some commanders, the misuse of riches, that of power,

the drunkenness of success, the distance from their country had changed the Portuguese. The religious fanaticism that had given them more force and activity to their courage, did not give more than atrocity. They did not have any scruples not to pillage, deceive, subjugate ["d'asservir"] idolaters. They thought that the pope, in giving to the kings of Portugal the kingdoms of Asia, did not refuse their subjects particular goods ("les biens des particuliers"). Tyrants of the seas of the Orient, they ransomed ("raçonnoient") the vessels of all nations. They ravaged the coasts, they insulted princes, and they became in a little while the horror and scourge of peoples.[114]

Raynal includes a critique of religion that became an opposition to the abuses of European history, in this case of Portuguese expansion overseas. Here is another opposition from within or at the very least a balancing of the historical accounts. For Raynal, the victory at Castro showed the vigor of the Portuguese, but this did not last for long: he considered the death of King Sebastian and the reign of Philip II of Spain to be detrimental, for each Portuguese in India came to work for his own fortune. Although this "little nation found itself at once the mistress of the richest and most widespread commerce on earth, ... she lost the foundation of all real power, agriculture, national industry and population."[115] Raynal took a backward glance and discovered that the Portuguese of that time did not understand the expansion in which they were involved and they allowed their customs (morals; "moeurs") to become depraved, so their "soldiers and officers were without discipline, without subordination, without love of glory" ("la gloire" being a prominent interest of the French).[116]

In Raynal's view, the corrupt Portuguese leaders could not suppress these vices, so what began, after the route round Africa to India, as "the emulation of the Portuguese," what might be called the instance of Portugal, ended with a shift in worldview and in the business of empire: "The Portuguese finally lost their grandeur, when a free, enlightened and tolerant nation, showed itself in India, and disputed the empire with them. It appeared that in the time of the discoveries of the Portuguese, the political principles based on commerce, on the real power of states, on the advantages of conquests, on the manner of establishing and maintaining colonies, and on the utility drawn from the metropole, were not then known."[117] Instead, Portugal wanted to conquer but did not have the means and population to carry this out because it "embraced an expanse of territory that no nation in Europe could maintain without weakening itself."[118] Raynal's progressive and "Whig" views of tolerance explained the demise of the Portuguese empire in terms of intolerance, indifference to commerce and submission to Spain, which contrasted to "the measured and reflective conduct of the Dutch."[119] The Netherlands came to represent the virtues needed for the kind of empire that Raynal described as a successor to that of Portugal, whose eschewing of commerce led them to change "projects of commerce into projects of conquest, the nation that never had a spirit of commerce took that of brigandage."[120] The new way of operation, then, required peace, prosperity, skilled labor and tolerance, all of which Portugal, a country of extremes of wealth and poverty, lacked: "Its intolerance does not allow it to admit to the rank of its citizens the peoples of the Orient and of Africa, and it must everywhere and all times combat its new subjects."[121] Whereas the Portuguese used force, the "Dutch were animated by the hope of founding a great commerce on the ruins of the commerce of their enemies. They conducted themselves with speed, with firmness. Their mildness and their good faith reconciled them to peoples. Soon several declared themselves against their ancient oppressors."[122] Raynal was creating, by design or not, a Black Legend of Portugal, but part of that legendary apparatus was also complicated by the attitude of Spain, "to which Portugal had then submitted, in desiring its debasement, and rejoicing in its defeats, as if they had not augmented the means of its enemies the Dutch" and sent men—as if to spite the Portuguese and in fear that if Portugal lacked the resources itself, Spain would have to fight its neighbor's wars—to fight in Italy, Flanders and elsewhere in Europe.[123] In the construction of such an interpretation, in which Raynal paid close attention to Portuguese expansion and gave Portugal its due while discussing its excesses, the author made his judgment and used the voice of someone from another culture: "the time finally arrived, when the Portuguese atoned for their perfidies, their robberies and their cruelties. Then the prophecy of a king of Persia came true. This prince, having asked a Portuguese ambassador how many governors his master had had decapitated since he had introduced his domination in the Indies: *none*, responded the ambassador. *Too bad*, replied the monarch; *his power in a country where he commits so many vexations and barbarities, will not endure long.*"[124] This kind of quotation from a "Native" source is something the enemies of Spain or those who wrote against the abuses or hubris of European colonization used as a means of chastising or exposing the offenders. Montaigne employed this technique, as did Jonathan Swift when the king of Brobdingnag leveled his searing attack against the English. Raynal also represented the Dutch attacks of the Portuguese—Négapatan in 1658 and Cochin in 1662— and their rivalry with the English in Asia: when the English tried to enter Japan, "the Japanese, instructed by the Dutch that the king of England had married the daughter of the king of Portugal, did not want to receive the English in their ports."[125] The more pressing rivalry by this time was between the English and the Dutch over the remnants and opportunities that Portugal left behind even as it continued to hold what it could.

The Black Legend of Spain was still strong and seems to have been more widespread and intense than a similar legend about Portugal. Long after the events, Jean-François Marmontel revisited the Spanish expansion into the western Atlantic: "All nations have had their brigands and their fanatics, their times of barbarism, their bouts of madness. The most esteemed are those who accuse themselves. The Spaniards have had this pride, worthy of their character. Never has a history traced anything more touching, more terrible than the misfortunes of the New World, in Las Casas' book."[126] The opposition from within, the critics of their own country, are a sign of high estimation. After praising the virtue and courage of Las Casas, Marmontel tells how this prelate "compares the Indians to lambs, and the Spaniards to tigers, to devouring wolves, to lions pressed with a long hunger."[127] The comparison here, as in the speech of the Persian king in Raynal, is between those native to the land and the European newcomers. Here, however, the lambs of the lamb of God are not the Christians but those they repress. Marmontel saw in Spain, a nation with rulers who listened to Las Casas's criticism publicly and whose rules and ordinances took care of the Indians: "Regarding these crimes, of which Spain washed itself, in publishing them herself and in devoting them to blame, one is going to see that everywhere moreover in the same circumstances men capable of the same excesses would be found."[128] Here, as in earlier representations of Spain, ambivalence informs this account: Spain is cruel but is absolved for recognizing the cruelty of some of its citizens acting beyond what court and people thought just.

Rather than concentrating on Portugal, Condorcet looked at current events—the American Revolution. More than Spain, the greatest rival to the French in the eighteenth century—England (as the French often still called it, but Britain by now)—was on Condorcet's mind. More importantly, it was, in the typology of the Old World and the New, something that reversed the usual point of view. In Condorcet what was most interesting about Britain was the loss of its colonies, whose revolution would have important implications and consequences for Europe. The colonies would change the centers of empire. First, however, were more immediate effects: "America had hardly declared its independence, and our politicians already saw clearly the ruin of England and the prosperity of France must have been the necessary consequence of this happy revolution."[129] An unspoken revenge perhaps for the Seven Years' War might well be part of this delight at the ruin of Britain. Condorcet admitted interest in the prize proposed by Raynal that involved a consideration of "the good and the bad that had resulted for Europe from the discovery of the New World" and that set out to examine "the influence of the independence of America would have on humanity, on Europe, on France in particular."[130] Like Raynal, Condorcet took an intellectual interest in how America influenced Europe and not the usual presumption that Europe had the principal effect on the New World. The birth of the United States intensified what some Europeans sensed from the beginning—the "discovery" of the lands in the western Atlantic would change Europe in a serious fashion.

Later, Alexis de Toqueville would also concentrate on the United States and its expression of democracy. His book would take on additional resonance in the conflict between monarchy and republic in France. The advertisement for the tenth edition of *Democracy in America* emphasized that the writing of the book was preoccupied with "the next, irresistible, universal advent of Democracy in the world."[131] The notice then became more explicit about the connection of America to France, which would bolster the importance of De Toqueville's book: "The institutions of America, which was a subject of curiosity for monarchical France, must be a subject of study for republican France."[132] The instance of Portugal and the example of Spain had given way to the model of the United States. This republic had, as the advertisement said, become an exemplum for republicans, an inspiration even if it should not be imitated with servility:

> For 60 years the principle of sovereignty of the people that we introduced yesterday among us reigns there without division. It is put into practice in the most direct, the most unlimited, the most absolute manner. For 60 years, the people who had made up the common source of all these laws grew incessantly in population, in territory, in richness; and note it well, it found itself to have been during this period not only the most prosperous, but the most stable of all the peoples of the earth. While all the nations of Europe were ravaged by war or torn by civil discord, the American people alone in the civilized world remained peaceful.[133]

Although this is a somewhat idealized version of the United States, it is a representation of an example for the Old World, which it has surpassed even at this early date. De Toqueville himself remarked in his opening words on "the egality of conditions" in the United States.[134] Moreover, he, too, saw an example in the United States for Europe: "Then I will report my thought toward our hemisphere, and it seemed to me that I distinguished in it something analogous to the spectacle that the New World offered me."[135] That model involved a democratic revolution of the kind operating among the French. De Toqueville also traced some of the American traits and institutions to England. For instance, "communal government, that fecund germ of free institutions, had already profoundly entered English habits, and with it the dogma of the sovereignty of the people was introduced even in the bosom of the Tudor monarchy."[136] Another aspect of this equality of conditions in the United States is like similar conditions in other places in the "New World" (the term De Toqueville favors). Each early European colony in the Americas, whether English, French, Spanish or something else, contained "at least the germ of a complete democracy" because the happy and powerful did not seek exile and poverty and misfortune "are the best guarantees of equality that we know among men."[137] The conditions in the New World were not conducive to aristocracy—the privileged class of the Europe. But, for a moment, before advancing to the United States, it would be worth, as De Toqueville himself thought, to step back to England, when it was on the brink of permanent settlements in the New World.

V

On December 31, 1600, Elizabeth I issued a charter for the founding of the East India Company, which had 218 subscribers and possessed a monopoly for English trade in Asia and the Pacific. The first four company ships left Woolich on February 13, 1601 and arrived in Bantam (now in Indonesia) on December 16, 1602 (over five years after the first Dutch ship reached there) and returned safely to England by September 1603. Along with a Dutch ship, the ship of James Lancaster, who had raided Portuguese ships in the early 1591 as far as Sumatra, fought and captured a Portuguese carrack in the Straits of Sumatra on October 3 and 4, 1602. The Portuguese and the Chinese traded in Bantam, which pepper had boosted, and, after landing that first time, the English rented accommodation in the Chinese quarter. Although Portuguese was a language the English employed at first to communicate in the area, they soon switched to Malay, which the Chinese had used as the *lingua franca* in Southeast Asia before the arrival of the Europeans. The first publications from the East India Company were manuals to learn to trade in Malay: *A true and large discourse of the voyage ... to the East Indies* (1603) and *Dialogues in the English and Malay* (1614). A number of voyages were made to Bantam thereafter, the voyage of 1612 being the most profitable with a return of 220 percent. The principal products of England were woolen broadcloth and lighter cloths like serges, kerseys and baize, something the merchants soon realized would not be in demand in extreme climates, although in *Discourse on Western Planting* (1584) Richard Hakluyt recorded the hope for sales of woolen cloth to the Natives in Canada.[138] The East India Company soon learned that bartering Asian goods, especially Indian textiles, for other Asian goods was the most profitable trade. They sailed the first English ships to India in 1608, but the Mughal governor at Surat, anxious not to anger the Portuguese, ordered the departure of an English fleet in 1610, an action that caused Sir Henry Middleton to intercept the annual Haj pilgrimage ships from Surat at the entrance to the Red Sea and, avoiding the name of pirate, forced an exchange of Indian cloth for broadcloth. In 1611, other ships opened relations with the other coast of India that was outside the Mughal Empire, and in 1613 the East India Company opened a factory at Hirado in Japan. An English pilot, William Adams, sailed in 1598 with a Dutch fleet en route to Indonesia via the Straits of Magellan and his ship alone reached Japan in April 1600. Imprisonment and interviews with the shogan Ieyasu, through a hostile interpreter, a Portuguese Jesuit, João Rodrigues, followed but in time Adams became a retainer of Ieyasu and replaced Rodrigues as official interpreter for Europeans in that region and thereby helped the Dutch East India Company to set up a factory at Hirado in 1609 and was friendly to the English four years later. Adams died in Japan in 1620.[139]

The Dutch were stronger than the Portuguese and English: in 1601, in the Bay of Bantam, they defeated a Portuguese fleet and, as Anthony Farrington has noted, the English found at Bantam and elsewhere that the Dutch had more money, ships, men and purpose.[140] To control the fine spice trade in Asia, the Dutch offered, through treaties, protection in exchange for a monopoly over the spices. The Dutch imitated the Portuguese example of Goa in India by establishing Batavia (now Jakarta) as a hub or rendezvous for its trade. The Dutch and English cooperated for a few years, but in February 1623 the Dutch governor, Herman van Speult, had put to death Gabriel Towerson, the English leader on Amboina, nine other Company employees, nine Japanese samurai, and a Portuguese. A propaganda battle broke out between London and Amsterdam, and in England something akin to the Black Legend of the Netherlands developed for 50 years or more, reflected in texts like *A True Relation of the Unjust, Cruell and Barbarous Proceeding against the English*. The English gave up Run in exchange for New Netherlands, which included Manhattan. There Anglo-Dutch Wars took place in 1652–54, 1665–67, 1672–74 and 1780–84. France invaded the Netherlands during the French revolution: on December 31, 1795 the Dutch East India Company, the European commercial power in East Asia for most of the seventeenth century, was dissolved.[141]

On the west coast of India the Portuguese had been present before Mughal control of the area. Bombay, 160 miles south of Surat, which the sultan of Gujarat ceded to the Portuguese in 1534, was part of the dowry Catherine of Braganza brought to Charles II in 1661, and he handed it over to the East India Company, which made it its headquarters in 1674. In 1700 the English had three strongholds—Madras, Bombay and Calcutta—amid their factories in India. In East Asia the English found that the Chinese dominated maritime trade from Sumatra and Java to Japan. Moreover, the English also saw that the Dutch were allowed to stay in Japan after the Portuguese were expelled and that after 1644 the Manchu invaders captured Beijing and established the Ch'ing Dynasty, and in resistance and flight Cheng Ch'eng-kung (Koxinga) drove the Dutch out of their stronghold of Fort Zeelandia in Taiwan. From 1699 English ships traded in Canton and were later joined by Dutch, French, Danish, Austrian, Swedish, Indian and (after the War of Independence) American ships. The language of trade there was first Portuguese and then pidgin: a British embassy to the emperor in 1793 had both sides communicating by writing in Latin.[142] The greatest change was a move from the power of trade to that of political dominion. As the Mughal Empire was collapsing in the 1750s, the Europeans fought their wars beyond the bounds of Europe. France had founded the Compagnie des Indes in 1664 and was a rival of Britain from the 1720s: these two powers battled in North America, the Indian Ocean and India. During the Seven Years' War, Clive began a string of victories for the British in India against the French and local rulers. In 1773, the British East India Company assumed the monopoly for growing opium in Bengal, and when France invaded the Netherlands, the company took Ceylon in 1796 and Java in 1811. The Chinese had prohibited the sale of opium in 1729, but by 1840 the Chinese state, trying to stem this drug trade, suffered a defeat and the British seized Hong Kong.[143] The ebb and flow of trading and political powers did not mean that the ascension of British power in Asia or in the world was a foregone conclusion. The rise and fall of empires was something that Edward Gibbon had observed in ancient Rome and came to be true of Britain. The challenges of France, Russia, Germany and the United States would prove too great for it, just as the Iberian powers, Portugal and Spain, had given way to Dutch, French and English power in trade and politics. The translation of empire was never entirely predictable—being able to tell which party would fall and which would rise—but the translation itself, at least thus far, is something that was sure to happen.

A translation of empire occurred slowly between England and its principal former colonies in North America. The English long had an ambivalent and contradictory relation to Spain and Columbus and this continued in the 13 colonies after their independence. For instance, in the 1680s, England was still challenging Spain and producing texts that mentioned or meditated on Columbus as an example. In *The English Empire* (1685), R. B. represented Columbus as an instance, "after whose example several others made further Discoveries, till at last this New World, is almost wholly come to the knowledge of the Old."[144] Nearly 200 years after Columbus's arrival in the western Atlantic, a volume on English imperialism praised in typological terms of Old World and New the great Italian explorer who sailed in the service of the Spanish crown. Although British America was breaking apart during the War of Independence, its texts also showed a persistent interest in Columbus and Spain. Cases in point about a hundred years after R. B.'s work are David Ramsey's *The History of the American Revolution* (1789) and Jeremy Belknap's consideration of the three hundredth anniversary of Columbus's landfall in which he could praise Columbus and blame Spain.[145]

As Belknap declared, "It is not pretended that Columbus was the only person of his age who had acquired these ideas of the form, dimensions and balancing of the globe; but he was one of the few who had begun to think for themselves, and he had a genius of that kind, which makes use of speculation and reasoning only as excitements to action."[146] Spain, on the other hand, did not measure up to Columbus, who inaugurated the settlement of America, to which the English Puritans had brought liberty from persecution and on which their liberty-loving descendants had improved with their revolutionary war against England. The Spanish were part of the Black Legend and "the first introduction of the negro slavery into America was occasioned by the previous destruction of the native inhabitants of the West-India islands, by the cruelty of their Spanish conquerors, in exacting of them more labour than they were able to perform"; contrary to the usual canonizing of Bartolomé de Las Casas in this Black Legend, Belknap's view blames him in part for being responsible for one of the horrors of the European expansion into the New World: "The most remarkable and unaccountable circumstance attending the beginning of this traffic, is, that it was recommended by a Spanish Bishop, one of the most benevolent friends of the Indians, whom he could not bear to see so wantonly destroyed by his countrymen."[147] Belknap argued for tolerance toward all religions—including Hindu, Muslim, Jewish, Christian—and found fault with proud notions of English liberty and the lack of tolerance in the constitution of his home state of Massachusetts.[148] In his typology of the New World improving on the Old World and extending a haven of liberty to the inhabitants of Europe, Belknap praised the United States because the federal constitution of the United States "leaves religion where all civil governments ought to leave it; to the consciences of individuals, under the control of the supreme Lord."[149]

The Columbian World Exposition in Chicago in 1893 (a year late but celebrating the four hundredth anniversary of Columbus's landfall nonetheless), showed the staying power of Columbus and Spain and their legacy. In addressing President Grover Cleveland of the United States at the exposition, William Boldenweck and Maier Weinchenk picked up, consciously or not, on themes that Belknap outlined in 1792: they represented Columbus as a bearer of Enlightenment. In addition, their Columbus of 1893 was an agent of progress who served in the fight against superstition, bigotry and feudalism: "When the dark clouds of political and religious bigotry were enshrouding the sun lit heavens of then benighted Europe, and freedom of thought and the expression thereof was regarded as the key-note of treachery and treason."[150] As Boldenweck and Weinchenk implied, the Whig history of England was now the Whig history of "America," which would outdo the mother country and all of Europe in the ways of freedom: "the discovery of America may well be called the cornerstone of the great bulwark of progress, the vanguard of the march of civilization, the promoter of the spirit of education which has blessed the centuries which followed."[151] While taking up the earlier empire, this new power would displace the ancient ways with progress.

The 1890s are a key point in the representation of Spain in the United States, and William Eleroy Curtis is an interesting figure in this context. At the World's fair, Curtis had assembled artifacts for the reproduction of the Convent Santa Maria de la Rabida, where Columbus had found shelter in time of trouble.[152] An article reported: "The reproduction and the collection of rare relics of the Noah of our nation are in more than a measure due to the indefatigable perseverance of the Hon. William Eleroy Curtis of the Bureau of American Republics, who traversed the whole of Europe searching for traces of the great Genoese admiral and procuring relics, maps, etc. for exhibition here."[153] Curtis, who showed an awareness of the history of the reception of Columbus (as in the events of 1792 and the interpretations then of the explorer's contribution), wrote about the Columbian World Exposition in Chicago in 1893, about the need for more open trade between the United States and Latin American countries and about other events such as the inauguration of Grover Cleveland on March 9, 1893. He also kept a scrapbook, so that Curtis was written about, wrote and collected—the representation of Columbus, America and other topics was a mixture in a framework that he brought together, sometimes with the dates and chronology, sometimes not. For instance, under one section on Cuba, Curtis displayed through the title "Reciprocity and the World's Fair," a link between culture and trade as well as establishing a ground in which Columbus is used as a means of connecting the various Latin American countries to the United States through a common figure and common past. The Columbian World Exposition was a way of showing the United States to the world but also enabling to place it at the head of a common "American" market and sphere of influence: America is the Americas and vice versa. A potpourri of interesting details emerge: for example, Thomas Jefferson ordered a portrait of Columbus (perhaps, like Belknap, he viewed Columbus as a natural philosopher and figure of the Enlightenment); there are notes on Columbus's descendant, the Duke of Veragua, who was to attend the Columbian Exposition; materials on the chains of Columbus and the first poem about Columbus, an Italian edition of his letter in verse in 1493.[154] Despite Curtis's enthusiasm for the importance of Columbian and Hispanic history and an advocacy for closer economic ties between the United States and Latin America, he would, along with his compatriots, face a war with Spain in 1898.

The Spanish-American War possesses a vast historiography in the United States, Spain, Cuba, Puerto Rico, the Philippines and elsewhere, so this brief discussion is meant to be suggestive, particularly in the context of the war in terms of colonialism and imperialism. Ambivalence is attached to this varied historiography, or these historiographies. For some historians in the United States, this was a war when their country came of age as a world power; for others it was accidental; or a war formed by public opinion; some historians in Spain have seen this war as a catastrophic denouement to an empire after 400 years; in Cuba and the Philippines the historiography tends to see this conflict as an interlude in the movement from colony to nation; in Puerto Rico, this transition is in abeyance or has taken a different route.[155]

Whatever interpretation is gleaned from the intricacies of the Spanish-American War, the United States was able to break Spain's hold and in some sense acquire or have influence over the remnants of the Spanish empire in the Pacific and Caribbean, something that had begun in earnest with Columbus.[156] Spain had long been on the minds of the English and then their American descendants. In 1823, Thomas Jefferson wrote to James Monroe, the author of the Munroe Doctrine proclaiming the influence of the United States in the western hemisphere, that adding Cuba "to our confederacy" would "round out our power as a nation."[157] Jefferson and others would have liked annexation—James Polk offered $100 million in 1848 and Franklin Pierce upped the offer to $130 million in 1854 (much more than the $7 million for Alaska in 1867)—he and his successors, if they could not have annexation, would tolerate Spanish sovereignty rather than have Spain sign over the island to a third party, including those who might govern it as an independent nation. Cuba had several local and isolated uprisings in 1879–80, 1885, 1892, but the revolt of 1895 spread across the island and on January 10, 1898, a Cuban home-rule government, under the auspices of Spain, assumed power, but many of the insurgent leaders, like General Máximo Gómez, rejected this arrangement and demanded independence. Less than two weeks later, Spanish troops rioting against home rule destroyed the presses of two publications. In response to this crisis, on January 25, 1898, the United States sent a warship, the *Maine* to Havana harbor. Many in Spain and the United States and among the Cuban separatists concluded, rightly or not, that Spain would lose Cuba, but the Americans were not willing to lose the Cuba they had wanted for so long.

Neither the Cleveland nor the McKinley administration favored an independent Cuba. Richard Olney, the secretary of state in the Cleveland administration, was not alone in thinking that Cuba was unfit for nationhood because of racial division that would be self-destructive. In March 1898 neither did Stewart L. Woolford, McKinley's minister to Spain, consider the Cuban populace to be "fit for self-government" and maintained that the insurgency was "confined almost entirely to negroes."[158] The United States Congress had issued periodic resolutions supporting the insurgents and threatening war on their behalf: the McKinley administration, on the other hand, now wanted an armistice, but the Cuban separatists refused it.

In February 1898 a letter of Enrique Dupuy de Lôme, the Spanish minister in Washington, that was uncomplimentary to President McKinley was leaked and published in the *New York Journal*. The sinking of the U.S. battleship, *Maine*, in Havana Harbor did little to improve relations among Spain, Cuba and the United States. Intervention was the path that the government of the United States chose.

The Spanish-American War lasted from the beginning of May, 1898 until the Treaty of Paris was signed that December.[159] In four months of fighting the United States was able (politically and militarily) to annex the following territories—Guam, Puerto Rico and the Philippines—and have supervision over an independent Cuba, whose annexation the Americans had foresworn in the Teller Amendment to the war resolutions of 1898. The end of the Spanish empire, just over 400 years after Columbus landed in the Caribbean, came quickly indeed. A translation from Portugal to Spain to the United States, a successor to Britain in the region, was something Hakluyt and Ralegh could only dream about. The Black Legend of Spain was at last widespread enough to make the triumph over this tyranny a righteous cause in the popular imagination in the United States. American imperialism beyond the North American landmass might well have begun in a paradox that if the United States would try to keep Spain in power rather than have third party or independent forces govern its colonial possessions and if it could not bolster Spanish power, it would have to defeat it to succeed it.

An opposition to war and expansion occurred in Europe in the fifteenth and seventeenth centuries: in the late eighteenth century, the nineteenth century and the opening two decades of the twentieth century, some influential Americans of different backgrounds and political parties opposed war and empire for their country. John Quincy Adams, for example, observed on July 4, 1821, that the heart, benedictions and prayers of the United States would be "Wherever the standard of freedom and independence has been unfurled" and that his country, which he personified as a woman (yet another image of America as a woman), should lead by her voice and example and would suffer if taking an interventionist course:

> She well knows that, by once enlisting under other banners than her own, were they even the banners of foreign independence, she would involve herself, beyond the power of extrication, in all the wars of interest and intrigue, of individual avarice, envy, and ambition, which assume the color and usurp the standard of freedom. The fundamental maxims of her policy would insensibly change from liberty to force. The frontlet upon her brows would no longer beam with the ineffable splendor of freedom and independence; but in its stead would soon be substituted an imperial diadem, flashing in false and tarnished lustre the murky radiance of dominion and power. She might become the dictatress of the world; she would no longer be the ruler of her own spirit.[160]

Adams's insight would have a bearing on the 1890s and beyond, the course of American foreign policy from that point onward. An allusion here, conscious or not, is to a verse that Christ speaks and appears in three variants in the New Testament: "For what is a man profited, if he shall gain the whole world, and lose his own soul? Or what shall a man give in exchange for his soul?"[161] Here then is the metonymy of a woman for a man and a synecdoche of a person for a country, but the echo appears to play a part in the resonance of Adams's image of America dictating to the world but not ruling her spirit.

During the period surrounding the Spanish-American War of 1898 a diverse group of people among leaders in government, education and business were anti-imperialist: ex-Presidents Benjamin Harrison and Grover Cleveland; Democrats like William Jennings Bryan and former secretary of state, Richard Olney; Republicans such as senators from New England, Eugene Hale, George F. Hoar and Justin Morrill and House Speaker, Thomas Brackett Reed; political independents like Carl Schurz and Jane Addams; William James and Charles Eliot Norton of Harvard; William Graham Sumner of Yale; labor leaders like Samuel Gompers and businessmen like Edward Atkinson, Andrew Carnegie, George F. Peabody and Henry Villard; abolitionists like Thomas Wentworth Higginson; the sons of Ralph Waldo Emerson; writers like Ambrose Pierce, William Dean Howells, Edwin Arlington Robinson and Mark Twain. Above all the mugwump and dissident Republicans were the most energetic critics of expansion and had a long history of this opposition, having criticized the administration of Andrew Johnson for expansionist policies during the 1860s. They did not like the annexation of Alaska in 1867 and helped to turn the public against the Grant administration's plan to annex Santo Domingo. Later they opposed the Anglo-German–American protectorate over Samoa in 1889, the war scare with Chile in 1891–92, and the attempt to annex Hawaii in 1893. The political origins of the mugwumps or independents who switched sides went back to the antislavery politics of the 1840s and 1850s. Some of the mugwumps had helped to form the Republican party at a time when it pressed for the abolition of slavery and stayed with a party as long as it was committed to their own principles and reforms.[162] A mugwump, Carl Schurz, congratulated President McKinley on Admiral George Dewey's victory at Manila harbor on May 1, 1898, but he was against the annexation of Hawaii, a move he argued would harm the international reputation of the United States, which had assured the world community that the Spanish-American War was one "of deliverance and not one of greedy ambition, conquest and self-aggrandizement."[163]

The theme that John Quincy Adams set out—that America would lose its soul if it sought to gain the world—recurs here but also, more explicitly, in the writing of William James, who complained: "the manner in which the McKinley administration railroaded the country into its policy of conquest was abominable, and the way the country puked up its ancient soul at the first touch of temptation, and followed, was sickening."[164] Born in Cambridge, Massachusetts in 1827, Charles Eliot Norton, whose parents had as visitors such as Francis Parkman and Henry Wadsworth Longfellow, had been a capable student at Harvard (class of 1846), worked in the East India trade, studied, traveled and lived in Europe for 20 years, and, after the death of his wife, returned in 1875 to become Harvard's first professor of fine arts, a post from which he retired in 1897. His view of the role of the United States in the world resembled that of John Quincy Adams and something he thought founded in the ideals of the institutions of the country: these goals were pursued "by the establishment of her own democracy in such wise as to make it a symbol of noble self-government, and by exercising the influence of a great, unarmed and peaceful power on the affairs and the moral temper of the world"; he lamented that the policies the United States was pursuing were tantamount to a desertion of those unselfish ideals, so that the country had "taken up her place simply as one of the grasping and selfish nations of the present day."[165] For Andrew Carnegie, American republicanism had allowed the United States to avoid the wrongs of conflict and imperialism.[166] Although these anti-imperialists might have been, despite their own short-comings or their reflection of the intolerance of their times, the conscience of their nation, their words were often ignored or did not affect the lasting reforms they sought—a little like the arguments and warnings of Las Casas in the Spanish empire during the sixteenth century.[167]

A few aspects—the economy, the Press and politics—should be touched upon here as a reminder of the many intricate strands of this war. That United States might derive economic benefits from its expansion was a possibility considered in the late 1890s. For instance, Charles Morris saw one of "the chief advantages of the liberation of Cuba" as being commercial.[168] Another beneficiary was supposed to be the Press, which supported the war and perhaps helped to cause the conflict. This contribution to the Spanish-American War—not to deny the power of media then and now—might not, as Charles H. Brown suggested in the 1960s when studying the role of news-papers in the conflict, be as great as some have thought, for public opinion in favor of the war at the time meant that the time was ripe for it, that it is too simple to reduce "the cause of the war with Spain" to a "circulation fight between a New York press lord and his challenger."[169]

In considering the build-up to the Spanish-American War, it is also important to remember the context of the arms race between Britain and Germany that was developing and the rivalry for imperial expansion that European powers had experience in, in the late nineteenth century. When in September, 1897 Stewart Lyndon Woodford argued that Spain should grant Cuba autonomy, Wilhelm II, kaiser of Germany, urged other monarchs to help the queen of Spain "in case the American-British Society for Theft and Warmongering looks as if it seriously intends to snatch Cuba from Spain."[170] Ultimately, neither Britain nor Germany, whose monarchs were related to María Cristina through Queen Victoria, would help; Britain especially, because of its great navy, would have been the greatest concern to the United States if it wanted to act in the Caribbean. At this point, the pope offered to mediate the differences between Madrid and Washington, a suggestion not without historical irony as the papacy had, in the 1490s, divided up—between Portugal and Spain—the world "unknown" to the Europeans. Assistant Secretary of State William R. Day accepted no new presentations to Spain.[171]

After the war, in the negotiations of the Treaty of Paris between the United States and Spain, Day favored more acquisitions for the United States than ever before. Nothing was linear, as the kaiser might have thought, for the British, who would not help Spain but were in a strong position to do so, were sometimes helpful to the Americans in the business of imperial expansion. As part of the decision to annex the Philippines, the United States received some support from John Foreman, a British expert on the Philippines, who was a strong advocate of American annexation during his interview with the commission. Day said that the American people favored annexation of all of the Philippines, even if an influential minority was against expansion overseas.[172] It is possible that Presidents Cleveland and McKinley, opposed to any adventurism in the Caribbean, had to take into account increased public interest in the Cuban conflict, which was, as David Trask has suggested, "a phenomenon that rekindled the congenital American aversion to the lingering Spanish presence in the New World."[173]

Las Casas, who had long been used in the Black Legend of Spain, was reprinted in the context of tensions between Spain and the United States in the late 1890s. On July 24, 1898 the "Sunday Comic Weekly" in *The World*, a newspaper in New York, represented under two figures, "By Day" and "By Night," a circle of images of Spanish crimes. Under the title, "This is Spanish Honor (?)," the images show clockwise the sinking of The Maine in Havana harbor, "Killing surgeons operating on the wounded," "Wounded Spaniard murdering the officer who went to his aid," "Lying to the Spanish People," "Killing women and babes," "The Reconcentrados," and "Firing on the Red Cross." In the middle of the picture and amid these circular images is a Spaniard dressed in black staring out, a bloody dagger in his exaggerated teeth, his gnarled hands in the foreground. Below him, in large red letters, is the caption: "All Is Lost Save Honor" and below that in smaller black letters: "Spain's Sunset." In this image from the popular press a direct and emotional appeal is designed to move the reader to indignation and patriotism. This picture impugns the much-vaunted Spanish honor. This image shows a contemporary image of the cruelty of Spain that was part of propaganda in the United States, something it had inherited from England and later Britain.[174]

Considering the great economic, political and cultural changes between the 1490s and the 1890s that had occurred for the English-speaking people living in England and then in northern America, it is surprising how enduring this trope of the cruel Spaniard and the more ambivalent and contradictory uses of the example of Spain were. A century before, Columbus had been the visionary who helped to bring modernity and Enlightenment to the world, adopted by the new United States of America, as a symbol of its connections with, and break from, the Old World. Just a few years before, the United States had thrown a party for the world in the name of Columbus and the Columbian. This coming of age paradoxically showed the very power the United States used to take over the vestiges of the Spanish empire.

When the Portuguese pushed south along the western coast of Africa, it would have been hard to predict that the center of world power would really shift west to a land unknown to them. Although the vestiges of Hong Kong in 1997 and Macao in 1999 returned to China, the trace of European culture, politics and economics can still be felt in all parts of the globe, perhaps most of all in the great colony that became a reluctant empire—the United States. It was in the United States itself in which a debate occurred on whether it was an oxymoron to be an imperial democracy. The translation of empire takes unexpected turns.

Notes

Chapter 1

1. There are many books on empire and empires over the centuries. Here are a few of interest on the English/British empire over the past three centuries and more: R. B. [pseudonym Richard Burton for Nathaniel Crouch], *The English Empire in America: Or a Prospect of his Majesties Dominions in the West-Indies* (London: the Bell, 1685); John Oldmixon, *The British Empire in America, Containing the History of the Discovery, Settlement, Progress and Present State of all the British Colonies, on the Continent and Islands of America*, 2 volumes (London: John Nicholson, 1708); John Seeley's *The Expansion of England* (London: Macmillan, 1884); Achille Viallate, *La Crise Anglaise: Impérialisme et Protection* (Paris: Dujarric et Cie., 1905).
2. T. O. Lloyd, *The British Empire 1558–1995*, 2nd edition (Oxford: Oxford University Press, 1996; rpt. 2000), v.
3. One of the key related texts we studied in school, which took the sea as one of its main themes, was J. H. Parry, *The Establishment of the European Hegemony: 1415–1715: Trade and Exploration in the Age of the Renaissance*, 3rd edition revised (1949; New York: Harper & Row, 1966).
4. See Richard Koebner, *Empire* (Cambridge: Cambridge University Press, 1961), 2; my translations.
5. Koebner, *Empire* 2–3; the Latin quotation comes from *Auctor ad Herennium*, IV, 9, 13. The translation below is Koebner's; see 298n1 for chapter 3.
6. Koebner, ibid., 18.
7. Ibid., 19.
8. Ibid., 27.
9. Rather than repeat my work that includes discussions of analogy, I am listing a selection; see "Stephen Greenblatt's *Shakespearean Negotiations*," *Textual Practice* 5 (1991): 429–48; *Theater and World: The Problematics of Shakespeare's History* (Boston: Northeastern University Press, 1992); "The New Historicism: Taking History into Account," *ARIEL* 22 (1991): 93–107; "New Historical Shakespeare: Reading as Political Ventriloquy," *English* 42 (Autumn 1993): 193–219. Like other methods that rely to some extent on analogy and comparison, such as new historicism, mine has a few places that have some give and play.

10. See my *Representing the New World; English and French Uses of the Example of Spain* (New York and London: Palgrave, 2001) and *Columbus, Shakespeare and the Interpretation of the New World* (New York and London: Palgrave, 2002), the earlier books in this series on the New World.

11. Hutcheson Macaulay Posnett, *Comparative Literature* (1886: New York and London: Johnson, rpt. 1970), 73.

12. Ibid., 73.

13. For various and often opposing views of difference, see the essays *Explorations in Difference: Law, Culture and Politics*, ed. Jonathan Hart and Richard Bauman (Toronto: University of Toronto Press, 1996).

14. Posnett, *Comparative Literature*, 81.

15. *Comparative Literature in the Age of Multiculturalism*, ed. Charles Bernheimer (Baltimore: The Johns Hopkins University Press, 1995), 1–17, 21–48; see 45. There were many responses to this collection, itself a response. For instance, see the many essays on the state of comparative literature in the Review of Scholarship in the *Canadian Review of Comparative Literature/Revue Canadienne de Littérature Comparée* 23 (March 1996). In this volume one essay concentrates on the difference between the object of study and the problem of definition; see Douwe Fokkema, "Comparative Literature and Canon Formation," 51–66, esp. 51–53; see also his *Issues in General & Comparative Literature: Selected Essays* (Calcutta: Papyrus, 1987); an early bibliographical study that begins with a few books in the late eighteenth century but concentrates most on the nineteenth is Louis-P. Betz, *La Littérature Comparée: Essai Bibliographique, introduction par Joseph Texte, Deuxième Édition Augmentée, Publiée, Avec Un Index Méthodique, par Fernand Baldensperger* (1904; New York: Greenwood Press, 1969); a few examples of books on the topic of comparative literature over the past 35 years or so are Harry Levin, *Refractions: Essays in Comparative Literature* (New York: Oxford University Press, 1966); *Comparative Literature: Matter and Method* (Urbana: University of Illinois Press, 1969); Henry Gifford, *Comparative Literature: Concepts of Literature* (London: Routledge & Kegan Paul, 1969); Robert J. Clements, *Comparative Literature as Academic Discipline: A Statement of Principles, Praxis, Standards* (New York: The Modern Language Association of America, 1978)—he sees ancient roots to the comparing of national literatures (see p. 2); Claudio Guillén, *The Challenge of Comparative Literature*, trans. Cola Franzen (Spanish original, 1985; Cambridge, MA: Harvard University Press, 1993); Yves Chevrel, *Comparative Literature Today: Methods & Perspectives*, trans. Farida Elizabeth Dahab (French original, 1989; Kirksville, MO: The Thomas Jefferson University Press, 1995).

16. H. C. Gutteridge, *Comparative Law: An Introduction to the Comparative Method of Legal Study & Research*, 2nd edition (Cambridge: Cambridge University Press, 1949), 12–13; the first edition was published in 1946. For other suggestive discussions of comparative law and its method see O. Kahn-Freund, *Comparative Law as an Academic Subject* (Oxford: Clarendon Press, 1965), esp. 5; George E. Gloss, *Comparative Law* (Littleton, CO: Fred B. Rothman, 1979);

Rudolf B. Schlesinger, *Comparative Law* (New York: The Foundation Press, 1980), esp. 1–45; Jeffrey Seitzer, *Comparative History and Legal Theory* (Westport, Connecticut and London: Greenwood Press, 2001), esp. xiii–xviii; Andrew Harding and Esin Örücü, eds., *Comparative Law in the 21st Century* (London, the Hague, New York: Kluwer Academic Publishers, 2002), esp. vii–xiii.

17. Gutteridge, *Comparative Law*, 1; see Foukema in *CRCL* (March 1996), 51–66, for a related argument about comparative literature.

18. Jerome Hall, *Comparative Law and Social Theory* ([Baton Rouge]: Louisiana State University Press, 1963), 3.

19. See, e.g., Hall, 14–16.

20. Gabriel A. Almond, G. Bingham Powell, Jr. and Robert J. Mundt, *Comparative Politics: A Theoretical Framework* (New York: HarperCollins, 1993), 3. This work builds on the earlier text, Gabriel A. Almond and G. Bingham Powell, Jr., *Comparative Politics: A Developmental Approach* (Boston: Little, Brown and Company, 1966).

21. See, e.g., Mosche M. Czudnowski, *Comparing Political Behavior* (Beverly Hills: Sage Publications, 1976), 11.

22. See, e.g., Philip Burnham, "Pastoralism and the Comparative Method," *Comparative Anthropology*, Ladislav Holy, ed. (Oxford: Basil Blackwell, 1987), 165.

23. J. D. Y Peel, "History, Culture and the Comparative Method: A West African Puzzle," in Holy, ed., 89 here and below. For a view of comparative history as a timeline of "facts," see Wilhelm II [of Germany], *Comparative History, 1878–1914*, trans. F. Appleby Holt (1921; Toronto: Ryerson Press [n.d.]).

24. Peel, *History, Culture and the Comparative Method*, 89. See John Stuart Mill, *System of Logic* (1843; Toronto: University of Toronto Press, 1973), ch. 6.

25. Peel, 112.

26. Mark Hobart, "Summer Days and Salad Days: The Coming of Age of Anthropology," in Holy, ed., 44; see Ladislav Holy, "Introduction: Description, Generalization and Comparison: Two Paradigms," in Holy, ed., 15.

27. Holy, Introduction, 2.

28. Michael Herzfeld, *Anthropology: Theoretical Practice in Culture and Society* (Oxford: Blackwell, 2001), 5, see 1–20.

29. Talal Asad, "Afterword: From the History of Colonial Anthropology to the Anthropology of Western Hegemony," ed. George Stocking, *Colonial Situations: Essays on the Contextualization of Ethnographic Knowledge* (Madison: University of Wisconsin Press, 1991), 314, see 315–24; see Herzfeld, *Anthropology*, 73.

30. Herzfeld, *Anthropology*, 76. On "thick description," see Clifford Geertz, *Interpretation of Cultures: Selected Essays* (New York: Basic Books, 1973); see also Natalie Zemon Davis, *The Return of Martin Guerre* (Cambridge, MA: Harvard University Press, 1973) and Robert Darnton, *The Great Cat Massacre and Other Episodes in French History* (New York: Basic Books, 1984); for microhistory, see Carlo Ginzburg, *The Cheese and the Worms: The Cosmos*

of a Sixteenth-Century Miller (Baltimore: The Johns Hopkins University Press, 1980).

31. See, e.g., the notes in *The Voyage of Pedro Álvares Cabral to Brazil and India from Contemporary Documents and Narratives*, trans. with an intro. by William Brooks Greenlee, Second Series No. 81 (London: Hakluyt Society 1938 for 1937), 34–36, 41–42, 53–56. The translation of this anonymous narrative comes from *Paesi* that appears in Greenlee.

32. *De Nouo Orbe, Or The Historie of the west Indies, Contayning the actes and aduentures of the Spanyardes, whuch haue conquered and peopled those Countries, inriched with varietie of plesant re-lation of the manners, Ceremonies, Lawes, Gouernments, and Warres of the Indians* (London: Thomas Adams, 1612).

33. See James E. Lewis, Jr., *The American Union and the Problem of Neighborhood: The United States and the Collapse of the Spanish Empire, 1783–1829* (Chapel Hill: University of North Carolina Press, 1998). On the position of Spain in an earlier period, see James Muldoon, *The Americas in the Spanish World Order: The Justification for the Conquest in the Seventeenth Century* (Philadelphia: University of Pennsylvania Press, 1994).

Chapter 2

1. See Frances Gardiner Davenport, *European Treaties Bearing on the History of the United States and Its Dependencies to 1648* (4 vols. Washington, D.C., 1917), I, 1, 9–10.

2. Davenport, *European Treaties*, 1, 10–12, 34. For the treaty of 1479 and its ratification, see ibid., 36–41 (trans. 42–48).

3. See Felipe Fernández-Armesto, *Before Columbus: Exploration and Colonisation from the Mediterranean to the Atlantic 1229–1402* (Philadelphia: University of Pennsylvania Press, 1987), 248, 250–51. Columbus's desire for gold in the service of God was textual and practical, for such dreams were also fed in his reading of Polo. *The Four Voyages of Columbus*, trans. and ed. Cecil Jane (2 vols., London, 1930, 1933; rpt. New York, 1988), 2 vols. in 1 vol., I, 11 n. 3; II, 3 n. 4, 5. See also Jane's Introduction, II, lvii. Marcel Trudel, "New France, 1524–1713," *Dictionary of Canadian Biography*, gen. ed. George W. Brown, vol. 1, 1000–1700 (Toronto and Québec, 1966), I, 26; see also 27–37. Fernández-Armesto, *Before Columbus*, 5–6, 218. His book concentrates mainly on the expansion of Portugal, Genoa and Castile.

4. Bailey W. Diffie, "Christopher Columbus: a Genoese Who Made a 'Potuguese' Voyage for Spain," in Bailey W. Diffie and George D. Winius, *Foundations of the Portuguese Empire, 1415–1580* (Minneapolis: University of Minnesota Press, 1977), 167; see Samuel Eliot Morison, *Christopher Columbus, Mariner* (Boston: Little Brown, 1955) 6–10 and T. O. Marcondes de Souza, *O descobriemento da América* (1912; São Paolo: Editoria Brasiliense, 1944), 102–11. As I mentioned in chapter 2 of *Columbus, Shakespeare and the Interpretation of the New World* (New York and London: Palgrave, 2003), Cecil Jane takes a contrary view that Columbus was illiterate or barely literate; see note 3 of this chapter for a reference to Jane's edition of Columbus.

In 1552 João de Barros called Columbus "a good Latinist"; Barros, *Da Ásia*, Dec. I, bk. 3, chap. 11 (1552; Lisbon, 1777–88), 24 vols.; see Diffie 171 who discusses this and other aspects of Barros). Diffie does not think that Columbus made a voyage to Bristol in 1477 and thence to Iceland (167).

5. Barros, *Ásia*, Dec. I, bk. 3, chap. 11, in Diffie, 169.
6. William D. Phillips, Jr., and Carla Rahn Phillips, *The Worlds of Christopher Columbus* (Cambridge: Cambridge University Press, 1992), 110–24.
7. Diffie, 171. Diffie also calls attention to the representatives of the Spanish view that Portuguese had in practice benefited from the Treaty of Alcáçovas, which had constrained Spain in the Indies.
8. Ibid., 171–72.
9. A. J. R. Russell-Wood, *The Portuguese Empire, 1415–1808: A World on the Move* (1992; Baltimore: Johns Hopkins University Press, 1998), 9. See A. H. de Oliveira Marques, *History of Portugal. Vol. 1. From Lusitania to Empire* (New York: Columbia University Press, 1972) and Bailey W. Diffie and George D. Winius, *Foundations of the Portuguese Empire, 1415–1580* (Minneapolis: University of Minnesota Press, 1977).
10. Russell-Wood, 9.
11. The bull *Romanus pontifex*, January 8, 1455, in Davenport, *European Treaties*, 21.
12. All the bulls and treaties mentioned here, as well as other documents, can be found in Davenport, *European Treaties*. Ibid., 77–78. Quotations of over seven lines in the notes will be indented.
13. This is Green's legal view in L. C. Green and Olive P. Dickason, *The Law of Nations and the New World* (Edmonton: University of Alberta Press, 1989), 7. This book provides a good discussion of the bulls and of the legal aspects of the colonization of the Americas; see esp. 4–6.
14. Whereas Biggar thinks the dispatch was the first from Raimondo di Soncino to the duke of Milan, Williamson provides convincing evidence that if the date is correct, it would have to be from someone else because the ambassador was still at Dover on August 24. Dispatch to the duke of Milan, August 24, 1497 in H. P. Biggar, *The Precursors of Jacques Cartier, 1497–1534* (Ottawa: Government Printing Bureau, 1911), Biggar, 15 (translation 15–16), translation also in J. A. Williamson, *The Cabot Voyages and Bristol Discovery Under Henry VII*, Hakluyt Society, 2nd series, no. 120 (Cambridge: Cambridge University Press, 1962), 29–30; and in *Calendar of State Papers, Milan*, vol. 1, ed. Allen B. Hinds (London, 1912), no. 535.
15. Raimondo de Soncino to the duke of Milan, December 18, 1497 in Biggar, *Precursors*, 17 (translation 19). A less grandiose translation appears in Hinds and Williamson: "Having observed that the sovereigns first of Portugal and then of Spain had occupied unknown islands, he decided to make a similar acquisition for his Majesty," in *Calendar*, ed. A. B. Hinds, I, no. 552; for reproduction of the English translation in Hinds, see Williamson, *Voyages*, 30–32.
16. Russell-Wood, 10.
17. Ibid., 11.

18. Francisco Alvares, *Do Preste Joam das indias. Verdadera informa* (Lisbon, 1540); Samuel Purchas included in his work, *Hakluytus Posthumous or Purchas His Pilgrimes*, Hakluyt Society extra series (Glasgow: James MacLehose & Sons, 1905–07), vol. 7: ch. 7; see Russell-Wood, 10–11.

19. Russell-Wood, 14, 18.

20. Ibid., 14–15, 18

21. Ibid., 16; see Duarte Pacheco Pereira's, *Esmeraldo de Situ Orbis*, trans. and ed. George H. T. Kimble, 2nd series, vol. 79 (London: Hakluyt Society, 1937).

22. Russell-Wood, 20, 209–10.

23. A. Da Silva Rego, *Portuguese Colonization in the Sixteenth Century: A Study of The Royal Ordinances (Regimentos)* (Johannesburg: Witwatersrand University Press, 1965), 2–8, 13–14.

24. Pereira, 63–64; also quoted more fully and discussed in Rego, 13–14.

25. Rego, 16–18.

26. Ibid., 20. In another context, see my discussion of this treaty (also spelt Tordesillas) in *Representing the New World* (New York and London: Palgrave, 2001), 20, 25, 27.

27. Rego, 9.

28. *Alguns Documentos do Archivo Nacional da Torre do Tombo*, 108–21, quoted in Rego, 31; see 32–33.

29. *The Voyage of Pedro Álvares Cabral to Brazil and India from Contemporary Documents and Narratives*, trans. with an intro. by William Brooks Greenlee, Second Series No. 81 (London: Hakluyt Society 1938 for 1937), xxxvii.

30. Greenlee, Introduction to *Cabral*, xxxv–xxxix.

31. "Letter of by Pedro Vaz de Caminha to King Manuel Written from Porto Seguro of Vera Cruz The Ist of May 1500," in Greenlee, ed., 3–33. Elsewhere I have written about Gonneville, the Norman explorer of Brazil, and so will not do so here in connection with the focus on Brazil in this chapter. See my *Representing the New World*, 27–31.

32. Caminha in Greenlee, ed., 5.

33. Caminha, 7 and 7n2.

34. Ibid., 8.

35. Ibid., 9.

36. Ibid., 10–11.

37. I discuss speech and signs with regard to Columbus in a volume once called "By Speech or Signs," a quotation from Columbus, which still provides the epigraph for the book, and now entitled (using the original subtitle)— *Columbus, Shakespeare and the Interpretation of the New World*.

38. Caminha, 12.

39. Ibid., 13.

40. Ibid., 13.

41. Ibid., 15.

42. Colin Heywood, *A History of Childhood: Children and Childhood in the West from Medieval to Modern Times* (Cambridge: Polity, 2001), 170.

43. Arnold Van Gennep, *Manuel de folklore français contemporain*, vol. 1 (Paris: Picard, 1972), 166–67; see Heywood, 37–38, 103–04. On sexuality in children

and youths, see André Burgière, "Repression and Change in the Sexual Life of Young People in Medieval and Early Modern Times," *Journal of Family History* 2 (1977), 196–210 and Stephen Kern, "Freud and the Discovery of Child Sexuality," *History of Childhood Quarterly* 1 (1973), 117–41. On the varying definitions of what constituted a legal minor across times, class, nations, roles and cultures, see Jerome Kroll, "The Concept of Childhood in the Middle Ages," *Journal of the History of Behavioural Sciences* 13 (1977), 388, see 384–93. On childhood, see Danièle Alexandre-Bidon and Didier Lett, *Les Enfants au Moyen Ages: Ve-Xve siècles* (Paris: Hachette, 1997), Philippe Ariès, *Centuries of Childhood*, trans. Robert Baldick (London: Pimlico, 1996); Egle Becchi and Dominique Julia, eds., *Histoire de l'enfance en Occident* (Paris: Editions du Seuil, 1996); Hugh Cunningham, *Children and Childhood in Western Society since 1500* (London: Longman, 1995); Jean-Louis Flandrin, *Families in Former Times: Kinship, Household and Sexuality*, trans. Richard Southern (Cambridge: Cambridge University Press, 1979); Pierre Riché and Danièle Alexandre-Bidon, *L'Enfance au Moyen Age* (Paris: Editions du Seuil, 1994); Lawrence Stone, *The Family, Sex and Marriage in England, 1500–1800* (London: Weidenfeld and Nicolson, 1977); and Keith Thomas, "Children in Early Modern England," in *Children and Their Books: A Celebration of the Work of Iona and Peter Opie*, ed. Gillian Avery and Julia Briggs (Oxford: Clarendon Press, 1989), 45–77.

44. Caminha, 15.
45. Ibid., 16.
46. Ibid., 16.
47. Ibid., 16.
48. Ibid., 16.
49. Ibid., 16.
50. Ibid., 17 and 17n1.
51. Ibid., 17.
52. Ibid., 19. A key phrase in the original that I have partly paraphrased here is "e preguntou asy a todos se nos parecia seer bem mandar a nova do achamento d esta terra a Vosa Alteza pelo navjo dos mantijmentos"; *Alguns Documentos do Archivo Nacional da Torre do Tombo* (Lisbon, 1892), 113; see Caminha, 19n1.
53. This matter of kidnapping and hostage taking, which I touch on here and later, I discuss briefly in *Representing the New World*, to some extent in "Mediation in the Exchange Between Europeans and Native Americans in the Early Modern Period," special issue, *CRCL/RCLC* 22 (1995), 319–43, and, in more detail, in the chapter, "Between Cultures," in *Columbus, Shakespeare and the Interpretation of the New World*.
54. Caminha, 19.
55. Ibid., 20.
56. Ibid., 20–21.
57. Ibid., 22.
58. Ibid., 23. The Portuguese is from the original manuscript and a transcription appear in Jaime Cortes ão, ed., "*A Carta De Pero Vaz De Caminha* (Rio de Janeiro: Livros de Janiero, 1943), Fol. 7v. and Fol. 8. The translation "timid" for "esqujvos" does not convey the sense of someone who is firm in

not wanting to be approached. "Standoffish" would be better. The phrase "como monteses" might imply "wild" but is really someone or some beast that climbs or lives in the mountains and "em alguûa parte amansasem" suggests more or less tamed. My thanks to Magali Sperling for her advice on the Portugese. In checking the original manuscript and a transmission, I am using the original spelling. The manuscript states: "pareçeme jemte de tal jnoçenta que se os homē emtendese e eles anos. que seriam logo xpaãos por que eles nõ teem nem emtendem em nhuña creemça segº pareçe" (Cortesão, ed., *A Carta*, Fol. 11). For the convenience of the reader, I have been using the Greenlee translation. This passage I translate as "It appears to me that these people are of such innocence that if we could comprehend them and they us, then they would soon be Christians because they neither understood nor have any belief, so it appears."

59. Ibid., 24.
60. Ibid., 26.
61. Ibid., 28.
62. Ibid., 29.
63. See *Alguns Documentos do Archivo Nacional* (Lisbon, 1892), 108–21. This text, like that of Columbus and a good number of early modern texts, has problems with provenance and transmission. In this case there may be fewer difficulties with attribution and provenance than with the Columbus texts or the letter of July 29, 1501 from King Manuel to Ferdinand and Isabella. That is one reason, as well as the emphasis on accounts written on voyages or stays, that I have chosen to discuss in some detail the Caminha text rather than the king's letter. On texts and editing, see the last book in my series, *Columbus, Shakespeare and the Interpretation of the New World*.
64. Caminha, 29.
65. Ibid., 29.
66. Ibid., 30. On comparative matters of possession, see Patricia Seed, *Ceremonies of Possession in Europe's Conquest of the New World, 1492–1640* (Cambridge: Cambridge University Press, 1995) and Jonathan Hart, "Rediscovering Alternative Critique of Europe in the New World," *Bulletin of Hispanic Studies* (Liverpool) 76: 4 (October 1999), 533–541.
67. Caminha, 30.
68. Ibid., 31.
69. Ibid., 31.
70. Ibid., 31.
71. Ibid., 31.
72. Ibid., 31–32.
73. Ibid., 32.
74. Ibid., 32.
75. Ibid., 33.
76. See, e.g., the notes in Greenlee's edition, 34–36, 41–42, 53–56. The translation of this anonymous narrative comes from *Paesi* that appears in Greenlee.
77. "The Anonymous Narrative," *The Voyage of Pedro Álvares Cabral to Brazil and India from Contemporary Documents and Narratives*, trans. with an intro. by

William Brooks Greenlee, Second Series No. 81 (London: Hakluyt Society, 1938 for 1937), 58. In *Paesi* this work has the title, *Navigatione de Lisbona a Callichut, de lengua Portogallese in taliana* and in the Contarini MS it appears as *Copia del viazo de lisbona a Cholocut de lengua portogalesse in lengua taliana.*

78. Anonymous, 58. The original title of my last book, *By Speech or Signs*, was dropped and the subtitle was left as the title: *Columbus, Shakespeare and the Interpretation of the New World*, because the distributor thought readers could not read its signs.
79. Anonymous, 60.
80. Ibid., 68, see 60–67.
81. Ibid., 68–69.
82. Ibid., 71.
83. Ibid., 72–73.
84. Ibid., 73.
85. Ibid., 76.
86. Greenlee, Introduction, xliii.
87. *Anonymous*, 79.
88. Ibid., 79.
89. Ibid., 79.
90. Ibid., 80.
91. Ibid., 81.
92. Ibid., 82, see 81n3.
93. Ibid., 82.
94. Ibid., 82.
95. Ibid., 84.
96. Ibid., 84–85.
97. Ibid., 85.
98. Ibid., 86.
99. Ibid., 86.
100. Ibid., 87.
101. Ibid., 87n3 on 88. See November 20, 23 and December 20, 1513, *Cartas de Albuquerque*, 3: 73–74.
102. *Anonymous*, 89.
103. Ibid., 89.
104. Ibid., 88 and 88n1.
105. In *Columbus, Shakespeare and the Interpretation of the New World*, I have discussed mediators or those between cultures extensively. These figures touch on ethnology, history and literature. There are a number of interesting scholars who have written on these liminal figures: James Axtell, Ross Chambers and Stephen Greenblatt, for instance, have made some suggestive contributions to the theoretical and historical aspects of this topic.
106. See Anonymous, 90 n1.
107. Ibid., 90–94.
108. Greenlee, 114–16 for this discussion and later. This letter exists in various versions, including that printed in *Paesi*, and manuscript copies are in the

Marciana Library, Venice, in *Viaggiatori antichi* (MS. Ital. Cl. 6, No. 208) and in Codex Contraini A (6.277); in the Museo Civico, Venice, manuscript; in the diaries of Marino Sanuto and Girolamo Priuli. Greenlee's translation is made from the text given in *Paesi* (Book 6, ch. 125) and compared with that in the Marciana codex and the texts of Marino Sanuto and Rinaldo Fulin. I have stuck with Greenlee's translation owing to its availability in keeping with the textual premises of *Comparing Empires*, which sometimes differs in degree with earlier volumes in my series on the New World. As with many medieval and early modern documents, the textual history is complex and an authoritative version is difficult if impossible to establish.

109. Greenlee, 116–18.
110. D. Cretico, letter of June 27, 1501, in Greenlee, 120.
111. Cretico, 120–21.
112. Cretico, 121.
113. Cretico, 121.
114. Cretico, 121, see 121n4.
115. Letter of Giovanni Francesco de Affaitadi to Domenico Pisani, June 26, 1501, in Greenlee, 125, see 124, 126 and 125n2–5; see Sanuto, *I Diarii*, vol. 4, cols. 66–67.
116. Affaitadi to Pisani, June 26, 1501, in Greenlee, 126.
117. Greenlee, xliin1, 126n3–4.
118. Affaitadi to Pisani, 126–27.
119. Ibid., 127.
120. Ibid., 127.
121. Ibid., 128.
122. Ibid., 128.
123. Ibid., 128–29.
124. Letter of Angelo Trevisan to Domenico Malipiero, December 3, 1501, in Greenlee, 124, see 124n1. Owing to this statement, some attribute the anonymous narrative on Cabral's voyage, discussed above, to Il Cretico.
125. Lorenzo Pasqualigo to his Brothers at Venice, August 23, 1497, in Biggar, *Precursors*, 13 (translation 14); the translation of this letter is also found in James A. Williamson, *The Voyages of the Cabots and the Discovery of North America under Henry VII and Henry VIII* (London, 1929), 29. Whereas Biggar thinks the dispatch was the first from Raimondo di Soncino to the duke of Milan, Williamson provided convincing evidence that if the date is correct, it would have to be from someone else because the ambassador was still in Dover on August 24. Dispatch to the Duke of Milan, August 24, 1497, in Biggar, *Precursors*, 15 (translation 15–16), translation also in Williamson, *Voyages*, 29–30; and in *Calendar of State Papers, Milan*, vol. 1, ed. Allen B. Hinds (London, 1912), no. 535. Raimondo de Soncino to the Duke of Milan, December 18, 1497, in H. P. Biggar, *The Precursors of Jacques Cartier 1497–1534* (Ottawa: Government Printing Bureau, 1911), 17 (translation 19). A less grandiose translation appears in *Calendar of*

State Papers, Milan, vol. 1, ed. Allen B. Hinds (London, 1912), no. 552; for reproduction of the English translation in Hinds, see Williamson, 30–32. Raimondo di Soncino to the Duke of Milan, December 18, 1497, in *Precursors*, 17 (translation 21); for another translation, see De Socino in *Calendar*, ed. Hinds, I, no. 552; and in Williamson, *Voyages*, 30–32. Cabot claimed the New World with a banner of St. Mark (Venice) and another for England. On this point, see Jeffrey Knapp, *An Empire Nowhere: England, America, and Literature from Utopia to The Tempest* (Berkeley: University of California Press, 1992), 28.

126. Girolamo Priuli, Diary, 1501—July, in Greenlee, 131–32; for the originals, see *Archivio Veneto*, vol. 28, part 1; or Rinaldo Fulin, *Diarii e diaristi Veneziani* (Venice, 1881), 155–64 for here and later.
127. Priuli in Greenlee, 132.
128. Ibid., 132.
129. Ibid., 132.
130. Ibid., 132–33.
131. Ibid., 133.
132. Ibid., 133–34.
133. Ibid., 134.
134. Ibid., 134–35.
135. Ibid., 135.
136. Ibid., 136.
137. Ibid., 136–37.
138. Ibid., 137–38.
139. Ibid., 138.
140. Sanuto in Greenlee, 139, see 138 and Marino Sanuto, *I Diarii*, ed. Rinaldó Fulin and Nicolò Barozzi (Venice, 1880), vol. 3, cols. 1593–95.
141. Sanuto in Greenlee, 141, see *Diarii*, vol. 4, col. 485.
142. Greenlee, 145–47. See Giuseppe Conestrini, "Relazioni commerciali di Fiorentini co' Portoghesi" in *Arch. Stor. Ital.*, 1846, appendix 3; Angelo de Gubernatis, *Storia dei viaggiatori italiani* (Leghorn, 1875), Francisco M. C. Ficalho, *Viagen de Pedro da Covilhan* (Lisbon, 1898).
143. Bartolomeo Marchioni, Letter to Florence, June 27, 1501, in Greenlee, 147.
144. Ibid., 147.
145. Ibid., 147–48.
146. Ibid., 148.
147. Ibid., 148.
148. Bartolomeo Marchioni, Letter to Florence, July, 1501, in Greenlee, 149.
149. Ibid., 150, see 149.
150. Greenlee, 151–53.
151. Amerigo Vespucci, Letter to Lorenzo de' Medici, Beseguiche, June 4, 1501, in Greenlee, 154; see 153; no original is known to be extant; the first copy, which dates before 1514, is found in the Riccardiana Library (MS. 1910), was first published in Baldelii Boni, *Il Milione di Marco Polo* (1827), vol. 1

and was reprinted in Francisco Adolpho de Varnhagen, *Amerígo Vespucci. Son caractère, ses écrits* (Lima, 1865), 78–82.

152. Vespucci, 155.
153. Ibid., 156–60.
154. Ibid., 161.
155. Ibid., 161.
156. Jean de Léry, *History of a Voyage to the Land of Brazil*, trans. and introduction by Janet Whatley (Berkeley: University of California Press, 1990), 4.
157. Max Savelle with the assistance of Margaret Anne Fisher, *The Origins of American Diplomacy: The International History of Angloamerica, 1492–1763* (New York: Macmillan, 1967), 17.
158. Ibid., 19–21.
159. André Thevet, *La Cosmographie vniverselle*, vol. 2, book 1, cap. 11, f. 498 verso; see A. C. de C. M. Saunders, *A Social History of Black Slaves and Freedmen in Portugal 1441–1555* (Cambridge: Cambridge University Press, 1982), 11–12, 33.
160. Léry, 9.
161. Savelle, 21.
162. Savelle, 21–22. See Frances Gardiner Davenport, *European Treaties Bearing on the History of the United States and its Dependencies to 1648* (Washington, D.C., Carnegie Institution of Washington, 1917): I: 213.
163. Léry, *History*, 12. Although I have consulted many of the French editions, I refer here to Jean de Léry, *Histoire D'Vn Voyage Fait En La Terre Dv Bresil, Autrement dite Amerique* ([Geneva]: Eustache Vignon, 1594), 17. This is a reprint of the 1580 edition on which Whatley bases her translation.
164. Léry, *History*, 13.
165. Ibid., 25–26.
166. Ibid., 28.
167. Ibid., 112.
168. Ibid., 76.
169. Ibid., 76.
170. Ibid., 171.
171. Ibid., 32, 51.
172. Ibid., 52–53.
173. Ibid., 59.
174. Ibid., 59.
175. Ibid., 86.
176. Ibid., 72. I have modified Whatley's translation, changing "presently" to "at present." For "Americans" Léry uses "Ameriquains" in the original French; see Léry, *Histoire* (1594), 135 and *History* (Whatley trans.), 80.
177. Léry, *History*, 106.
178. Ibid., 106–07.
179. Ibid., 130.
180. Ibid., 131.
181. Ibid., 131.
182. Ibid., 131.

183. Ibid., 131.
184. Ibid., 131–32.
185. H. V. Livermore, "Portuguese History," *Portugal and Brazil: An Introduction*, ed. H. V. Livermore (Oxford: The Clarendon Press, 1953), 50–54.
186. Livermore, 55–62 here and later.
187. Vitorino Magalhães Godinho, *Ensaios*, vol. 2 (Lisbon: Sá da Costa, 1968) and A. H. Oliveira Marques, *History of Portugal, Volume 1: From Lusitania to Empire* (New York: Columbia University Press, 1972), 306–22.
188. Livermore, 62–64.
189. For a discussion of law and the European settlement of the New World, see Green and Dickason. My thanks to my research assistant, Len Falkenstein, for his bibliographical work on Hakluyt for this chapter. For an earlier version of this discussion, see my "Portugal and the Making of the English Empire: the Case of Richard Hakluyt the Younger," *Literatura de Viagen* (Lisboa: Cosmos, 1997), 155–68.
190. Geoffrey Bullough, introduction, 10–11.
191. A. H. Oliveira Marques, *History of Portugal*, I: 302. For a useful and lively general and popular account of the censorship and the difficult career of Camões, see John Dos Passos, *The Portugal Story: Three Centuries of Exploration and Discovery* (1969; London: Robert Hale & Company, 1970), 344–51.
192. Dos Passos, 344, 348.
193. Marques, I: 309.
194. Bullough, 14, 17.
195. Ibid., 13.
196. David Beers Quinn, *England and the Discovery of America, 1481–1620* (New York: Alfred A. Knopf, 1974), 51–52.
197. Ibid., 57.
198. Ibid., 58.
199. Ibid., 60.
200. Ibid., 68.
201. Ibid., 68–69.
202. Ibid., 82.
203. Quoted in *ibid.*, 9; see *Calendar of State Papers, Spanish, 1485–1509* (London, 1862), 177; H. P. Biggar, *The Precursors of Jacques Cartier, 1497–1534* (Ottawa, 1911), 27–29; J. A. Williamson, *The Cabot Voyages and Bristol Discovery Under Henry VII*, Hakluyt Society, 2nd series, no. 120 (Cambridge, 1962), 228–29.
204. Quinn, 10.
205. Ibid., 11–14.
206. Ibid., 15, see Williamson, 216.
207. Quinn, 15.
208. For instance, I would like to sketch out briefly the Western tradition or trope of the *translatio imperii*, or the translation of empire. In the search for continuity and identity and as a result of an anxiety over the relation of

past, present and future, historians from classical times to the eighteenth century and beyond have used allegory, prefiguration and typology. While portraying themselves as heirs to the Greek empire, the Romans were anxious to differentiate themselves from their predecessors. Although Rome enlisted Greek culture, it also distanced itself from that influence. Aeneas was a Trojan who escaped the Greek destruction of his city, but Romulus and Remus were also founders in the Roman mythological universe. Jordanes found a Scythian origin for the Goths and connected them with the Roman empire, while the *Chronicle of Fredegar* gave a Trojan ancestry to the Franks. In the integration of the Germans into the classical world, it was difficult to maintain "eternal Rome," so that the Divine Providence of Christianity became a way to represent continuity, stability and meaning in history. But translating new peoples into Latin historiography persisted. Whereas Richer called the Norman Richard I the *dux pyratorum* (the duke of pirates), Dudo, his contemporary, gave the Normans Trojan ancestry. About three centuries later, in *Les Grandes Chroniques de France*, France was also given a Trojan origin. Many English chroniclers of the Middle Ages adopted the *Brut*, which traced the English past to Brutus of Troy in a translation and adaptation of a French narrative. This Trojan myth that was modified and translated from the Romans to various later European nations shows the desire for continuity and the building of a national narrative. Narratives about nations change over time, and the great tension, long before the modern era, was between the translation of empire and the discovery of unique origins for a great nation. Robert Gaguin (1433–1501), who wanted to draw on the work of Italian humanists of the 1480s and 1490s to write a humanist history of France but could find no sponsors, expressed doubts over the Trojan origin of the French, doubts that Paolo Emilio, a humanist from Verona, made more explicitly. Emilio said the Franks were German. Soon the French looked to the Gauls for their origins. Geoffrey of Monmouth had ignored the Anglo-Norman claims to England and focused on the Celts, whereas, later, in *Britannia* William Camden did not take seriously the Trojan origin of the English and instead celebrated the Roman heritage of England.

My contention is that the European contact with America soon revealed that this translation of empire and this assimilation of new peoples into a successor to the Greek and Roman empires would be a difficult if not new balancing act. The Amerindians represented new peoples whom the Europeans knew nothing about. Even though the American experience was novel, many of the Europeans tried, for obvious reasons, to fit the Amerindians and their lands into the framework of European experience. I have talked about Columbus elsewhere, and so much has been said about Columbus to mark the five hundredth year since he first saw the new lands to the west, that I shall move on to other figures. In 1519 Charles of Spain became Emperor Charles the Fifth of the Holy Roman Empire. In 1521 Magellan's voyage around the globe uncovered a world of diverse peoples that the classical chronicler, Eusebius (ca. 263–339), and his successors did not know. Still the idea of a universal Spanish monarchy persisted into the 1700s, a rule in which universal meant European. The universality of the past was not the same as the universality of the future, and this was a problem that the Spanish and Europeans generally had a hard time facing. Peter Martyr (ca. 1455–1526), an Italian humanist, wondered whether the Amerindians were inhabitants of the Golden Age who had escaped corruption as their land had long ago been severed from Europe. Gonzalo Fernández de Oviedo wrote his universal history with an understanding of "empire" in its traditional Mediterranean and Western European meaning and spoke of Charles as being part of a direct line of emperors from Caesar. But Oviedo and colonial administrators and missionaries came to see that the Amerindians had their own traditions. See Ernst Breisach, *Historiography: Ancient, Medieval & Modern* (Chicago: University of Chicago Press, 1983), 178–79. Throughout I draw heavily on his references to the translation of empire.

The debate between Bartolomé de Las Casas and Juan Ginés de Sepúlveda over the treatment of the Amerindians represented two ways of incorporating America into European history. Las Casas saw the contact as fulfiling Christian universal history in the conversion of the Indians, who were human and had souls to be saved. Sepúlveda argued for the growth of the Spanish monarchy and empire and did not consider important the conversion of the Indians, whom he thought were not completely human. See Anthony Pagden, *The Fall of Natural Man: The American Indian and the Origins of Comparative Ethnography* (Cambridge: Cambridge University Press, 1982, rev. 1986), 10, see 11–26; see also Jonathan Hart "Images of the Native in Renaissance Encounter Narratives," *ARIEL* 25 (October 1994), 55–76. This topic also appeared in my lecture, "Some Theoretical 'Dilemmas' in Post-Colonial Studies," Centre for Critical and Cultural Theory, University of Wales, Cardiff, January 31, 1994.

209. Loren E. Pennington, "The Amerindian in English Promotional Literature, 1575–1625," *The Western Enterprise: English Activities in Ireland, the Atlantic, and America 1480–1650*, ed. K. R. Andrews, N. P. Canny and P. E. H. Hair (Liverpool: Liverpool University Press, 1978), 179; see Hart, "Images", 55 f.
210. Pennington, 179–80.
211. M. M. S., *Spanish colonie*, sigs q2^r–qq^r cited in Pennington, 183.
212. Richard Hakluyt, *Virginia Richly Valued*, facsimile of 1609 edition (Ann Arbor: University Microfilms, 1966); see Anonymous foreword, *Virginia Richly Valued*, March of America Facsimile Series, No. 12 (Ann Arbor: University Microfilms, 1966), no pagination.
213. Richard Hakluyt, *Voyages: In Eight Volumes*, vol. 1. 1907 (London: Dent, 1967).
214. Pennington, 180–83.
215. See Walter Ralegh, *The discoverie of the large and bewtiful empire of Guiana*, ed. V. T. Harlow (London, 1928), 138–49, 71, see Pennington, 185–87.
216. Hakluyt, *Voyages*, 1: 2.

217. Ibid., 1: 6.
218. Ibid., 1: 7.
219. Ibid., 1: 7.
220. Ibid., 1: 9.
221. Ibid., 1: 12.
222. Ibid., 1: 15.
223. Ibid., 1: 20.
224. Ibid., 1: 22.
225. Ibid., 1: 22.
226. Ibid., 1: 23.
227. Ibid., 1: 42.
228. Ibid., 1: 43.
229. Ibid., 1: 44.
230. Ibid., 1: 44.
231. Ibid., 1: 47–50.
232. Ibid., 1: 49.
233. Anonymous foreword, *Virginia Richly Valued.*
234. I discussed this theme in "Some Theoretical 'Dilemmas' in Post-Colonial Studies," Centre for Critical and Cultural Theory, University of Wales, Cardiff, January 31,1994.
235. Anonymous foreword, *Virginia Richly Valued.*
236. Luís de Camões, *Os Lusiadas,* ed. Frank Pierce (Oxford: Clarendon Press, 1973). Canto X 143: 1–2; *The Lusiads,* trans. Richard Fanshawe, ed. Geoffrey Bullough (Carbondale: Southern Illinois University Press, 1963), 334.
237. Livermore, 64–66. See also P. E. Russell, *The English Intervention in Spain and Portugal in the Time of Edward III and Richard II* (Oxford: Oxford University Press, 1955).
238. *The Luciad, Or Portugalls Historicall Poem: Written In the Portingall Language By Lvis De Camoens; And Now newly put into English* By *Richard Fanshaw* Esq; *Horat. Dignum laude virum Musa vetat mori; Carmen amat quisquis, Carmine digna facit* (London: Humphrey Moseley, 1655). Taylor, 700–13 in Firestone Rare Books, Princeton University, Canto 1, Stanzas 8–18, Canto 10, Stanzas 145–56. For a fine recent edition, see *The Poems and Translations of Sir Richard Fanshawe,* ed. Peter Davidson, 2 volumes (Oxford: Clarendon Press, 1997–99).
239. Roger Walker, "General Note," in *The Poems,* ed. P. Davidson, 581.
240. Fanshawe uses this description of Portuguese in the first sentence of his dedication to the earl of Strafford; see *The Luciad,* trans. Fanshawe, 1655. On context, see Walker, 581–82; see also Madonna Letzring, "The Influence of Camões in English Literature," *Revista Camoniana* 1 (1964), 158–80. Roger M. Walker argues that Fanshawe knew Manuel de Faria e Sousa's *Lusiadas de Luis de Camoens, principe de los poetas de España* (Madrid, 1639), the Spanish scholarly edition in which a prose translation and notes and commentary follow each stanza in Portuguese [Walker, "Sir Richarde Fanshawe's *Luciad* and Manuel de Faria e Sousa's *Lusíadas*

Comentadas: New Documentary Evidence," *Portuguese Studies* 10 (1994), 44–64].

241. Gareth Alban Davies, "Sir Richard Fanshawe, Hispanist Cavalier," *University of Leeds Review* 20 (1977), 87–119 and Walker, 583.

242. *The Luciad*, trans. Fanshawe,1655, Firestone Rare Books, Princeton University, poem facing the title page.

243. Ibid., A2.

244. Ibid., A2 verso. The text calls attention to Hor. Lib. 3. Epist 2.

245. Ibid., A2 verso.

246. Ibid., A2 verso.

247. Ibid., A4. The authoritative and original Latin also appears on A3 verso:

> Orbem jam totum victor Romanus habebat:
> Qua mare, qua terræ, qua fidus currit utrumque:
> Nec satiatus erat. Gravidis freta pulsa carinis
> Jam peragrabantur. Siquis Sinus abditus ultra,
> Siqua foret tellus quæ fulvum mitteret aurum,
> Hostis erat: fatisque in tristia bella paratis
> Quærebantur opes.

248. Ibid., A4. The English translation of "Out of Satyr of Petronius Arbitrer, pag 48."

249. Jonathan Swift, *Gulliver's Travels*, ed. Philip Pinkus (Toronto: Macmillan, 1968), 126. I discuss Swift in more detail in *Columbus, Shakespeare and the New World*, ch. 2.

250. At length, I discuss Hakluyt and his representation of Spain, particularly in this text, in *Representing the New World*.

251. *The Luciad*, trans. Fanshawe, b2 verso.

252. Ibid., b2 verso.

253. Ibid., b2 verso.

254. Ibid., b3verso.

255. Ibid., b4 recto.

256. Ibid., b5 verso.

257. Ibid., B recto, Canto 1, Stanza 1.

258. Ibid., B recto.

259. Ibid., B verso.

260. Ibid., Canto 1, Stanza 8.

261. Ibid., Ee2.

262. Ibid., Canto 10, 92.

263. Ibid., Canto 10, 93.

264. Ibid., Canto 10, 146.

265. Ibid., Canto 10, 138.

266. Ibid., Canto 10, 140.

267. Ibid., Canto 10, 139.

268. Ibid., Canto 10, 150.

269. Ibid., Canto 10, 152.

270. Ibid., Canto 10, 154.

271. Ibid., Canto 10, 156.
272. Walker, "Commentary," 584–85. The Latin is "Testis adsit Poetarum Princeps Camoenus, qui licet patria Lusitanus, sermone tament perite admodum a te edoctus modulari Anglo\;" for a full text and translation, see Roger M. Walker and W. H. Liddell, "'Mercurius Anglus': Sir Richard Fanshawe's Reception as Ambassador in Lisbon," *Portuguese Studies* 6 (1990), 126–37. For Melo's sentiments, see Walker, 586 and for a full Spanish text, see Roger M. Walker, "A Rediscovered Seventeenth-Century Literary Friendship: Sir Richard Fanshawe and Dom Francisco Manuel de Melo," *The Seventeenth Century* 7 (1992), 15–25.
273. Walker, "Commentary," 587–89. The literary reception of Camões's epic, as Walker has noted, includes John Anderson's Memoirs of the *Life and Writings of Luis de Camoens* and Robert Southey's review of it in *The Quarterly Review* (volume 27, April 1822, 1–39).
274. C. R. Boxer, *The Portuguese Seaborne Empire 1415–1825* (1969; London: Carcenet, 1991), 105.
275. Boxer, 106–10.
276. Ibid., 113, see 111–12.
277. Ibid., 113–18
278. De Oliveira Marques, I: 329–33.
279. See Ibid., 120–27; in 1659, Governor General Johan Maetsuyker and his council at Batavia and, at the end of the seventeenth century, Pieter van Dam, stated such views in works prepared for the directors of the Dutch East India Company. For more on Brazil, see C. R. Boxer, *The Dutch in Brazil, 1624–1654* (Oxford: Clarendon Press, 1957).

Chapter 3

1. *De Nouo Orbe, Or The Historie of the west Indies, Contayning the actes and aduentures of the Spanyardes, whuch haue conquered and peopled those Countries, inriched with varietie of plesant re-lation of the manners, Ceremonies, Lawes, Gouernments, and Warres of the Indians* (London: Thomas Adams, 1612).
2. Ibid., B verso.
3. Ibid., B verso.
4. William Bradford, *Of Plymouth Plantation 1620–1647*, ed. Samuel Eliot Morison (New York: Knopf, 1952, rpt. 1991), 23, 23n1, 26n8. Morison, the editor of this edition, notes that the truce between Spain and the Netherlands, which began on March 30, 1609, was due to end in 1621, so that the Pilgrims, a small minority of the Pilgrim church in Leyden, left just before hostilities might resume; see ibid., 19n7.
5. Bradford, 25.
6. Ibid., 26.
7. Ibid., 27.
8. Ibid., 28.

9. Ibid., 28–29.
10. Ibid., 122.
11. Ibid., 122.
12. Ibid. here and later.
13. Ibid., 19. The Pilgrims and the English they deal with seem to trade in Spain (see ibid., 237n, 241n, 250). John Clarke, later one of the pilots on the Mayflower, had sailed to Virginia in 1610, and the following year had been taken back to Spain and imprisoned for four years after the English in Virginia had held some Spaniards who had come ashore (366n1).
14. Ibid., 345.
15. Ibid., 347 and 347n4.
16. "Appendix VI" in ibid., 378.
17. Ibid, 380.
18. Ibid., 380.
19. Philip P. Boucher, *Les Nouvelles Frances: France in America, 1500–1815: An Imperial Perspective* (Providence: John Carter Brown Library, 1989), 27.
20. Sagard said that America was named after Vespucci but reminded his reader that the honor was due to Columbus, who discovered the New World five years before. Gabriel Sagard, *Histoire dv Canada et voyages qve les freres mineurs Recollets y ont faicts pour la conuersion des Infidelles* (Paris, 1636), 627. Another example that raised expectations amongst the French were the riches of Peru. Sagard described it as perhaps having the richest deposit of gold and silver in the world as a means of talking about the Spanish possession of that country and the ransom King Atabaliba offered the Spaniards. This description might seem out of place in a history of Canada, but the reason for its presence becomes readily apparent. The anxiety Sagard anticipated in his readers was the inadequacy of New France beside the Spanish colonies. Ibid., 787. The success of Spanish Recollets, real and imagined, in conversion in America and the Far East became a model that the French amongst the Hurons in Canada sought to imitate.
21. On the torture of the Jesuits, Jean de Brébeuf and Gabriel Lalemant, and the acts of anthropophagy by the Iroquois in that instance, see Frank Lestringant, *Le Cannibale: Grandeur et décadence* (Paris: Perrin, 1994), 218–23. The cruelty was not always Spanish but could be Native. The complication is that such cruelty led to martyrdom in the view of the Catholic Church, which

involved an imitation of Christ. Another example of a discussion of the cruelty and barbarity of cannibalism occurred in the work of Claude d'Abbeville, someone, in Lestringant's view, that Léry influenced; see ibid., 208–11 and Claude d'Abbeville, *Histoire de la mission des Peres Capucins en l'Isle de Maragnan et terres circonvoysines* (Paris, 1614), 294–96 and Yves d'Evreux, *Suitte de l'Histoire des choses memorables advenues en Maragnan es annees 1613 et 1614* (Paris, 1615). D'Evreux was d'Abbeville's successor. More generally, see Charles Arpine, *Histoire generale de l'origine mineurs de S. François* (Paris, 1631), which looked at the Recollets from 1486 to 1606, and Philippe de Bethune, comte de Selles et de Charost, *Le Conseiller d'estat* (Paris? 1632), which in chapter 15, examined the Christianization of peoples of Brazil, Mexico and Peru.

22. From Huronia, Paul Le Jeune could write in 1637 about the success of turning the Paraquais from cruel cannibals to gentle lambs of God and of the good results of Portuguese conversions of the American Indians. Paul Le Jeune, "Le Jeune's Relation, 1637" (Rouen, 1638) in *The Jesuit Relations and Allied Documents*, ed. Reuben Gold Thwaites (73 vols., Cleveland, 1898), XII, 221.

23. Boucher, *Les Nouvelles*, 27.

24. Boucher, *Les Nouvelles*, 28. On Le Jeune, see Peter A. Goddard, "Christianization and Civilization in Seventeenth-Century French Colonial Thought" (unpublished D.Phil. dissertation, University of Oxford, 1990), 57–119; Rémi Ferland, "Procédés de rhétorique et fonction conative dans les Relations du Père Paul LeJeune" (unpublished Ph.D. dissertation, Université Laval, 1991); Yvon Le Bras, *L'Amérindien dans les Relations du Père Paul Le Jeune* and Pierre Dostie, *Le Lecteur suborné dans cinq textes missionaires de la Nouvelle-France*, 2 vols. in 1 vol. (Sainte-Foy, Québec: Éditions de la Huit, 1994); Dostie begins at 159. Ferland, who is interested in rhetoric and discourse analysis, examines Le Jeune's work in terms of one of Roman Jakobson's six inalienable factors of communication—"la fonction 'conative' "—or the orientation toward addressee to modify his comportment or opinion, the purest form of which occurs in the imperative or vocative; ibid., 4. Le Bras and Dostie are both interested in exploring the Amerindian as other in Le Jeune and various French missionaries like Gabriel Sagard and Louis Hennepin. Neither of these authors touches on the example of Spain

or any other topics concerning Spain. Apparently, from the first years of the existence of the Society of Jesus (founded in 1540 through a bull by Paul III, Ignatius Loyola, the Spanish founder of the Jesuits, encouraged his companions dispersed in Italy to write him regularly, so that he set a precedent for the whole notion of relations; Léon Pouliot, *Étude sur les Relations des jésuites de la Nouvelle-France (1632–72)* (Montréal, 1940), 3, cited in Le Bras, *L'Amérindien*, 15; see Ferland, "Procédés," 6.

25. Paul Le Jeune, "Le Jeune's Relation, 1637" (Rouen, 1638) in *The Jesuit Relations and Allied Documents*, ed. Reuben Gold Thwaites (73 vols., Cleveland, 1898), XII, 221.

26. Dominique Deslandres, "Le modèle français d'intégration socio-religieuse, 1660–1650. Missions intérieurs et premières missions Canadiennes" (unpublished Ph.D. dissertation, Université de Montréal, 1990), 247, 255–56.

27. Ibid., 16–24.

28. Sagard, "Av Lecteur," 12. All translations of Sagard in the notes are mine.

29. Ibid., 627.

30. Ibid., 629–30.

31. Ibid., 631.

32. Ibid., 632.

33. Sagard thought in 1632 that even the most successful Jesuit missions in New France, like the one in Ouendake or Huronia, "was very far away from the ten of million souls that our confrères have baptised ... the East and West Indies"; Gabriel Sagard, *Le Grand Voyage du Pays des Hurons*, ed. Réal Ouellet and Jack Warwick (Montréal: Les Presses de l'Université de Montréal, 1990), quoted and translated in Codignola, 215. On Sagard's view of the Natives, see Dickason, *Myth*, 78–79.

34. For a helpful discussion of the geographical and cultural contexts that shaped Spain before the emigration to the western Atlantic, see Ida Altman, "Spain in the Era of Exploration," *1492: An Ongoing Voyage*, ed. John R. Hébert (Washington: Library of Congress, 1992), 64–77.

35. Claude Charles Le Roy Bacqueville de la Potherie, "A Monseigneur Le Duc d'Orleans, Regent du Royaume" to *Histoire de L'Amerique Septentrionale* (Paris, 1722), ã recto- ã verso.

36. Ibid., ã recto- ã verso.

37. Benjamin Martyn, "Number 7," August 10, 1737, *An Account, Shewing the Progress of the Colony of Georgia in America, from its First Establishment* (London, 1741) in *Tracts and Other Papers, Origin, Settlement, and Progress of the Colonies in North America, from the Discovery of the Country to the Year 1776*, collected by Peter Force (4 vols., Washington, 1836–46), I, 50–51.

38. Ibid., I, 50–51.

39. Peter Burke, *Montaigne* (Oxford: Oxford University Press, 1981), 46. Burke aptly points out the temptation to describe someone like Montaigne as an anthropologist or as a precursor of social anthropology, but that it is also important to distinguish between the cultural context of the founding of that

172 Notes, pp. 89–95

discipline at the end of the nineteenth century and that of Montaigne's time. Ibid., 44.

40. Anonymous, *The British Sailor's Discovery: Or the Spaniards Pretensions Confuted* (London, 1739), 2–3.

41. Ibid., 2–3

42. Philip Boucher, *Les Nouvelles*, 22.

43. Ibid., 33. For an account of the expedition of 1643, see Paul Boyer, *Véritable relation de tout ce qui s'est fait et passé* (Paris, 1654).

44. For a description of the French war with the Iroquois, see Paul Le Jeune, *Relation de ce qui s'est passé en la Nouvelle France, es années 1640 et 1641* (Paris, 1642), ch. 11.

45. John Winthrop in Green and Dickason, *The Law of Nations* (Edmonton: University of Alberta Press, 1989), 235; the other term used is *vacuum domicilium.*

46. Ramsey, *The History* (1789), 3, cited in Pagden, *Lords*, 75.

47. Patricia Seed, *Ceremonies of Possession* (Cambridge: Cambridge University Press, 1995). For a discussion of the *Requerimento*, and the *encomiendas*, which were not feudatories like the lands granted in the French colonies or the quasi-independent occupation in English America, see Pagden, *Lords*, 91.

48. For a different view of Le Challeux and for a brief account of Gourges, see Boucher, *Les Nouvelles*, 13.

49. I use the words "in part" because in *Les trois mondes* (Paris, 1582) La Popelinière had helped to publicize Le Challeux's horrific description of the treatment of Ribault's severed head and to bring out Laudonnière's *L'Histoire notable de la Floride* (Paris, 1586); see Philip Boucher, *Les Nouvelles*, 14–15.

50. Samuel de Champlain, *Voyages de la Nouvelle France occidentale, dicte Canada* (Paris, 1632). The conflict occurred between Huguenots companies and Catholic missionaries; see Boucher, *Les Nouvelles*, 24.

51. Pierre Boucher, *Histoire veritable et natvrelle des moevrs et prodvctions dv pays de la Novvelle France, vvlgairement dite le Canada* (Paris, 1664).

52. Bacqueville, *Histoire*, ã ii recto.

53. See Boucher, *Les Nouvelles*, 38. See Jean Baptiste Du Tertre, *L'Histoire générale des isles de S. Christophe* (Paris, 1654) and *L'Histoire générale des Antilles* (Paris, 1667–71). On Du Tertre and representations of Natives, see Olive Dickason, *The Myth of the Savage* (Edmonton: University of Alberta Press, 1989), 79, 82. The Jesuits in New France, on the other hand, appealed for French soldiers to attack Iroquois villages; Boucher, *Les Nouvelles*, 41; see Jérôme Lallement, *Relation de ce qui s'est passé de plus remarquable* (Paris, 1661) and Paul Le Jeune, *Relation de ce qui s'est passé de plus remarquable* (Paris, 1662). Pierre Boucher was sent on a mission to see Louis XIV. See Pierre Boucher, "Epistre," *Histoire veritable.*

54. Marc Lescarbot, *L'Histoire de la Nouvelle France* (Paris 1609), quoted in Boucher, *Les Nouvelles*, 17. There were other calls for labor rather than living off the avails of the work of others. See, e.g., Antoine Joseph Le Febvre de la Barre, *La Description de la France équinoctale* (Paris, 1666).

55. John Smith, *New Englands Trials*, 2nd edition (London 1622) in *Tracts*, ed. Force, II, 23.

56. Justus Lipsius in Alejandro Ramírez, *Epistolario de Justo Lipsio y los Españoles* (Saint Louis: Washington University Press, 1966), 374, cited in J. H. Elliott, *Spain and Its World, 1500–1700* (New Haven: Yale University Press, 1989), 25.

57. Although they recognized this lag (the English and the French still revisiting earlier examples from Spain into the eighteenth century), Anthony Pagden and David Armitage do not emphasize it as much as I do. This lag or unevenness, and its pervasiveness, has been one of the surprises in these texts. There was, then, more of an archeology, where the layers of uses of the example of Spain occurred at different levels. Pagden recognizes an important aspect of this irony: in *Histoire et description générale de la Nouvelle France* (Paris, 1744) Pierre Charlevoix, a French Jesuit, wrote that the French, unlike the Spanish, had had no conquerors in America, and in 1784 the Spanish Jesuit exile, Juan Nuix, asked rhetorically whether other Europeans would have despised and abandoned the New World had it been given to them; see Anthony Pagden, *Lords of all the World: Ideologies of Empire in Spain, Britain and France c. 1500–c. 1800* (New Haven: Yale University Press, 1995), 86, see 72. One of the fascinating points that Pagden makes in his chapter "Conquest and Settlement" is that increasingly from the late seventeenth century onward the Spanish moved away from the earlier Spanish model of conquest; ibid., 71–73, 101–02.

58. *Les Voyages Dv Sievr De Champlain Xaintongeois, Capitaine ordinaire pou le Roy, en la marine* (Paris: Iean Berjon, 1613), ã ij, ãi ij. All translations of Champlain here and later are mine. The edition I consulted at Princeton has literary connections as it came from the collection of W. Beckford (1760–1844), author of "*Vathek*," and is the first edition of the first three voyages—1604, 1610, 1611. The fourth voyage of 1613 occurs first in this book. One of the interesting things about this literature of voyages, exploration and settlement, which is a key part of travel literature, is the comparative nature of writers, readers and collectors: they read and write outside their culture and there is an intertextuality and cross-cultural reach to the enterprise from its beginnings.

59. Ibid., ã ij verso.

60. Ibid.; the first page recto and verso of this poem, "AUX FRANCOIS," has no pagination and the next pages begin with ê. The fourth to sixth lines read: "*C'est ce monde nouueau don't l'Espagne rostie / Ialouse de mon los, seule se glorifie / Mon nom plus que le sien y doit estre planté.*" This "doit" also seems to imply something deserved.

61. Ibid.; see especially e iij recto, line 57f.

62. 1612 voyage, Livre Premier, chap. VI, in ibid., 53–55. The Princeton copy has the fourth voyage—"Qvatriesme Voyage Dv Sr De Champlain Capitaine Ordinaire Povr Le Roy En La Marine, Et Lieutenant de Monseigneur le Prince de Condé en la Nouuelle France, fait en l'annee 1613"—misbound, so that it comes before the main text rather than after it. The binder followed the rule of binding gathering—signed lower case before those signed in upper

case. The heading on p. 161 of this volume is a caption title and is not uncommon at this time. My thanks to Stephen Ferguson in Rare Books at Princeton for this explanation, and also for sending me to the following description: "1 unnumbered leaf and 50 (3–52) pages. The signature-marks begin with 'a.' This fourth voyage is not mentioned on the title, but is always found with this volume"; see *Catalogue of the John Carter Brown Library in Brown University, Providence, Rhode Island* (Providence: The Library, 1919–31), II: 93. The reader has to pay close attention to this situation or risk confusion over the chronology of events in Champlain's narratives.

63. *Voyages 1608–1612*, Livre Second, chap. III, in ibid., 177.

64. Ibid., chap. III, 184; see 183. This conspiracy has some affinities to the one in Bermuda that Strachey reports and that Shakespeare echoes in *The Tempest*.

65. Ibid., chap. III, 184.

66. 26 X^bre 1669, pp. 16 verso–17 recto; see 22 recto–verso; all these documents here and later in this section are from l'Archive d'Outre Mer in Aix-en-Provence, France. The translations are mine here and later.

67. M. de Baar, le 24 de feburier 1670, Martinique, 36 verso. "Souliers de corde": my thanks to Nicole Mallet for making additional suggestions concerning these shoes. She said that "the phrase right away evoked the 'espadrilles' to me, that is the special sort of sandals (canvas top and soles made of braided rope) made in Roussillon and worn in the South of France. I am sure you have seen them in stores in Cassis! Interestingly enough, here is what I found in "Le Dictionnaire universel" de Furetière (1690. Slatkine reprint 1970) at "CORDE" : 'On fait aussi des souliers de corde que les Espagnols nomment des 'Alpargates' et dont on fait grand trafic aux Indes.' " The effect of trade between the Spanish and the French, no matter how great the rivalry, also changed the dos, objects and culture of everyday life. The shipment of slaves is prominent in these documents.

68. M. d'Oregon, Memoire, "Auantages et utilités quon peut tirer de la Collonie de la Floride," la Floride 1669, no pagination, so I will refer to the document in the body of my main text in terms of the numbers of its articles. Some of these officials share similar concerns with Philippe Duplessis-Mornay, a Huguenot leader Richard Hakluyt the younger had known. See my *Contesting Empires: Promotion, Opposition, Slavery* (New York and London: Palgrave, forthcoming) for discussions of Duplessis-Mornay and of Hakluyt.

69. November 2, 1669, [1]; no pagination; the document has seven pages, so I will create my own numbers in square brackets. M. d'Oregon [one source has the name as Oregeon] was governor.

70. Ibid., [1].

71. Ibid., [2]. "Chasseurs de boeufs." I wish to thank Nicole Mallet for calling my attention to additional possibilities to certain key words in this passage, such as the instances in "*Le Dictionnaire Robert*" (7 volumes), there is "BOUCANIER": "se disait desaventuriers coureurs de bois de Saint-Domingue qui chassaient les boeufs sauvages pour en boucaner la viande." and "BOUCANER": "Faire sècher à la fumée." "Aller à la chasse aux boeufs sauvages pour en recueillir les peaux" (hides). Professor Mallet favors the idea

of catching these wild oxen to get their skins, a practice that when performed by the "aventuriers" did not exclude poaching.

72. Ibid., [5].
73. Ibid., [5].
74. Ibid., [6–7].
75. Monsieur de Louançay, February 28, 1678, [1–2]; this is a three-page document that is unpaginated.
76. Ibid., [3].
77. Ibid., [3].
78. De Louançay, January 9, 1679, [2]; this document is four pages without pagination.
79. Ibid., [2–4]. See the next Spanish document for the copy of the letter of the Spanish governor: the notation and title are in French, perhaps by the scribe.
80. "Coppie de la lettre de Monsieur le gouuerneur et president de la ville de St. domingue escrite A Monsieur de Louancay gouuerneur de la Tortue et Coste St. domingue," [1–2]; this two-page document is in Spanish, except for the title.
81. De Louançay, July 27, 1680, [1]; three-page unpaginated document.
82. Ibid., [1–3]. From the coast of St. Domingue, on September 25, 1682, De Louançay continued to discuss relations with Spain; see [3] in unpaginated document.
83. De Louançay, memorandum 1682, [5–6].
84. On October 18, 1685 Le Sieur de Cussy, from St. Domingue, [1–4]; four-page unpaginated document.
85. Don Alvero Romero [V]enegas to Le Sieur de Cussy, July 3, 1688, [1–2]; two-page document unpaginated. There is also a French translation, August 22, 1688, [1–3]; three-page document unnumbered.
86. Pierre François-Xavier Charlevoix, *Histoire et description générale de la Nouvelle-France avec le journal historique d'un voyage fait par ordre du Roi dans L'Amérique Septentrionale* (3 vols., Paris, 1744), I, 2, quoted in ibid., 86.
87. Charlevoix, I, iii–iv. On Charlevoix, see Bruce Trigger, "The Historian's Indian: Native-Americans in Canadian Historical Writing from Charlevoix to the Present," *Canadian Historical Review* 67 (1986), 315–42.
88. On settlement of the Caribbean by Norman and Breton nobles, see Boucher, *Les Nouvelles*, 37. The French population of Canada later referred to Wolfe's victory over Montcalm at Québec in 1759, which ultimately led to France ceding Canada to Britain, as "La Conquête" or the conquest.
89. See Alexandre Exquemelin's [Oexmelin] *Histoire des avanturiers* (3 vols., Paris, 1686).
90. Ibid., ã ij verso– ã iij recto; my translations here and later.
91. Ibid., ã iij recto.
92. Ibid., n.p. [page 2 verso of the preface].
93. Ibid., ê iiij recto.
94. Anonymous, "The Preface," *The Travels of Several Learned Missioners of the Society of Jesus, into Divers Parts of the Archipelago, India, China, and America* (London, 1714), A 4 verso.

95. Ibid., A 5 recto.
96. See ibid., 243–44, 252.
97. See ibid., 254–59.
98. See ibid., especially 284.
99. Joseph François Lafitau, *Mémoire… concernant le précieuse plante de Gin seng… concernant le précieuse plante de Gin seng de Tartarie* (Paris, 1718), 12–13.
100. Boucher, *Les Nouvelles*, 49–51.
101. *Loix et constitutions des colonies françoises*, ed. Médéric Louis Elie Moreau de Saint-Méry (Paris, 1784–90), (March 1685), 415, reproduced in ibid., 51; my translation.
102. Boucher, *Les Nouvelles*, 53.
103. Blaise François de Pagan, Comte de Merveilles, *Relation historique et géographique* (Paris, 1655); see also Boucher, *Les Nouvelles*, 37.
104. Blaise François de Pagan, *An Historical & Geographical Description of the Great Country & River of the Amazones in America*, trans. William Hamilton (London, 1661), A 3 recto.
105. Ibid., A 3 verso.
106. Ibid., A 3 verso.
107. Ibid., A 3 verso–A 4 verso.
108. Étienne Taillemite, Préface in Raymonde Litalien, *Les explorateurs de l'Amérique du Nord 1492–1795* (Sillery, Québec: Septenrion, 1993), 8; my translation here and later.
109. Ibid., 8.
110. Ibid., 8.

Chapter 4

1. Marco Polo, *The Travels of Marco Polo: The Complete Yule-Cordier Edition: Including the unabridged third edition (1903) of Henry Yule's annotated translation, as revised by Henri Cordier; together with Cordier's later volume of notes and addenda (120): In Two Volumes: Volume I: Containing the first volume of the 1903 edition* (New York: Dover Publications, 1992), 15–17; see Cordier's notes, volume 2: 109; Lyle N. McAlister, *Spain and Portugal in the New World 1492–1700* (Minneapolis: University of Minnesota Press, 1984), 41.
2. See my *Columbus, Shakespeare and the Interpretation of the New World* (New York and London: Palgrave, 2003). On Polo's portrait, see Henry Yule, introduction, in Polo I: 75–77.
3. Yule, introduction, in Polo I: 55–64, 80–104.
4. This account is indebted to McAlister, 42–45.
5. McAlister, 51–52.
6. Carter G. Woodson, "Attitudes of the Iberian Peninsula," *Journal of Negro History* 20 (1935), 202; Margaret T. Hogden, *Early Anthropology in the Sixteenth and Seventeenth Centuries* (Philadelphia: University of Pennsylvania Press, 1964); Winthrop D. Jordan, *White Over Black: American*

Attitudes toward the Negro, 1550–1812 (Chapel Hill, NC: University of North Carolina Press, 1968); McAlister, 54–55.

7. For a more detailed discussion, see my *Representing the New World: English and French Uses of the Example of Spain* (New York and London: Palgrave, 2001), 15–48.

8. Pope Alexander VI, *Copia dela bula dela concession* (Logroño [1511]).

9. See, e.g., Abraham ben Samuel Zacuto, *Almanach perpetuum exactissime nuper emendatum* (Venice, 1502).

10. Amerigo Vespucci, *Van de nieuwer werelt oft landtscap nieuwelicx gheounden* (Antwerp, 1508).

11. Benedetto Bordone, *Isolario di Benedetto Bordone nel qual si ragiona di tutte l'isole del mondo* (Venice, 1534). For an early account of the settlement of Madeira, the Canaries, the Azores and Cape Verde, see Edgar Prestage, *The Portuguese Pioneers* (London: Adam & Charles Black, 1933; rpt. 1966), 35–75.

12. Hans Staden, *Warhaftige Historia und Beschreibung einer Landtschaft der wilden nacketen grimmigen Menschenfresser Leuthen in der Newenwelt America gelegen* (Marburg, 1557); Jean de Léry, *Histoire d'vn voyage fait en la terre du Bresil, autrement dite Amerique* (La Rochelle, 1578).

13. Pedro de Magalhães Gandavo, *Historia da provincia sācta Cruz a que vulgarmente chamamos Brasil* (Lisboa, 1576).

14. Simão de Vasconcellos, *Chronica da Companhia de Jesu do estado do Brasil: e do que obrarão seus filhos nesta parte do Nouo Mundo* (Lisboa, 1663).

15. André de Barros, *Vida do apostolico padre Antonio Vieyra da Companhia de Jesus, chamado por antonomasia o Grande* (Lisboa, 1746).

16. Willem Piso, *De Indiae utriusque re naturali et medica libri quatuordecim* (Amsterdam, 1658).

17. Michael Hemmersam, *West-Indianische Reissbeschreibung* (Nuremburg, 1663). For a helpful catalogue of this and other related books once exhibited at the John Carter Brown Library in 1988, see Dagmar Schäffer, *Portuguese Exploration to the West and the Formation of Brazil 1450–1800* (Providence, RI: The John Carter Brown Library, 1988), esp. 65–66. A key study remains important; see Charles R. Boxer, *The Dutch in Brazil, 1624–1654* (Oxford: Clarendon Press, 1957).

18. G. R. Crone, "Introduction," *The Voyages of Cadamosto and Other Documents on Western Africa in the Second Half of the Fifteenth Century* (London: The Hakluyt Society, 1937), xix.

19. Crone, xxx–xlv. It is possible that Cadamosto wrote some parts before 1460. The apparently late fourteenth-century manuscript is in a cursive semi-Gothic hand, probably that of a copyist and not in Cadamosto's autograph. See *Paesi novamente retrovati* (Vicenza, 1507).

20. Crone, xliii–iv. Crone's translation is based on the *Paesi.*

21. Cadamosto, *Voyages*, 1.

22. Ibid., 1, see 2.

23. Ibid., 3–4.

24. Ibid., 8, 13.

25. Ibid., 13.

26. Ibid., 13–14.
27. Ibid., 16.
28. Ibid., 17.
29. Ibid., 17.
30. Ibid., 17.
31. Ibid., 18. See Gomes Eannes de Azurara, *The Chronicle of the Discovery and Conquest of Guinea*, trans. and ed. C. R. Beazley and E. Prestage (London: Hakluyt Society, 1896–99).
32. Cadamosto, *Voyages*, 18.
33. Ibid., 18–19.
34. Ibid., 19, see 20–32 for later.
35. Ibid., 31, see 33–34 for later.
36. Ibid., 35–39.
37. Ibid., 41.
38. Ibid., 41.
39. Ibid., 44–45.
40. Ibid., 49.
41. Ibid., 49.
42. Ibid., 49; for later, see 50n1.
43. Ibid., 50.
44. Ibid., 51.
45. Ibid., 54, see 55.
46. On interpreters and medicators, see the chapter, "Between Cultures," in my *Columbus, Shakespeare and the Interpretation of the New World*.
47. Cadamosto, *Voyages*, 55.
48. Ibid., 55.
49. Ibid., 55–56.
50. Ibid., 56.
51. Ibid., 56.
52. Ibid., 57.
53. Ibid., 57–58.
54. Ibid., 60.
55. Ibid., 61.
56. Ibid., 62–63.
57. Ibid., 67.
58. Ibid., 68.
59. Ibid., 68.
60. Ibid., 69.
61. Ibid., 76, see 70–77.
62. Ibid., 84, see 78–83.
63. Ibid., 84.
64. Ibid., 84.
65. See Anthony Farrington, *Trading Places: The East India Company and Asia 1600–1834* (London: The British Library, 2002), 10–19; this paragraph is indebted to this fine and clear account.

66. Andrew Marvell, "The Character of Holland," *The Complete Poems*, ed. Elizabeth Story Donno (Harmondsworth: Penguin, 1972; rpt. 1996), 112–16; see 263.
67. See Marvell, 264 note for line 26.
68. See ibid., 264 note for line 28.
69. See ibid., 264 notes for lines 32, 62.
70. See ibid., 264, notes for lines 78 and 80.
71. See ibid., 265, note for line 107.
72. See ibid., 265, note for line 113.
73. See ibid., 265, notes for lines 120, 124, 137–38.
74. Domingo Fernández de Navarrete, *The Travels and Controversies of Friar Domingo Navarrete 1618–1686*, ed. J. S. Cummins (Cambridge: for the Hakluyt Society at the University Press, 1962), 2 vols., continuous pagination; see Cummins, introduction, xx–xxviii.
75. Cummins, introduction, xxxv.
76. My analysis, in keeping with my wish for this book to reach general readers as well as scholars and owing to the availability of Cummins's translation for the reader (it is based on the Churchill version in English of 1704 but offers corrections), concentrates on book 6 of the Tratados. In later work I might concentrate as well on the parts of the Tratados included in the collection by Awnsham and John Churchill in 1704. See Cummins cxv–cxx.
77. Ibid., 113.
78. Ibid., 124–25.
79. Ibid., 125.
80. Ibid., 126.
81. Ibid., 367.
82. Ibid., 368.
83. Ibid., 273.
84. Ibid., 265–66.
85. Ibid., 266.
86. Ibid., 266, see 266n2 for what follows.
87. Ibid., 266.
88. Ibid., 266.
89. Ibid., 267, see 266.
90. Ibid., 267.
91. Ibid., 267.
92. Ibid., 268, see 270.
93. The outline of the Dutch in Brazil, although not many of the points of interpretation, at the beginning of this section derive from one of the standard works in English in the field, C. R. Boxer's *The Dutch in Brazil 1624–1654* (1957; Hamden, CT: Archon Books, 1973), esp. 1–3. See also J. F. Jameson, *Willem Usselincx, Founder of the Dutch and Swedish West India Companies* (New York, 1887) and C. Ligtenberg, *Willem Usselincx* (Utrecht, 1915).
94. Walter Ralegh, *The Discouerie of the Large, Rich, and Bewtiful Empyre of Guiana, with a Relation of the Great and Golden Citie of Manoa (which the Spanyards call El Dorado* (London, 1596), A 4 recto. For a good example

of Willem Usselincx's views, see his anonymously published *Vertoogh hoe nootwendich, nut ende profijtelich het sy… te behouden de vryheyt van te handelen op West-Indien* (1608).

95. Boxer, 4–9.
96. Ibid., 10–28.
97. Ibid., 31, 43–48.
98. Ibid., 73–74, 82–83, 108–20, 251–58.
99. François Valentijn, *François Valentijn's Description of Ceylon*, trans. and ed. Sinnappah Arasaratnam (London: Hakluyt Society, 1978), 226, 231, 258–60. Two helpful books on the Dutch colonies are W. Ph. Coolhaus, *A Critical Survey of Studies on Dutch Colonial History* (S-Gravenhage: Martinus Nijhoff, 1960) and Om Prakash, *The Dutch East India Company and the Economy of Bengal, 1630–1720* (Princeton: Princeton University Press, 1985). On the Portuguese, e.g., see Sanjay Subrahmanyam, *The Portuguese Empire in Asia, 1500–1700: A Political and Economic History* (London: Longman, 1993). A useful general work is *Historiography of Europeans in Africa and Asia, 1450–1800*, ed. Anthony Disney (Aldershot: Variorum, 1995).
100. Valentijn, 262.
101. Ibid., 270–73.
102. Ibid., 274.
103. Denis Diderot, *Oeuvres complètes…, tome quatorzième* (Paris: Garnier frères, 1876), 14: 6. My translations of the French texts here and later.
104. Diderot, 14: 28. The fascination with sex, love, lust and marriage is something that occurred in a number of Europeans about exotic peoples and places, and not just in the New World; see chapter 4, "Sexing America," in my *Columbus, Shakespeare*.
105. Diderot, 14: 29.
106. Ibid., 14: 40.
107. Ibid., 14: 40.
108. Guillaume-Thomas Raynal, *Histoire philosophique et politique des établissemens et du commerce des Européens dans les deux Indes*, tome 1 (La Haye: Gosse fils, 1776), 1: 1.
109. Raynal, 1: 47, see 44–46.
110. Ibid., 1: 60, see 58–59.
111. Ibid., 1: 66.
112. Ibid., 1: 71.
113. Ibid., 1: 73–47, 78–79, 82.
114. Ibid., 1: 108–09.
115. Ibid., 1: 119, see 1: 113–14, 118.
116. Ibid., 1: 119.
117. Ibid., 1: 119.
118. Ibid., 1: 119–20.
119. Ibid., 1: 120.
120. Ibid., 1: 120.

121. Ibid., 1: 120.
122. Ibid., 1: 139.
123. Ibid., 1: 139.
124. Ibid., 1: 139–40.
125. Ibid., 1: 290; see I: 174–76. See also A. F. Prévost d'Exiles, *Histoire générale des voyages*, 20 vols. (Paris, 1746–70).
126. Jean-François Marmontel, *[Les] Incas, ou La destruction de l'empire du Pérou* (Paris: Lacombe, 1777), xi.
127. Marmontel, xi.
128. Ibid., xi.
129. Jean-Antione-Nicolas de Carita, marquis de Condorcet, "De L'Infuence de la Révolution d'Amérique sur l'Europe," *Oeuvres de Condorcet*, ed. A. Condorcet O'Connor and M. F. Arago, tome huitième (Paris: Firmin Didot frères, 1847), 3. On British views of politics and the American Revolution, see Eliga Gould, *The Persistence of Empire: British Political Culture in the Age of the American Revolution* (Chapel Hill: University of North Carolina Press, 2000).
130. Condorcet, 4.
131. Alexis de Toqueville, *De la Démocracie en Amérique, douzième édition, tome premier* (Paris: Pagnerre, Éditeur, 1848), i. The twelfth edition also contains the advertisement (notice) for the tenth edition.
132. De Toqueville, 1: ii.
133. Ibid., 1: iii–iv.
134. Ibid., 1: 1.
135. Ibid., 1: 2.
136. Ibid., 1: 44.
137. Ibid., 1: 45.
138. Farrington, 17–22, 34–39. See Richard Hakluyt, *Discourse of Western Planting*, ed. David B. Quinn and Alison M. Quinn (London: Hakluyt Society, 1993), 28, 31.
139. Farrington, 41–47.
140. Ibid., 48.
141. Ibid., 48–53.
142. Ibid., 64, 80–86.
143. Ibid., 98–106.
144. R. B. [pseudonym Richard Burton for Nathaniel Crouch], *The English Empire in America: Or a Prospect of His Majesties Dominions in the West-Indies* (London: the Bell, 1685). I have consulted the first edition in the British Library, whose copy had been misplaced but is now back in circulation. In chapter 2 of *Columbus, Shakespeare and the Interpretation of the New World*, I discuss this aspect of the representation of Spain and Columbus; on the representation of Spain more generally, see also my first book in this series, *Representing the New World: The English and French Uses of the Example of Spain* (New York and London: Palgrave, 2001).

145. David Ramsey, *The History of the American Revolution*, 2 vols. (Philadelphia, 1789).

146. Jeremy Belknap, *A Discourse, Intended to Commemorate the Discovery of America by Christopher Columbus; Delivered at the Request of the Historical Society in Massachusetts, on the 23rd Day of October 1792, Being the Completion of the Third Century Since that Memorable Event* (Boston: Belknap and Hall, 1792), 19.

147. Ibid., 46–47.

148. Ibid., 41.

149. Ibid., 41.

150. William Boldenweck and Maier Weinchenk, "*An Address to His Excellency, Grover Cleveland, President of the United States in Presenting the Historical World's Fair Medal in Gold at the Dedication of the World's Columbian Exposition at Chicago, on May 1st. 1893. By William Boldenweck and Maier Weinchenk*," 2–3. This is the copy that Grover Cleveland presented to the Princeton Library. He retired to Princeton after his presidency.

151. Ibid., 4–5.

152. *Rand, McNally & Co.'s A Week at the Fair* (Chicago: Rand McNally & Co., 1893), 111.

153. Ibid., 113.

154. See William Eleroy Curtis, *Scrapbooks*, especially for the years 1890–94, in the Princeton archives; these scrapbooks do not have a standard way of classification (the dates with a scrapbook can be a mixture of years), but one of them has on the inside cover "1892 AM 15237 Scrapbook on Christopher Columbus."

155. For an interesting and detailed discussion of the relation between U.S. and Cuban historiographies, see Louis A. Pérez, Jr., *The War of 1898: The United States and Cuba and Historiography* (Chapel Hill: The University of North Carolina Press, 1998); for a general view of the historiography of the war, see especially ix–xiii. For a few other useful recent essays on the historiography of the war, see Edward P. Crapol, "Coming to Terms with Empire: The Historiography of Late-Nineteenth-Century American Foreign Relations," *Diplomatic History* 16 (1992), 573–97; Thomas G. Paterson, "United States Intervention in Cuba, 1898: Interpretation of the Spanish-American-Cuban-Filipino War," *History Teacher* 29 (1996), 341–61.

156. Pérez talks about the difficulty of discovering the meaning of the war of 1898; see 2–3.

157. Thomas Jefferson to James Munroe, June 11, 1823, in H. A. Washington, ed., *The Works of Thomas Jefferson*, 9 vols. (New York, 1884), 7: 300, quoted in Pérez, 5.

158. Pérez, 5–14. See Richard B. Olney to Enrique Dupuy de Lôme (the Spanish minister in Washington), April 4, 1896, *FRUS*: 1897, 543, quoted in Pérez, 13 and Stewart L. Woolford to William McKinley, March 9, 1898, *Dispatches from U.S. Consuls to Spain, U.S. Department of State,*

General Records, 1792–1906, Record Group 59, National Archives, Washington, D. C., quoted in Pérez, 14. On the Maine, see, e.g., Captain Charles D. Sigsbee, *The "Maine": An Account of Her Destruction in Havana Harbor* (New York, 1899); John Edward Weems, *The Fate of the "Maine"* (New York, 1899); David F. Trask, *The War with Spain in 1898* (New York: Macmillan, 1981), 24–29 and Michael Blow, *A Ship to Remember: The Maine and the Spanish-American War* (New York: William Morrow and Company, 1992).

159. Pérez, 16–22.

160. John Quincy Adams, quoted in Robert L. Beisner, *Twelve Against Empire: The Anti-Imperialists 1898–1900* (New York: McGraw-Hill, 1968), iii.

161. St. Matthew 16: 26, The Holy Bible ... The Authorized King James Version (Cleveland and New York: The World Publishing Company, n.d.). The other variants are: "For what shall it profit a man, if he shall gain the whole world, and lose his own soul?" (Mark 8: 36) and "For what is a man advantaged, if he gain the whole world, and lose himself, or be cast away?" (Luke 9: 25).

162. Beisner, iv–ix, 6–17.

163. Carl Schurz to William McKinley, May 9, 1898, Frederic Bancroft, ed., *Speeches, Correspondence and Political Papers of Carl Schurz* (New York: G. P. Putnam's Sons, 1913), 5: 465–66.

164. William James to W. Cameron Forbes, June 11, 1907, Henry James, ed., *The Letters of William James* (Boston: The Atlantic Monthly Press, 1920), 2: 289, quoted in Beisner, 48.

165. Charles Eliot Norton to William Roscoe Thayer, August 16, 1898, quoted in William Roscoe Thayer, "The Sage of Shady Hill," *The Unpartizan Review* 15 (1921), 84; see Beisner, 81 and 56–83.

166. Andrew Carnegie, *Triumphant Democracy or Fifty Years' March of The Republic* (Garden City, NY: Doubleday, 1933), 210; see Beisner, 167–68.

167. On some of the drawbacks of the anti-imperialists, see Beisner, 230–39.

168. Charles Morris, *Our Island Empire* (Philadelphia, 1899), 162–64. See Philip S. Foner, *The Spanish-Cuban-American War and the Birth of American Imperialism 1895–1902* (New York and London: Monthly Review Press, 1972), 2: 466–83.

169. Charles H. Brown, *The Correspondents' War: Journalists in the Spanish-American War* (New York: Charles Scribner's Sons, 1967), 443.

170. Kaiser Wilhelm II, quoted in Ernest R. May, *Imperial Democracy: The Emergence of America as a Great Power* (New York, 1961), 196; see Trask, 45.

171. Trask, 48–49.

172. Ibid., 449–51.

173. Ibid., 473.

174. *The World*, July 24, 1898. This image courtesy of Nicholson Baker, American Newspaper Repository, Rollinsford, N.H. (www.oldpapers.org). My thanks also to Steve Ferguson for calling this image to my attention

and for making it available to me. For some studies of the Spanish-American War, see Brooks Adams, "The Spanish War and the Equilibrium of the World," *Forum* 25 (1898), 641–51; Richard Challener, *Admirals, Generals, and American Foreign Policy 1898–1914* (Princeton: Princeton University Press, 1963); James A. Field Jr., "American Imperialism: The 'Worst Chapter' in Almost Any Book," *American Historical Review* 83 (1978), 644–68. My thanks to Richard Challener, whose office I shared in the Department of History at Princeton and whose library I admired there. In the final stages of the book Professor Challener died and I wish to remember him for what he did for Canadian Studies at Princeton and what that meant to me personally.

Index